£29.99

Niche Tourism

Contemporary issues, trends and cases

Niche Tourism

Contemporary issues, trends and cases

Edited by

Marina Novelli (PhD)

*Senior Lecturer in Tourism Development and Management
Centre for Tourism Policy Studies, University of Brighton*

ELSEVIER

AMSTERDAM • BOSTON • HEIDELBERG • LONDON • NEW YORK • OXFORD
PARIS • SAN DIEGO • SAN FRANCISCO • SINGAPORE • SYDNEY • TOKYO

Elsevier Butterworth-Heinemann
Linacre House, Jordan Hill, Oxford OX2 8DP
30 Corporate Drive, Burlington, MA 01803

First published 2005
Reprinted 2005

British Library Cataloguing in Publication Data
A catalogue record for this book is available from the British Library

Library of Congress Cataloguing in Publication Data
A catalogue record for this book is available from the Library of Congress

ISBN 0 7506 6133 X

For information on all Elsevier Butterworth-Heinemann
publications visit our website at www.bh.com

Working together to grow
libraries in developing countries

www.elsevier.com | www.bookaid.org | www.sabre.org

ELSEVIER   BOOK AID International   Sabre Foundation

Typset by Keyword Group, Wallington, UK
Printed and bound in Great Britain

To my parents and Kemi, for their priceless and endless support

Preface

This book is the result of the desire of the author to provide a set of case studies from around the world focusing on a growing segment of the tourism industry: *niche tourism*. The aim is to offer a theoretical framework underpinned by contemporary issues and cases written by specialists with an emphasis on linking niche tourism theory to practice.

Owing to the nature of the case studies, this book is designed for use as reference for the academic and practitioners' markets, for undergraduate and graduate tourism courses.

The number of tourism qualifications, and in particular the growing set of niche tourism related modules, have exploded in the last decade. This text may be used for a better understanding of a selection of tourism scenarios, characterised by issues such as special interest, impacts, planning, marketing, fragile destinations, ethics and sustainability; identified as common areas of study to the majority of tourism courses.

In writing and editing this book, the author discovered the existence of great interest in defining niche tourism as a recognised discipline, based on research on a variety of niche tourism products, services and markets, by fellow academic researchers from all over the world. The existence of extensive research being undertaken in the field of niche tourism was witnessed by the response to the call for contributions to this book, which attracted an unexpected number of proposed topics; these were then limited to its actual content.

Contents

Contributors

David Arnold is Dean of the Faculty of Management and Information Sciences and Professor of Computing Science at the University of Brighton, UK. He has been involved in 30 years of research in the design of interactive computer graphics systems and their applications in architecture, engineering, cartography, scientific visualisation, health and most recently cultural heritage. He is co-ordinator of a Network of Excellence called EPOCH under the EC Framework 6 program, which focuses on the interaction between technology and cultural heritage and brings together 86 partners. He was educated at the University of Cambridge and has an MA in Engineering and Computer Science and a PhD in Architecture. Following a brief spell at the Royal Naval Engineering College, he moved to the University of East Anglia, Norwich, UK, for 24 years, where he was Dean of Information Systems, and led the university's contributions to a number of projects in European Framework programs. Between his several academic and professional involvements David is currently on the Council of the UK Parliamentary Information Technology Committee (PITCOM).

Angela Benson is Senior Lecturer in Tourism at the Centre for Tourism Policy Studies (CENTOPS), University of Brighton, UK. She holds a Masters degree in Leisure and Tourism, and her research interests concentrate upon volunteer, research and scientific tourism and the consequences of both the organisations and the participants for tourism destinations. At present the focus of her work is in Asia, and particularly Indonesia.

Moira Birtwistle is a Lecturer in Tourism and Rural Tourism at the Scottish Agricultural College in Ayr, Scotland, where she teaches on a range of leisure and tourism courses at undergraduate and postgraduate level. Moira represents the Higher Education sector on the Executive of the Ayrshire and Arran Tourism Forum and has worked on industry-related projects developing and delivering training courses and providing consultancy and research to local tourism businesses. Recent projects include 'Family History Training' and 'Burns Familiarisation' developed to strengthen the local tourism product.

Peter Burns is Professor of International Tourism and Development at the School of Service Management, University of Brighton. He leads research in the school and co-ordinates the Centre for Tourism Policy Studies (CENTOPS). His research interests include: destination master planning with a focus on the interaction between local social structures (including pro-poor tourism measures); tourism and small island destinations (special problems of impacts on social structures);

changing nature of tourism consumption (tourists' responses to globalisation and consumerism); tourism in the Arab world. He is Associate Editor (research section), *Tourism Recreation Research*, invited guest editor for special edition on the role of NGOs in the development and monitoring of tourism (Autumn, 1999), Associate Editor *Journal of Hospitality and Tourism Planning*, member World Tourism Organisation Education Council, Organiser of Tourism and Sustainability conference series, regular peer reviewer for *Progress in Tourism & Hospitality Research*, *Tourism Management* and *Annals of Tourism Research*. He has an extensive consultancy expertise in over 26 countries including: Saudi Arabia (with Ernst & Young: Tourism Master Plan), Mauritius (with Deloitte and Touche: EU funded Tourism Master Plan), Libya (with World Tourism Organisation: Tourism Master Plan) and Oman (with World Tourism Organisation: Tourism Society Awareness Programme).

Michelle Callanan is the Co-ordinator of Tourism Management Programmes at Birmingham College of Food, Tourism and Creative Studies, and is a recognised lecturer of the University of Birmingham. Michelle originally qualified as a teacher of Geography, Sociology and Maths (at St Patricks College, Maynooth, Ireland) and spent the next 3 years teaching in the USA. In 1991, Michelle moved to Birmingham to undertake the BSocSc (Hons) Tourism Management degree at Birmingham College of Food, Tourism and Creative Studies, followed by an MSocSc in Cultural Studies at the University of Birmingham. Throughout her career, Michelle has had the opportunity of gaining extensive experience in tour operations and consultancy. Michelle currently lectures on both undergraduate and postgraduate programmes in tourism at Birmingham College of Food, Tourism and Creative Studies. Her main areas of interest include international tourism policy, motivational studies, 'new tourism' and cultural tourism studies.

Ngaire Douglas holds a BA and a PhD from the University of Queensland, and is Associate Professor in the School of Tourism and Hospitality at Southern Cross University. She is also Visiting Associate Professor of Special Interest Tourism at the Norwegian School of Hotel Management, Stavanger, Norway. She has held scholarships to pursue research on tourism at the School of Oriental and African Studies in London, and the International Institute for Asian Studies in Leiden, The Netherlands. She is author, co-author or editor of a dozen books, numerous journal articles and book chapters on various aspects of tourism in the Pacific Asia region, and is a former editor-in-chief of the multi-disciplinary journal *Pacific Tourism Review*. Her knowledge of the Pacific region has been recognised through consultancies with Asia Pacific Economic Cooperation (APEC), the Pacific Asia Travel Association (PATA), and Cruise Down Under Inc (CDU). Research interests include: histories of tourism, tourism development in Southeast Asia and the South Pacific, and cruise tourism. Her latest co-authored book is *The Cruise Experience: Global and Regional Issues in Cruising*, Pearson Education, Frenchs Forest, 2004.

Norman Douglas holds a BA (Hons) from Newcastle University and a PhD from the Australian National University. He has taught at universities in Australia, Fiji and the USA, in subjects that include Modern History, Pacific Studies and Media

Studies. He is author, co-author or editor of 14 books and scores of articles in both academic and popular publications on topics ranging from missionary history to tourism and film analysis. As director of the research consultancy Pacific Profiles, he has undertaken consultancies for a variety of organisations, including the University of the South Pacific, the South Pacific Regional Environment Programme, the International Development Programme of Australian Universities and Colleges and Southern Cross University Press. His research interests include: visual and verbal imagery in travel and tourism, tourism history and cruising as a socio-cultural phenomenon. A keen and persistent photographer, his work has appeared on the covers of a number of books and magazines and within the pages of many more. His latest co-authored book is *The Cruise Experience: Global and Regional Issues in Cruising*, Pearson Education, Frenchs Forest, 2004.

David Timothy Duval is a Lecturer in the Department of Tourism at the University of Otago. His research interests include transnationalism and migration in the context of travel and mobilities, the role of transport in tourism development, and tourism in small island states in the Caribbean and the Pacific. He recently edited *Tourism in the Caribbean: trends, development prospects* (Routledge, 2004).

Sarah Evans is sales manager with a leading UK Business Travel Company. Since completing her degree in Tourism Management at the University of Brighton, she has had a continuing interest in both niche tourism and adventure travel and has undertaken several adventure travel trips both in Europe and the United States.

Yana Figurova was a student at the Centre for Tourism Policy Studies, University of Brighton, and graduated in 2002 with a BA (Hons) in Tourism Management and now works for a major tour operating company in the UK.

Rosalina Grumo is Research Fellow at the Department of Scienze Geografiche e Merceologiche of the University of Bari (Italy). She completed a PhD in Economic Geography and she has interests and research publications in Innovation, Tourism Enterprises and Planning, as well as experience in EU Programs. She has been Lecturer of Planning and of Tourism in various courses as well as expert and consultant in International and European Programs development.

Derek Hall is Professor of Regional Development and Head of the Leisure and Tourism Management Department at the Scottish Agricultural College (SAC). He has interests in both niche tourism and transport development and has published widely on both, often in relation to development in Central and Eastern Europe. He has the dubious distinction of being one of the few scholars to have published an article on North Korean trolleybuses. He once also had film confiscated after photographing a helicopter landing pad in a residential area of Cuba.

Michael Hall is Professor at the Department of Tourism, School of Business, University of Otago, New Zealand. He is also Honorary Professor in the Department of Marketing at Stirling University, Scotland. Co-editor of *Current Issues in Tourism*, he has written widely in the fields of tourism, leisure and environmental history. Current research interests include tourism policy processes, contemporary mobility, regional development and innovation in peripheral areas, and cool climate wines and food.

Tom Hose, initially an earth scientist (University of London) and a Fellow of the Geological Society, is a principal lecturer in tourism and a consultant on geology-focused interpretation. He has extensive experience as a field naturalist and geologist, conservationist and environmental educationalist. He has worked in schools as a head of geology and museums as a head of natural history, education officer at an inner city nature reserve and head of a county museum education service, eventually gaining his MA in museum and gallery administration (City University). He undertook extensive fieldwork in the UK, Europe and the USA in developing the geotourism concept, the focus of his doctoral thesis (University of Birmingham). He has authored chapters for three Geological Society books and numerous articles, reports and conference papers on geotourism. He contributes, often by invitation, geotourism keynote conference addresses and practitioner workshops in the UK and Europe.

Michael N. Humavindu is an economist within the National Bank of Namibia. At the time of contributing to this publication, he was employed at the Environmental Economic Unit (EEU) of the Directorate of Environmental Affairs in Namibia. He also serves as the deputy co-ordinator of the EEU as well as sitting on the Ministerial Economising Committee. His research is mainly focused on the economics of community based natural resource tourism as well as trophy hunting research. He was educated at the University of Namibia and the University of Stellenbosch, South Africa.

Antonietta Ivona is Research Fellow at the Department of Scienze Geografiche e Merceologiche of the University of Bari (Italy). She completed a PhD in Economic Geography and she has interests and research publications in tourism and sustainability and rural geography. Before joining academia, she worked as director of a travel agency, consultant for tourism enterprises and lecturer of tourism in various courses.

Jo-Anne Lester is a Senior Lecturer at the Centre for Tourism Policy Studies, University of Brighton. Key interests in teaching and research include cruise tourism, visual representation of tourism and travel products and tourism and visual culture, specifically exploring the relationship between photography and tourism. Current research projects, in collaboration with Dr Catherine Palmer, include investigating the symbolic significance of the act of taking photographs. Prior to entering education, she gained considerable operational experience working in tour operating and on cruise ships.

Richard Mitchell is a Senior Lecturer in the Department of Tourism, School of Business, University of Otago, New Zealand. He has formerly worked at the University of Western Sydney and La Trobe University in Australia. Current research interests include tourist consumer behaviour, wine marketing and tourism, urban cycling hazards, and innovation strategies in alpine goat farming in southern New Zealand. His research on wine tourism includes conduct of a long-term study of post-winery visit purchasing behaviour as well as an ongoing sensory analysis of Central Otago wines.

Marina Novelli is Senior Lecturer in Tourism Development and Management at the Centre for Tourism Policy Studies (CENTOPS), University of Brighton, UK. She completed a PhD on 'Rural and Farm Tourism: a comparative study of Apulia (Italy) and the West Country (UK)' at the University of Bari, Italy. Her main research interests include regional development and tourism, niche tourism markets such as wine and food, festival and events and eco-tourism, tourism planning and management. Her most recent research activity focuses on consumptive vs non-consumptive forms of tourism in the natural environment, Trophy Hunting Tourism, Tourism Clusters and Regional Development, Integrated Quality Management and Tourism, Consumers' Behaviour and Tourism Impacts. She has been involved in a variety of European regional planning and tourism management and consulting projects. She is currently co-ordinator of the special interest group 'Tourism and the Local Economy' and of a project funded by the South East England Development Agency (SEEDA) named 'Healthy Lifestyle Tourism Cluster'.

Catherine Palmer is a Principal Lecturer at the Centre for Tourism Policy Studies, University of Brighton. Her PhD examined the relationship between heritage tourism and English national identity. Her research interests are focused on anthropology and tourism, specifically the role of objects in identity formation, visual culture, tourism and identity. Current research projects include investigating the symbolic significance of the act of taking photographs (with Jo-Anne Lester) and the culture of the chef (with Professor Peter Burns). She is a Fellow of the Royal Anthropological Institute and a Consulting Editor for the *International Journal of Tourism Research*. She is widely published and makes regular conference presentations, both in the UK and overseas.

Greg Richards is Research Fellow, Department of History and Geography, Universitat Rovira i Virgili, Tarragona, Spain, and Fundació Interarts, Barcelona, Spain. He obtained a PhD in Geography from University College London in 1982, and entered market research with RPA Marketing Communications. He has worked on surveys of the UK conference and exhibition industry, hotel feasibility studies and tourism development and marketing consultancy for local government. In 1984 he became a partner in Tourism Research and Marketing (TRAM), a consultancy specialising in tourism and event marketing. With TRAM he has worked on projects for the British Tourist Authority, the English Tourist Board, the Scottish Tourist Board and numerous local authorities. He has also worked for 10 years in The Netherlands, developing research on cultural tourism and consumer behaviour. He is a European Executive Member of the Association for Tourism and Leisure Education (ATLAS) and has directed a number of ATLAS projects for the European Commission on topics including cultural tourism, crafts tourism, sustainable tourism, tourism education and labour mobility in the tourism industry.

Brent Ritchie is Director of the Centre for Tourism Research at the University of Canberra, Australia. He has research interests in the area of sport tourism related to his PhD research programme and the publication of referred journal articles and conference proceedings related to the development and management of cycle tourism in New Zealand. He also has an interest in event sport tourism concerning masters games events and rural event development. Brent has also published and edited a special issue of the journal *Current Issues in Tourism* concerning the subject of sport tourism and organised an international conference on sport tourism in 2000 in Australia. He teaches sport events tourism as a second-year undergraduate subject for tourism, travel and leisure students.

Mike Robinson is Professor and holds the Chair of Tourism Studies. He is also Director of the Centre for Tourism and Cultural Change at Sheffield Hallam University, UK. His work is focused upon research in the field of tourism and culture relationships. Previously he was Reader and Director of the Centre for Travel and Tourism Research Unit at the University of Northumbria at Newcastle for 8 years and was also Tourism Research and Development Officer at New College Durham. He has a PhD in Environmental Politics from the University of East Anglia. He is Editor in Chief of the *Journal of Tourism and Cultural Change* and is an Associate Editor of the Scandinavian *Journal of Hospitality and Tourism*. He is Series Editor of *Tourism and Cultural Change* with Channel View Publications. He has been chief editor of several books on tourism's inter-relationships with the cultural domain and has authored numerous chapters and articles on tourism and cultural issues. His research interests include heritage tourism, tourism and cultural change, tourism's relationships with the arts, tourism and identity making, image, international tourism policy, sustainable tourism development and tourist behaviour. He also chairs the research committee of the International Festivals and Events Association Europe.

Graham Shephard is a Senior Lecturer in Travel and Tourism at the School of Service Management, University of Brighton. He initially spent 10 years working in the ski industry both in Europe and in the United States and has had a long association with sports and adventure travel. With an overwhelming interest in the outdoors and wild places, he is currently undertaking research into niche and special interest tourism in Europe.

Peter E. Tarlow is a sociologist specialising in the impact of crime and terrorism on the tourism industry and also in tourism and economic development. He completed a PhD in sociology from Texas A&M University. In 1990, he introduced one of the nation's first courses on the Sociology of Tourism, and in 1994 he designed and taught a groundbreaking course on Tourism, Crime and Security. Since 1997, he has also taught tourism security courses for the International Association of Chiefs of Police. He is a member of the Distance Learning Faculty of the George Washington University in Washington, DC, and he is an adjunct faculty member of Colorado State University and a honorary professor at the Universidad de Especialidades Turísticas (Quito, Ecuador) and of the Universidad de la Policia Federal (Buenos Aires, Argentina). He lectures at numerous other universities around the world. He has worked with government agencies such as the FBI, the Royal Canadian Mounted Police, and the US Park Service, and the World

Tourism Organisation. Since September 11 2001 he has been actively involved in various US government meetings on terrorism. He lectures on current and future trends in the tourism industry, rural tourism economic development, the gaming industry, issues of crime and terrorism, the role of police departments in urban economic development, and international trade. He is a founder and president of Tourism & More Inc. (T&M), and writes and publishes "Tourism Tidbits", an electronic newsletter on tourism and travel.

Sarah Thomas [BA (Hons) PhD] began teaching at Birmingham College of Food, Tourism and Creative Studies in 1994 after working as a Conference and Banqueting Manager in the hospitality industry. Currently she is employed as Coordinator of Research (External) where she has engaged and directed several large research projects in recent years and conducted a range of consultancy activities for the private and public sector. Sarah is a recognised lecturer of the University of Birmingham and currently lectures on both undergraduate and postgraduate programmes, specialising in service operations management, research methods and human resources management within the hospitality and tourism sectors. Personal research interests and publications focus on the areas of: managerial cognition, customer and volunteer behaviour, operations and revenue management.

Clare Weeden is a Senior Lecturer in the School of Service Management at the University of Brighton. She specialises in the marketing of tourism but her wider research interests include consumer psychology and cruise tourism. Clare is currently completing her PhD which is exploring decision-making and the UK consumer, with particular emphasis on the purchasing of ethical holidays.

Eugenia Wickens (PhD) is Reader in Tourism at the Faculty of Leisure and Tourism, Buckinghamshire Chilterns University College, High Wycombe, UK, and has a special interest in tourists' experiences and travel motivation. She has published extensively on Cultural Tourism, Tourist Typologies, Tourism and Health, and more recently on Rural Tourism Development. Her current research is on understanding undergraduate students' learning experiences and student retention.

Julie Wilson is Research Fellow, Department of History and Geography, Universitat Rovira i Virgili, Tarragona, Spain, and University of the West of England, Bristol, UK. She completed a PhD in Human Geography and specialised in the field of tourism geography, with research and teaching interests in youth and independent travel and tourism imagery. She has held visiting fellowships at the University of Barcelona (Spain), the Autonomous University of Barcelona (Spain) and Aalborg University (Denmark). She has directed a range of research projects including *The Effect of Cultural Tourism Experiences on the Attitudes and Behaviour of Young Travellers, The Impact of Major Cultural Events on City Image* and *The Social Construction of Backpacker Travel*, with support from the British Academy, Anglo-Catalan Batista i Roca programme, EU Marie Curie Intra-European Fellowships programme, the Royal Geographical Society/HSBC Holdings, Royal Society/Dudley Stamp Memorial Trust and the British Council Netherlands/NWO

UK–Netherlands Partnership Programme in Science. Collaborations on major research projects include *International Co-operation in the Field of Cultural Tourism Education IBERTUR* (EU ALFA), *Participation, Leadership, and Urban Sustainability PLUS* (EU FP5) and *Marine Ecotourism for the Atlantic Area META* (EU Interreg IIC).

Foreword

Despite sustained, serious academic interest in tourism over the past few decades, there is no doubt that there still remains much of this pervasive global phenomenon to be explored. Superficial and mechanistic studies of tourism have long given way to more penetrative analyses of what is now recognised to be a highly complex aspect of human life. Indeed, it is human life but in a temporary context, a different place, a different time; but human life all the same with all its attendant experiences and impacts, subtleties and sensitivities. As such, tourism requires to be examined from an interior, subjective perspective as well as a positivistic, external objective position, relating as it does to central human emotions and conscious feelings of joy, sorrow, desire, lust, envy, etc. Furthermore, tourism also requires to be examined in a multi-disciplinary way and with the dynamic of change constantly in the background. This is both a necessity and a challenge.

If one strips away much of the hardware of tourism and travel we find that the human imagination is at its core. The imaginative faculty – what Swift, in literature, termed the 'power of invention' – provides tourism with a transformative power both at the point of its production and consumption. Tourists imagine themselves, and others, inside and outside of quotidian realities, fantastical realms, exotic contexts. Tourists draw upon their own imaginations and the collective imagination that runs through societies and are integral to constructions of that society and of identity.

Assisted by the superstructures of technology and tacit traditions of story telling, the tourism industry taps into the realms of the imagination to create 'worlds' for the tourist to visit. Thus the most prosaic places are transformed into destinations that attract the curious and inspire the apathetic. It is imagination that fuels both the organisation of tours – to the sewers of Paris or Vienna, the public toilets of London, the underground tunnels of the Viet-Cong in Vietnam, etc. – and, the willing participation of tourists on such tours. Sites of mass murder, homes of the living rich and famous dead, old diner cars, visitor attractions dedicated to tinned meat, have all, to various degrees, been packaged for the ever-curious tourist. At one level, such touristic practices represent the edges of what we would generally take to be mainstream tourism and are likely to remain so. At another level they demonstrate the ever growing power of a consuming public (albeit a highly selective public in global terms) that continues to free itself from the impediments to living out its dreams and wishes, or in Bauman's words (2003: 14), borrowing from Freud, 'the liberation of the pleasure principle'.

Whatever the deceptions and contestability of the term 'niche tourism', as a form of speciality tourism, it nonetheless reflects the power, or at least the apparition of power, of the consumer. It speaks to us of a relationship that is increasingly being forged between producer and consumer, between reality and imagination, and between wishing and fulfilment. Niche tourism is an economy of imagination, where individual preferences and practices are co-ordinated, packaged and sold. The wants and wishes of the bird watcher, the golfer, the genealogist, the railway enthusiast, can now be purchased; indeed, the fullest stretches of the imagination can now be catered for. For the tourist, niche tourism legitimates our most human and intimate proclivities. For the scholar, it provides yet another layer for investigation, as each variety of niche tourism leads us to a series of fundamental questions about the human condition and provides us with opportunities to move ever deeper into understanding the complexities of the relationships tourists form with people and objects, places and pasts.

Mike Robinson
Chair, Tourism Studies
Director, Centre for Tourism and Cultural Change
Sheffield Hallam University

Reference

Bauman, Z. (2003) Consuming life. *Journal of Consumer Culture*, 1(1), 9–29.

Acknowledgements

A number of people have contributed significantly to the realisation of this book. First of all, it is only thanks to the enthusiasm and the professional support of Sally North and her team at Elsevier, that this book became reality.

While several colleagues have offered valuable comments and suggestions at different stages, Professor Peter Burns deserves a particular mention for his patience and support throughout the editing process.

I am particularly grateful to all those who have believed in this project and have contributed with chapters and general comments, making this book a possible platform for further discussion.

Niche tourism: an introduction

Mike Robinson and Marina Novelli

The concept of 'niche tourism' has emerged in recent years in counter-point to what is commonly referred to as 'mass tourism'. It implies a more sophisticated set of practices that distinguish and differentiate tourists. In a globalising world of increasing sameness, niche tourism represents diversity and ways of marking difference. It plays on the pejorative connotations that have accompanied the evolution of mass and package tourism and their, often cited, negative impacts in relation to environmental degradation and socio-cultural disturbance. For destination managers and planners seeking to utilise tourism as a mechanism for economic development, the niche tourism approach appears to offer greater opportunities and a tourism that is more sustainable, less damaging and, importantly, more capable of delivering high-spending tourists. For tourists, niche tourism appears to offer a more meaningful set of experiences in the knowledge that their needs and wants are being met. But what exactly is niche tourism? What is its genealogy? What are its drivers and how does it relate to the experience of the tourist?

'Niche' production, consumption and complexity

Common characterisations of contemporary international tourism continue to relate to the notion of mass production and consumption. This locates tourism strongly as a feature of modernity; a phenomenon that has taken on some attributes of what are widely termed Fordist economies. The term 'mass tourism' is problematic to define with any precision but certainly there is a common-sense understanding that the development of tourism over the past 40 years can be depicted by the growth of tourist resorts, agglomerations of hotel developments, growth in the number of attractions designed for significant numbers of visitors, larger aircraft, an increase in air traffic and a general expansion of infrastructure to support some 700 million international trips in 2002 (World Tourism Organisation, 2003). Here, 'mass' is equated with magnitude and despite recent lulls in international travel, forecasts are generally unanimous in their long-term predictions of increased volumes of touristic activity.

But mass tourism also refers to the production, structure and organisation of tourism akin to an industrial process whereby economies of scale are sought to meet market needs. Poon (1993) defines 'mass' tourism as a large-scale phenomenon, packaging and selling standardised leisure services at fixed prices to a mass clientele. Large-scale packaging has been via tour operators, airlines and multinational hotel groups who hold significant power and influence with regard to the political economies of destinations and host communities around the globe. Despite more recent attempts to promote issues of quality and value, competition between the major producers has largely been based upon price supported by strong branding and mass marketing. The application of Fordist-type principles to the delivery of tourism for an expanding market signalled an important process of democratisation of travel, particularly in Europe during the mid-1960s and 1970s, increasing access to a wide variety of packaged destinations. On closer inspection the production, or more accurately, the organisation of international travel and tourism, has always significantly differed from manufacturing in respect of its delivery of intangible and perishable service products rather than physical goods. Further to this, in tourism, the production and consumption of services are, in effect, inseparable. The evolution of the tourism industry to service large-scale demand for travel has involved the development of practices that are designed to maximise efficiencies and production reflecting the spirit of Taylorism and Fordism. More specifically, the development of such practices has been led by a relatively small number of large companies. In the UK, for instance, the 'inclusive' tour, or package holiday, is produced by a small number of vertically and horizontally integrated operators who dominate the market. Integration provides a series of benefits in terms of economies of scale, purchasing power, considerable control over retailing and marketing and competitive advantage.

The consumption of goods and services has been widely taken to be a secondary process following on from production (Miller, 1987). From the perspective of the tourism industry engaged in the project of production to meet the needs of the masses, there has been an implicit assumption that the market somehow behaves in an undifferentiated way and is price led. In the early days of packaged holidays the inexperience of consumers and their unfamiliarity with cross-cultural travel, coupled with a lack of organisational infrastructure and relative high costs against incomes, generated a need to provide systems that could deliver cost-effective, predictable forms of tourism that generated homogeneous holidays. On the surface, it is easy to see how such systems have influenced market behaviour. Such standardised systems produced a certain rhythm for holidaymakers over 1 or 2 weeks (Lofgren, 1999) consisting of well-ordered excursions, regular and predictable meals and organised but superficial encounters with the host community. Those wedded to romanticised conceptions of travel as a search for international peace (Hunziker, 1961), social therapy (Krippendorf, 1987), cultural inquiry (Fussell, 1980) and aesthetic enchantment (Featherstone, 1992) have, to varying degrees, railed against the mechanistic mobilisation of the masses (see for instance: Enzensberger, 1958; Turner and Ash, 1975; Fussell, 1980 and Boorstin, 1987). However, critics reluctantly accepted that this industrial-type standardisation was now required to meet demand. As Krippendorf (1987), for instance, sadly reflected: 'assembly line techniques are the only way of dealing with huge numbers'.

International tourism as identified by both structure and agency has matured over the past 40 years or so into an incredibly complex phenomenon. Indeed, tourism reflects the hyper-complexity of society (Qvortrup, 1998) with its layerings of connections not solely in terms of hard-wired information technologies, but also in the ways that societies have become transnational and cross-cultural in the ways they relate to one another. Behind apparently simple practices such as buying an airline ticket, there lies a complex system of global economic transactions, social exchanges and political negotiations that also produce a series of impacts. Jacobsen (2003: 76) refers to the development of 'complicated abstract systems' as an essential part of international European tourism. Such systems, although complex in themselves, nonetheless act to make tourism less complicated. In addition to the systems of production that the tourism industry has designed for itself, there are other adjunct factors of production that have emerged to assist the development of mass international tourism. Jacobsen cites the examples of, for instance, the growth of automatic cash point machines with multilingual instructions and the introduction of the Euro as a multinational currency. The net effect is one of 'standardised commodities and homogenised services' which are promoted by the tourism industry (Jacobsen, 2003: 77).

The horizons of tourist experience

By and large, tourists have readily bought into these complex systems because it makes the processes of holidaying easier. As Chaney (2002: 145) observes 'tourists are, however, in general conforming – and complacent in their conformity – to the expectations of their role and the programmes of their holiday organisers'. Added to this, tourists, via normative processes of socialisation, have adapted to the holidaying mode through, for example, the frequent experiences of actual and virtual travel and increasing multilinguism (Giddens, 1990). However, tourists would swiftly dismiss any notion that they are merely outputs of some vast inter-connected global machinery. The 'mass-ness' and complexity involved with the production of contemporary tourism can be contrasted with the individual and intimate experiences that are actually being consumed. What has emerged over recent years is a greater awareness of this amongst the producers of tourism. We can interpret this as symptomatic of a re-fashioning of modernity; a move to post-industrial/post-Fordist economies where consumption no longer follows on from production, but rather drives the production process as consumers increasingly consume material objects, signs and symbols to extract value, meaning, and status (see for instance: Urry, 1992, 1994, 1995; Bocock, 1993; Pretes, 1995; Lury, 1996). Seeing tourism in the context of a wider 'culture' of consumption is helpful as it highlights its role in the processes of social differentiation and status seeking, particularly amongst the 'new middle classes'.

The notion that the market extends beyond the concept of mass tourists as envisioned by producers is not new of course. Cohen (1972), partly in direct recognition of the growth of the packaged holiday at the time, pointed to a basic two-fold typology of 'tourism roles'; institutionalised tourists which included the individual mass tourist and organised mass tourist, and non-institutionalised tourists which included 'explorers' and 'drifters'. Whilst it was clear that there was a mass market, Cohen highlighted that tourists had needs beyond this. Broadly this analysis holds true today. Mass tourism continues to dominate and characterise the patterns of tourist flows, but with a larger number of more specialised forms of tourism. Visitors are increasingly interested in visiting the places, as much as in discovering, experiencing, participating in, learning about and more intimately being included in the everyday life of the destinations. Moreover, a larger number of tourists would probably argue themselves out of the 'mass tourism' category despite engaging in inclusive tours as they like to see themselves as 'individuals' even though they are engaging in 'mass practices'.

Always at the core of tourism, however, are a series of subjective, emotional experiences that actually begin with the first decision and opportunity to travel. Such experiences vary considerably but all tourists seek them, and have them, whether we are considering young tourists getting drunk in the streets of Ibiza, or tourists confronting the Himalayas, or the Mona Lisa for the first time. In this way, in the context of tourism at least, it becomes more meaningful to *avoid* speaking of discrete breaks between modernity and post-modernity (Harvey, 1989), or any discrete shifts from so-called 'mass tourists', to what Feifer (1985) terms, 'post-tourists'. Though there have clearly been economic and social structural shifts in both the way that tourism is produced and consumed, and there are useful frameworks we can use to understand the shifting meanings of tourism – in real and symbolic terms – it is also important to note the continuity around the nature of tourist experiences.

Niche tourism as a contested concept

The term 'niche tourism' is largely borrowed from the term 'niche marketing', which in turn has appropriated the niche concept from the language of the relatively recent discipline of ecology. Hutchinson (1957) is widely credited with introducing the concept of 'niche' referring, in its widest sense, to a region in a multidimensional space characterised by environmental factors that affect the welfare of the species. Thus, in broad terms, niche refers to an optimum location, which an organism can exploit in terms of resources in the presence of its competitors. It is easy to see the analogy to the world of business and so we may talk, for instance, of a company finding its particular or appropriate niche. Indeed, the use of the term 'niche' is part of a wider usage of biological/ecological metaphors that informs business theory and practice (see for instance, Lambkin and Day, 1989).

In marketing terms, niche refers to two inter-related ideas. First that there is a place in the market for a product, and second, there is an audience for this product, where both place and audience are seen to be particular entities. This can be extended further to refer to a specific product tailored to meet the needs of a particular audience/market segment. The clear premise is that the market should not be seen as some simplistic homogeneous whole with general needs, but rather as sets of individuals with specific needs relating to the qualities and features of particular products. Thus we can speak of a 'niche market' as a more narrowly defined group whereby the individuals in the group are identifiable by the same specialised needs or interests and are defined as having a strong desire for the products on offer. The size of a niche market can vary considerably but effectively it needs to be balanced between being large enough to produce sufficient business and small enough so that it is overlooked by competitors. Behind the idea of a niche market lies a knowledge process that involves producers, researching, identifying and targeting specific audiences and maintaining a relationship with them in the face of competition. Following Hannan and Freeman (1977) the 'niche' term is rooted in ideas of competitiveness where, in ecological terms, a distinction can be made between 'fundamental' niches which would refer to the size of the *potential* niche or market segment, and *realised* niches, which refer to the *actual* size of the market in the face of competition.

Not surprisingly, the discourses surrounding the niche tourism idea borrow heavily from the niche marketing idea. Thus we hear the terms 'niche tourism products' and 'niche tourist markets'; each related to the other. Importantly perhaps, the discourse is constructed by the producers of tourism rather than consumers; the former more eager to categorise and structure than the latter. There are, of course, no formal rules for what can, or what cannot, be referred to as niche tourism and there exists considerable variation under this broad term. The term 'cultural tourism', for instance, is frequently cited as a form of niche tourism with 'cultural tourists' forming the niche market. Now, while we may be able to identify travel preferences as they are aligned to broad motivations and desires to experience particular cultural forms and expressions – art, music, folklore, gastronomy, etc. – it is clear that this category can be further segmented. Smith (2003: 37) for instance highlights a typology of cultural tourists that is largely defined by 'typical places' tourists visit and 'activities of interest' that tourists engage in. Thus, the 'arts tourist' goes to the theatre, attends concerts, festivals and events, visits galleries and literary sites, whilst the 'popular cultural tourist' may visit main heritage sites, themed attractions, shopping malls as well as pop concerts and sporting events. Tourism producers are increasingly keen to focus-in upon particular activities that are practised by particular groups that can be identified and contacted (macro-niches). In this way, someone as a cultural tourist may also be an arts tourist, a literary tourist, a dedicated follower of a particular author or of their genealogy in relation to the places visited. Tourism marketers frequently act on assumptions that products that would have an appeal to one interest group (say, those that attend galleries), will also have appeal to another group (say, those who go to the theatre). Of course, in actuality, tourists seldom define their own typologies with any precision, nor with any fixity. Rather they are able to engage in a wide variety of touristic activities so that in one instance they will be happy to take a short break in a heritage town and visit the theatre, while on another occasion they may visit a mass resort complex as part of a packaged holiday.

At one end of the spectrum then niche tourism can be defined as breaking down into still relatively large market sectors (macro-niches – i.e. cultural tourism, rural tourism, sport tourism, etc.), each capable of further segmentation (micro-niches – i.e. geo-tourism, gastronomy tourism, cycling tourism, etc.). At the other end of the spectrum, niche tourism is focused on very precise small markets that would be difficult to split further. But as well as niche tourism based around what tourists do, there is also a *geographical dimension* by which locations with highly specific offers are able to establish themselves as niche destinations. Thus for instance, a wine growing region can position itself as a niche destination offering tours of its specific wines.

The way that niche tourism has been frequently referred to in tourism policy and strategy documents over recent years, in opposition to mass tourism, almost provides it with a moral legitimacy. The connotations of a more tailored and individualised service carries its own cachet relating to features like the small scale of operations, implied care and selectivity regarding discerning markets, and a suggested sensitivity of tourists. Such features provide a more apt fit with planning and development policies relating to environmentally sustainable and socially caring tourism. For these reasons, organisations such as the World Tourism Organisation (WTO) and the World Travel and Tourism Council (WTTC) view niche tourism consumption as more beneficial to the host communities as compared to the more traditional forms of mass tourism (Hall and Weiler, 1992; Hall and Lew, 1998). In addition, niche tourism is also seen as a mechanism for attracting high spending tourists, which labels it as a rather elite form of tourism as opposed to implied crass and cheap mass packaged tourism. For tourists themselves, in their engagement with social life, niche tourism allows them to become 'cosmopolitans' (Hannerz, 1996), establishing a selective distance between them and 'other' tourists. Seaton (2002) in his discussion of tourist typologies, for instance, plays to the implicit selectivity accorded to the cultural tourist when he refers to tourist types such as the aesthete, the litterateur and the epicurean. This sort of typologising of tourists, particularly with regard to whether they belong to the 'masses' or are independent travellers is inevitable to some extent, but it has tended to perpetuate the fallacy that somehow good behaviour and responsible action resides in the latter rather than the former.

A further important association with the niche idea is one of intimacy in terms of process. There is almost a tinge of amateurism connected with the niche tourism idea. Holidays for photography or steam engine enthusiasts and the like invoke a certain feeling of 'anorakism'. Beneath the surface, however, niche tourism is far from intimate and amateur in its operations. Indeed, it generally is representative of a highly sophisticated approach to marketing which allows a marked degree of segmentation and ongoing relationships built with a client base. Niche tourism may be a packaged form of tourism and in terms of the potential numbers of niches it can fill comes close to a mass phenomenon. At one level this is operated through a network of small firms (tour operators, hotels, etc.), making use of the low barriers to entry that are a feature of the tourism industry, and employing information technology almost as a form of 'cottage industry'. At another level, niche tourism can be operated through very large, transnational firms (that also deliver mass tourism packages) using highly developed expert systems that can deliver product variety but in an effective, standardised way. From the perspective of the tourist, the product appears to be 'niched' to their highly individual needs, but is delivered to what can be an exceedingly large number of individual tourists sharing similar interests and needs. This then can be interpreted not as some 'post-Fordist' fragmentation of production, but rather as a neo-Fordist move towards flexible specialisation, developed using available technologies to deliver product types, product variants, brands and sub-brands.

The drivers for niche tourism

As this book of case studies indicates, the development of niche tourism is widely acknowledged as a major trajectory in contemporary tourism. And as we have seen, the usage of the term is not without its semantic problems. However, it has taken on a common-sense meaning and demands further examination regarding its evolution.

It is clear that tourists, as consumers, have developed increasing levels of expertise and experience of being tourists. Whilst this developmental pattern of tourists may not always be linear, or simplistic as portrayed, for instance, in Pearce's Travel Career (1988, 1991), it is evident that tourists are increasingly sophisticated in their needs and preferences, and similarly adept in ensuring that their needs are met. Tourists have, as Robinson and Phipps (2003) argue, adopted the practices and discourses of tourism and have embedded them in everyday life. As part of this emergent culture of tourism, tourists have recognised their role and influence as consumers of the world. Featherstone (1990) highlights that consumption is more than a functional process that responds to the demands of the economy. Rather, following social theorists such as Giddens (1990) and Beck (1991), Featherstone speaks of consumption as a means of creating social bonds and distinction, its associated emotional pleasures and the states of desire it generates. 'Being' a tourist is closely bound to the issue of identity (Desforges, 2000; Lanfant, 1995), thus the choosing of holiday type and destination can also be seen as part of identity-making (see also Macleod, 2003). As Holden (2000) and Sharpley and Telfer (2002) highlight, tourists' consumer behaviour has produced a more segmented, specialised and sophisticated market and we can conceive of the development of niche tourism as a response to consumer needs; as a way of allowing the development and expression of identity through specific activities that also overlap with other consumer preferences. In other words, if cycling as a home leisure phenomenon provides a way of social and individual identification/distinction (complete with the purchases of clothing, equipment, attendance at cycling events, etc.), such a market will also seek to express itself in its holiday choices such as looking for destinations and resorts with a cycling friendly environment. Of course this in itself may not always amount to a specific 'niche' holiday built solely around cycling; it nonetheless provides the tourism industry with a specific market to target for 'cycling holidays'. Similar scenarios may be presented in relation to other sport activities like golf, climbing, walking, water rafting, etc.

The notion of an increasingly experienced group of tourists demanding specialist holidays to meet their specific desires provides a necessary condition for the growth of niche tourism, but it is far from sufficient. Amongst tourism businesses the creation of niche tourism can be seen as an element of competitive strategy. As tourism has grown as a business, companies have increasingly sought to gain competitive advantage in an expanding, yet often crowded marketplace. In basic terms competitive advantage relates to a company being able to generate higher profits as a proportion of sales than does its competitors. The growth of tourist markets was accompanied with the growth of providers and increased competition, particularly in the delivery of all-inclusive holidays. Although increasing turnover, market share and price-wars have been dominant features of tour operators' strategies, profit margins amongst large and medium sized tour operators, particularly in the UK, have been narrow. The development of niche products has been part of a wider structural process of diversification as the tourism industry has sought to capture new, more profitable markets, either by internal development and building a new customer base or by acquiring other (usually smaller) companies that specialise in high value tailored products. Central to this diversification process is the development and utilisation of ever more sophisticated information technology in order to offer specific products almost directly to consumers known to want those products.

The existence of low barriers of entry to the business sector has tended to polarise a relatively small number of very large, increasingly transnational, companies, and a large number of small businesses. It is from the latter that considerable momentum has come over the years with regard to niche tourism. Establishing, often very precise, market niches has allowed small businesses to gain their own edge in a highly competitive and generally price-sensitive market. In their abilities to be close to their market and offer personalised service and high levels of product knowledge, such businesses have been able to carve out specialist tours and holiday packages. A cursory glance at the UK's Association of Independent Tour Operators Directory reveals the full range of niche tourism products on offer – from battlefield tours to tailored natural history tours to the Galapagos Islands. On initial inquiry there appears to be a strong correlation between the growth of niche tourism products and a steady growth in levels of entrepreneurial activity that builds upon the special interests of enthusiasts who frequently seek to transform these interests into a business venture. However, little research has been carried out in this field.

Issues of whether niche tourism is product led or consumer led are in many ways in danger of overlooking the realities of a form of tourism that is increasingly able to deliver a wide range of experiences to ever growing numbers of tourists. Whatever the mechanisms behind niche tourism, whatever its deceptions and contestability, it provides a connection between tourist dreams, desires, imaginings and experience. No longer can we understand tourism as some composite and solid whole with its implications of composite and easily definable markets and mainstream tourists. Dig a little deeper of course and tourism has never been like this; mass tourism, despite some unifying characteristics, has always been an amalgam of highly varied experiences, tastes and behaviours. Now, even the most extreme corners of human imagination can be catered for in a packaged way.

Case studies

The examples and cases of niche tourism considered in the chapters of this volume address a wide variety of motivations, behaviours and experiences from both the perspective of production and consumption. They provide an integrated picture of niche tourism as a whole, looking at specific scenarios, offering a comprehensive theoretical framework and discussing initiatives, policies and strategies adopted internationally. With an emphasis on linking theory to

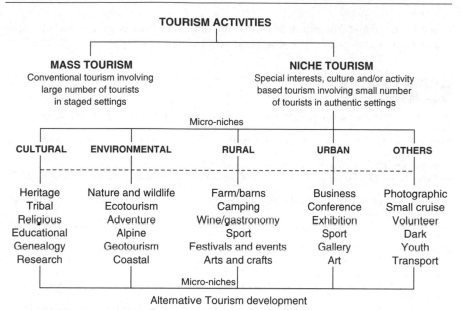

Figure 0.1 Niche tourism components.

practice, the following chapters are underpinned by up-to-date international case studies from around the world. Within certain tourism macro-niches contexts, it is possible to identify a variety of micro-niches emerging from the most appealing and vibrant characteristics, locations of destinations and specific tourists' interests (Figure 0.1). Given the diverse nature of niche tourism and related products, it may be appropriate to employ different general definition approaches, such as:

- *A geographical and demographic approach* – the location and the population involved where the tourism consumption process takes place plays a key role. These may belong to an urban, rural, coastal or alpine environment, within a developed or a developing context; but what matters is its relevance to the *specific activity* that the tourists want to engage in.
- *A product-related approach* – the presence of activities, attractions, settlements, food and other amenities is emphasised. These constitute the key parts of the niche tourism destination mix, which is shaped in accordance with *specific tourists' needs and wants.*
- *A customer-related approach* – tourist requirements and expectations are the focus of the niche tourism marketing approach. Attention is placed on the relations between the demand and the supply side; it looks at what *specialty activities* tourists are seeking in order to have a satisfactory holiday experience, whether a simple observation of nature or the direct participation in the unique lifestyle of the hosting community.

Divided into four main parts, this volume covers a variety of aspects under the headings of Special interest tourism; Tradition and culture based tourism; Activity based tourism; and The future of niche tourism. Some final consideration on niche tourism and sustainability are also presented in the last chapter.

References

Beck, U. (1991) *Risk Society: Towards a New Modernity*. London: Sage Publications.

Bocock, R. (1993) *Consumption*. London: Routledge.

Boorstin, D.J. (1987) *The Image, A Guide to Pseudo Events in America*. New York: Atheneum.

Chaney, D. (2002) *Cultural Change and Everyday Life*. London: Palgrave.

Cohen, E. (1972) Towards a sociology of international tourism. *Social Research*, 39(2), 64–82.

Desforges, L. (2000) Travelling the world: identity and travel biography. *Annals of Tourism Research*, 27(4), 926–945.

Enzensberger, H.M. (1958) reprinted (1996) A theory of tourism. *New German Critique*, 68, 117–135.

Featherstone, M. (1990) Perspectives on consumer culture. *Sociology*, 24(1), 5–22.

Featherstone, M. (1992) *Cultural Theory and Cultural Change*. London: Sage Publications.

Feifer, M. (1985) *Going Places*. London: Macmillan.

Fussell, P. (1980) *Abroad: British Literary Travelling Between the Wars*. Oxford: Oxford University Press.

Giddens, A. (1990) *The Consequences of Modernity*. Cambridge: Cambridge University Press.

Hall, C.M. and Lew, A.A. (1998) *Sustainable Tourism: A Geographical Perspective*. Harlow: Addison Wesley Longman.

Hall, C.M. and Weiler, B. (eds) (1992) *Special Interest Tourism*. London: Belhaven Press.

Hannan, M.T. and Freeman, J. (1977) The population ecology of organisations. *American Journal of Sociology*, 82(5), 929–964.

Hannerz, U. (1996) *Transnational Connections – Culture, People, Places*. London: Routledge.

Harvey, D. (1989) *The Condition of Postmodernity*. Oxford: Blackwell.

Holden, A. (2000) *Environment and Tourism*. London: Routledge.

Hunziker, W. (1961) Human relations in tourism development. *Revue de Tourisme*, 1(3), 90.

Hutchinson, G.E. (1957) Concluding remarks. *Cold Spring Harbour Symposium on Quantitative Biology*, 22, 415–427.

Jacobsen, J.K.S. (2003) The tourist bubble and the europeanisation of holiday travel. *Journal of Tourism and Cultural Change*, 1(1), 71–87.

Krippendorf, J. (1987) *The Holiday Makers*. Oxford: Heinemann.

Lambkin, M. and Day, G.S. (1989) Evolutionary processes in competitive markets: beyond the product life cycle. *Journal of Marketing*, 53, July, 4–20.

Lanfant, M.F. (1995) International tourism, internationalization and the challenge to identity. In M.F. Lanfant, J.B. Allcock and E.M. Bruner (eds) *International Tourism: Identity and Change*. London: Sage, pp. 24–43.

Lofgren, O. (1999) *On Holiday: A History of Vacationing*. Berkeley: University of California Press.

Lury, C. (1996) *Consumer Culture*. Cambridge: Polity Press.

Macleod, D.V.L. (2003) Culture and the construction of a niche market destination. In D.V.L. Macleod (2003) (ed.) *Niche Tourism in Question*. Dumfries: University of Glasgow Chrichton Publications, pp. 30–44.

Miller, D. (1987) *Material Culture and Mass Consumption*. Oxford: Blackwell.

Pearce, P.L. (1988) *The Ulysses Factor: Evaluating Visitors in Tourist Settings*. New York: Springer-Verlag.

Pearce, P.L. (1991) Analysing tourist attractions. *Journal of Tourism Studies*, 2(1), 46–55.

Poon, A. (1993) *Tourism, Technology and Competitive Strategies*. Wallingford: CAB International.

Pretes, M. (1995) Postmodern tourism: the Santa Claus industry. *Annals of Tourism Research*, 22(1), 1–15.

Qvortrup, L. (1998) *The Hypercomplex Society: Fourteen Stories about the Information Society*. Copenhagen: Gyldendal.

Robinson, M. and Phipps, A. (2003) Worlds passing by: journeys of culture and cultural journeys. *Journal of Tourism and Cultural Change*, 1(1), 1–10.

Seaton, A. (2002) Tourism as metempsychosis and metensomatosis: the personae of eternal recurrence. In G.M.S. Dann (ed.) *The Tourist as a Metaphor for the Social World*. Wallingford: CAB International.

Sharpley, R. and Telfer, D.J. (2002) *Tourism and Development. Concept and Issues.* Clevendon: Channel View.

Smith, M.K. (2003) *Issues in Cultural Tourism Studies*. London: Routledge.

Turner, L. and Ash, J. (1975) *The Golden Hordes*. London: Constable.

Urry, J. (1992) The tourist gaze and the environment. *Theory, Culture and Society*, 9, 1–26.

Urry, J. (1994) Cultural change and contemporary tourism. *Leisure Studies*, 13, 233–238.

Urry, J. (1995) *Consuming Places*. London: Routledge.

World Tourism Organisation (2003) *Tourism Highlights 2003*. Madrid: World Tourism Organization.

Part I
Special interest tourism

The tourism patterns previously highlighted have led to the rise of what is commonly recognised as 'special interest tourism' (see also Hall, C.M. and Weiler, B. 1992, *Special Interest Tourism*, London: Belhaven Press; Douglas, N., Douglas, N. and Derret, R. 2001, *Special Interest Tourism*, Brisbane: Wiley). The tourism consumption process has become increasingly based on an advanced level of travelling experiences and on a selective and knowledgeable set of choices of destinations according to particular needs and interests. The desire for new locality and authentic products becomes part of the motivation of visiting a place. The past and the present of those places are part of the unique experience sought by the tourist. *Special interest tourism* may be defined as a form of tourism which involves consumers whose holiday choice is inspired by specific motivations and whose level of satisfaction is determined by the experience they pursue. These elements will be reflected in the chapters presented in this part of the book, highlighting a variety of theoretical issues, practically explaining needs and wants of certain customers and discussing case studies on special interest tourism. 'Photography', 'geology', 'youth', 'dark', 'genealogy', 'gastronomy' and 'transport' will be the main themes of this section offering an extremely interesting international perspective and a rich set of inputs for future further discussion.

1

Photographic tourism
Shooting the innocuous, making meaning of tourist photographic behaviour

Catherine Palmer and Jo-Anne Lester

Introduction

Edensor (1998: 128) has described the iconic image of the tourist easily identified by the prominent existence of a camera as a 'banal and familiar' sight. The stereotypical image of tourists taking pictures of all that they encounter highlights the ongoing relationship between photography and tourism; a relationship that can be traced back to the significant technological developments of the nineteenth century which saw the invention of photography closely followed by key advancements in travel and tourism. Within the tourism literature there is much debate about this relationship (Chalfen, 1979; Cohen et al., 1992; Crawshaw and Urry, 1997; Osborne, 2000) and indeed it has been stated that travel is the 'search for the photogenic' (Urry, 1990: 139) or as Sontag puts it 'a strategy for accumulating photographs' (1977: 9). The interrelationship between tourism and photography is also evident when one looks at the forecasted expenditure for consumer spending on photographic equipment. Key Note (1999) estimated that in the UK £2,366m were going to be spent on photographic equipment in 2003, and that a large part of this figure is attributable to tourism; however, no confirmation of this is yet available.

Given the above comments, this chapter examines the current state of the market for specialist photographic holidays, and discusses some of the main issues and challenges to be faced. Relevant demand and supply factors will be considered together with the key motivational indicators underpinning the market for this type of tourism. Case studies of two specialist companies will be presented to illustrate the scope and diversity of this niche sector. Operational issues for management will be discussed such as environmental and socio-cultural impacts, codes of conduct and relevant ethical concerns pertaining to the taking of photographs.

Defining photographic holidays as a niche tourism product

One of the first challenges to be faced in any investigation of the market for photographic holidays is that of definition. It is necessary to make a distinction between those types of tourism where the act of photography plays a supportive or ancillary role, and those types of tourism where the whole purpose of the trip is geared around the need to take photographs. This distinction is important because the second example requires a distinct response from the tourism industry in terms of facilities offered relevant to tourist needs and expectations. It is difficult to assess the size, scope and economic value of this type of tourism because the taking of photographs is seen as part and parcel of what all tourists do and not as a reason for travelling in its own right. So, while some forms of tourism can be easily measured (for example, business tourism, visiting family and friends, cruise tourism), limited analysis can be made of photographic holidays because it is not yet seen as a distinct market.

Derret describes special interest tourism as 'the provision of customised leisure and recreational experiences driven by the specific expressed interests of individuals and groups' (2001: 3). Mintel (2002) state that these specific interests frequently embrace inert activities centred on specific pastimes. This is interesting as photographic holidays have evolved out of the pastime, or hobby, of taking photographs. Hence, a shared interest in photography unites members of a tour group, photographic tips are exchanged, tour guides offer expert advice and select photographic opportunities based on their ability to intensify the photographic activity. While such elements are common to nearly all photographic holidays there are various types of photographic holidays; for example, the photographic safari and guided photo-shoots of landscapes, flora, attractions and people. Some tours are unique in that they combine photographic opportunities at selected destinations with technical tuition and photographic workshops covering subjects as diverse as photographic analysis and historical and anthropological issues.

While acknowledging the fact that photography is an element of most holidays, companies specializing in photographic tours differentiate themselves by emphasizing the specific features of the trip, such as the opportunity to engage in the act of photography; the photographic subjects; personal tuition or workshops; and the provision of services unique to the holiday such as the inclusion of professional nature photographers as team leaders or as 'resident experts' accompanying the tour. Although the sharing of expertise and tuition from professionals is a key aspect of many tours it does mean that relatively small numbers of people can be accommodated at any one time. This has the effect of pushing up the cost of this type of holiday, which reinforces the exclusivity label often associated with niche products.

The above illustrates some of the issues involved in establishing a clear definition of what separates a holiday where photography is a common activity for tourists, from a holiday where the focus and purpose is to take photographs. This, coupled with the extensive selection of special interest holidays that exist both in the domestic and overseas market, contributes to the challenges for those endeavouring to calculate accurately the size and scope of the sector for photographic tours.

Measuring the market estimate

It is calculated that over one-third of UK consumers have, at some stage in their lives, participated in a special interest holiday, and estimated figures for 2002 showed that some nine million special interest holidays would have been taken by British consumers (Mintel, 2002); however, no recent data are available to confirm this. Within the UK market this represents an overall rise in demand for these types of holidays of 17% since 1996 (Mintel, 2002). However, it is difficult to measure the extent to which photographic holidays have contributed to this percentage increase because Mintel places special interest holidays into several sub-categories. Photographic holidays appear in the category labelled arts participation. This category includes not only photographic holidays but also activities involving music, poetry and crafts. Moreover, Mintel (2002) forecasts that by 2006 the special interest holiday market will have risen by an overall 10%. While this may serve as a positive indicator of growth in this sector, there is still limited data easily available that accurately measures the market for photographic holidays. It is therefore difficult to determine the growth and economic value of this market and as a consequence obtain a clear picture of the operators involved in providing photographic holidays. It is interesting that given what appears to be a general shift from mass homogenized tourism to that of consumers seeking a more individualized, flexible holiday experience (Mowforth and Munt, 1998) the industry is somewhat myopic in its approach to the analysis of such tourism products. There appears to be a focus on the more visible tourism products such as business tourism, visiting family and friends and cruise tourism at the expense of the less visible but still highly significant niche sectors in the industry. Table 1.1 provides examples from the current provision of photographic holidays.

The selection in Table 1.1 serves to illustrate the diversity of provision, offering wide-ranging experiences to many parts of the world. What it does not do, however, is provide any real insights into why people choose specific types of photographic holiday.

Tourist photographic motivations

The increase in the uptake of specialist holidays both at home and abroad (Mintel, 2002) may in part be explained by the growth in demand for the individualized and flexible holidays that are characteristic of what Urry (2002[1990]) refers to as post-Fordism. For Urry, Western society has undergone such significant changes that consumption rather than production is the dominant economic force. This has

Table 1.1 Examples of photographic holidays

Light and Land: Landscape and Wildlife Photographic Tours	*Web address: www.lightandland.co.uk*

Operators of landscape and wildlife photographic tours. Described as the 'perfect blend of holiday and hobby' the company operates overseas in destinations ranging from Portugal, Tuscany and Venice to further afield in Cuba, Namibia and Hawaii. UK destinations include: the Yorkshire Dales, Lake District, Dartmoor and Cornwall. The target market encompasses both beginners and experts with individual expert tuition available. Light and Land also run short courses in photography, for example, 'Panoramic Photography' and 'Landscape Technique'. Prices for the tours range from around £290 for a 3-day trip to Dartmoor in Devon, England, to £3,100 for a 2-week trip to Namibia. Prices do not include flights for overseas trips (Travel brochure 2003).

Joseph Van Os Photo Safaris	*Web address: www.photosafaris.com*

Providers of worldwide photographic tours marketed to nature and outdoor photography enthusiasts. The tours encompass visiting national parks, wildlife reserves, private ranches, tribal lands, deserts, rain forests, wildlife migration stopovers and areas of significant cultural interest. Destinations include Africa, Asia, Europe, North and South America, Antarctica and the Pacific. Tours include: photo cruises of Antarctica, New Zealand flying safaris and African wildlife and landscape photo safaris. Prices differ significantly depending on the type and duration of tour; for example, the New Zealand flying safari is quoted in the region of $7,995 for 15 days whilst a 6-day wildlife shoot of the predatory animals of North America costs in the region of $1,895 (Travel brochure 2003).

Lakeland Photographic Holidays	*Web address: www.lakelandphotohols.com*

Providers of specialist photographic holidays in the English Lake District. Targeted to all age groups with varying levels of photographic ability, the holidays include guided photographic walks around the Lake District providing 'personalised coaching and tuition in all aspects of landscape photography'. A 3–6 day holiday would cost in the region of £65 per person per day, which would include accommodation, food, photographic excursions, tuition and discussions (www.lakelandphotohols.com).

resulted in a consumer who is less inclined to be seen as part of any 'mass' consumer movement, preferring a more tailored, individualized consumption experience (Urry, 1990, 1995). While this may support the demand for niche markets it does not fully contribute to our understanding of why there is a demand for photographic holidays.

To obscure the issue further, even the question of why tourists take photographs is not an easy one to answer, compounded as it is by the fact that different types of tourists will engage in different types of photography (Chalfen, 1979; Redfoot, 1984). However, understanding some of the complex reasons that drive individuals to take photographs will help illuminate why there is a market for this type of tourism. In Bourdieu's social and cultural analysis of photography, he refers to the results of a survey into the psychology of photography carried out by a market research company. The reasons that drive individuals to take photographs are categorized into five areas, a summary of which is presented in Table 1.2.

Table 1.2 Psychological benefits of photographic holidays

Protection against time	The power of photography to capture and preserve time and space in a visual way by providing a tangible reminder of past memories and experiences in the form of a photograph.
Communication with others and expression of feelings	Symbolic reminders that resurrect past times together, and express interest or affection for another (i.e. you mean something to me because I kept a photograph of you . . .).
Self-realization	The power of the photographer to take or appropriate people, places and objects and to control how an image is represented as a result of his/her artistic and technical skills.
Social prestige	Technical ability linked to a journey made or event attended, serve as evidence of conspicuous consumption in relation to the cost of the trip or equipment.
Distraction or escape	To engage in an activity that serves as a distraction from the routines and responsibilities of everyday life.

Adapted from Bourdieu (1990: 14 15).

The motivations highlighted above serve to reinforce the complexity of the act of photography and subsequently the market for this type of tourism. While the findings emerge from rather dated research, there is significant current thinking and opinion in this area that points to their continued relevance (Wang, 2000; Todd, 2001; Garlick, 2002). The seeming obsession of some tourists with having to photograph everything they encounter creates a cycle of consumption driven by the logic that the more photographs we take the more we need in order to satisfy our greed, our hunger for consumption (Sontag, 1977; Flusser, 2000). Booking a photographic holiday certainly enables the individual to lay claim to a degree of social status and prestige based upon the high cost of the trip, the limited number of participants and the skills associated with capturing the perfect image. Consumption as a sign of status and the use of photographs to construct a person's exclusive visual biography may go some way towards explaining the 'photo-mania' behaviour of some tourists; reflecting the accepted creed that taking photographs is part of what being a tourist means. It is almost unthinkable not to take photographs while on holiday. The extent to which this is so is certainly worthy of further investigation.

Several authors make reference to the ritualistic characteristics of tourist photography (Crawshaw and Urry, 1997; Osborne, 2000; Slater, 1999), an activity that sees groups of tourists gathering at specific sights for the same reason, to take photographs of the same limited number of sights. This ritualistic behaviour whereby tourists photographically immortalize all that they encounter, may bring about a sense of 'communitas' (Turner and Turner, 1978) among the group participants based upon their shared interests. Communitas can be defined as a sense of communal togetherness that serves to establish and reinforce social relationships while on holiday (see Franklin, 2003). In his study of a tour group on a nature-based excursion Markwell (1997) made some interesting observations. For example, there was an increased degree of discussion about cameras, films and photographic techniques amongst those participants that used relatively sophisticated equipment, as opposed to those using less expensive fully automatic cameras with fixed lenses. The desire to view and reflect on the photographs of others after the trip was over was also noted. Thus the shared interest and activity of taking pictures contributed to the overall social cohesion of the tour group.

All the above issues highlight the complexity of factors underpinning why people choose to take a photographic holiday. Understanding the motivations of tourists is crucial to any operator in terms of product development and sales, but also understanding the wants and needs of tourists may contribute positively to a company's pre-tour organization and on-tour management and subsequent success of their holidays. In addition to understanding the consumer, consideration must also be given to the potential impacts that these types of holidays may have on particular destinations and their people.

Tourists' photographic behaviour and responsible tourism

Some of the destinations that play host to specialist photographic holidays may be in varying stages of development with many having fragile eco-systems. For example, the Antarctic, the Arctic, the Falkland Islands and Alaska have ecologically fragile environments that serve as excellent terrain for photographic opportunities. Given that the purpose of many of the photographic trips is to capture the wonders of the natural world on film, then ensuring the protection of the ecological environment as well as minimizing impacts on the socio-cultural environment, is essential to the long-term sustainability of this type of specialist holiday.

Many companies limit the numbers they take on each tour. However, with the growth and popularity of special interest holidays, the danger is not that group sizes will increase but rather that several providers of photographic tours will embark on the same destination at the same time. This may result in exceeding acceptable carrying capacities of particular sights and their attractions. Operators will need to liaise closely with local providers and remain vigilant in their organization and scheduling of itineraries in order to minimize any undue strain on the natural environment or negative impact on the indigenous populations.

In terms of photography and socio-cultural impacts, the photographic behaviour of tourists has stirred debates regarding what is and what is not appropriate for tourists to photograph; particularly in relation to indigenous people (Scharwtz, 1996; Human, 1999; Sturken and Cartwright, 2001; Wearing and Wearing, 2001). According to Teymur (1993) the locals may begin to see themselves in terms of how they are represented by the tourism industry. Such a view would benefit from further research to establish whether and to what extent this may occur. Some of the ethical issues arising from taking pictures while travelling are detailed in Table 1.3.

Other cultural issues that need to be carefully understood while on tour include those of prohibited photography, some of which include military sights, religious

Table 1.3 A photographic code of conduct

Appropriate photography	• Be sensitive to the situation in which the photograph is being taken • Be aware of cultural values • Avoid religious ceremonies, taking pictures in temples and other private situations • Be aware of the intrusion of flashes in some circumstances
Seek permission	• It is polite to ask before taking someone's picture • Remember to say thank you
Respect people's wishes	• If someone objects, don't take the photograph • Some people believe that the camera steals the soul
Research the local do's and don'ts	• Read up about the local culture prior to travelling, especially attitudes towards photography • In Asia it is rude to touch someone on the head or step over their legs to get your photograph

Adapted from Young (2001: 62–63).

temples and shrines, and in some countries it is viewed as offensive to photograph women. The seriousness of these restrictions is highlighted by the 2003 incident in which a group of British 'plane spotting' tourists photographing airplanes were arrested on suspicion of espionage in Greece. Although these tourists were not part of an organized tour this incident highlights the need for tour companies to be aware of the laws and cultural differences of particular destinations, so as to avoid offence or contravening local and national laws.

One of the key management issues for operators and leaders of photographic holidays is to understand the environment that they are consuming and convey the local norms pertaining to sensitive photography appropriately. If tourists 'religiously' seek out and 'gaze' at sights already predetermined by the marketing of destinations, responsibility for this lies in the pre-consumption stage of tourism, in effect with the marketing of destinations. Good guidance and on-trip management, which to some extent is made easier by the relatively small group sizes, will go someway to alleviate any problems. The following case studies, based on interviews conducted with the owners of the companies, provide examples of good practice among providers of specialist photographic holidays.

Case study 1   Photoventures

Photoventures is a small UK-based company that offers specialist photographic holidays to a variety of worldwide destinations, including the United States, Africa, South America and India. Inspired by the interest they and others had for photography, Roger Reynolds and Peter Morss set up the business in 1999 and now organize and operate on average six trips per year. This in itself highlights the highly specialized nature of their holidays. The company also enjoys high levels of repeat business.

Essentially the tours entail taking people to places where opportunities to take photographs are maximized. While the tours do not necessarily entail the teaching of photography, Roger, Peter or both always lead the tours and participants are able to benefit from the wealth of photographic expertise that they can provide, although participants are encouraged to do their own photography, as the underlying philosophy is that people learn by doing. Participants on the tours have varied levels of photographic expertise, from beginners to professional experts in the field of photography; there is also a wide age range, from the youngest participant at age 17 to the oldest at age 82. However, people on the tours are typically those individuals in the upper age range who are retired, with both the disposable income and the time to engage in this type of holiday. Photoventures have more men than women touring with them and this suggests an interesting avenue of research in terms of the gender implications in the choice of photographic holidays.

Motivating factors for those participating in the tours are attributed to a general enjoyment of taking photographs. While acknowledging that some participants do lecture in photography and exhibit their work, Roger Reynolds believes that most people on the tours want to return from holiday with a record of their trip and a set of 'good' photographs taken by themselves. Tour participants are responsible for paying for their own flights; however, Photoventures will arrange the flight itineraries and advise customers who to contact to secure the flights. Participants are also responsible for arranging their own travel insurance.

As a small operator Photoventures is highly susceptible to external environmental factors. For example, in 2003 the company had to cancel tours to China and Alaska due to the SARS outbreak. Other operational and financial constraints for a company of this size include the limited number of participants that make up the tour groups and the financial outlay on advertising and marketing.

Limitations on the number of people accommodated on a tour are due in part to Photoventures' desire to enhance and maintain the personal service that their customers receive while on tour. The company also believes that maintaining a high ratio of tour guides to tour participants is essential to the efficient management and organization of the tours. Other constraints on group sizes are unique to particular holidays, for example Yellowstone numbers are dictated by the number of available seats on the snow coaches. Marketing and advertising are limited to periodic advertisements in the national press and specialist national magazines such as *Practical Photography*.

Photoventures maintain that reputation is everything to a small company as it generates repeat business and positive word of mouth. The organization of the trip is crucial to this reputation and tour itineraries are carefully planned and mapped, taking into account the particular desires of tour participants. Roger Reynolds believes that the structure and planning of the tours, with the ability to be flexible, is an essential planning ingredient. As he states: 'Photography is a funny thing . . . it happens in front of you. You can never plan all of it, and sometimes you've got to react to what's going on. If we're going somewhere and a photo opportunity appears we'll stop and do that.'

Managing customer expectations and communicating the unique elements of the tours are achieved by holding pre-tour meetings. The group meet up before the holiday and this contributes to embedding social relations between tour participants, thereby enhancing the degree of social interaction while on tour. Roger Reynolds believes that the success of a tour can be as much about the social dynamics of the group as it is about how a tour is organized.

Examples of tour prices: £1,500 for 17 days to Texas and £2,800 for a 19-day tour to China. Prices do not include flights. (www.photoventures.net)

Case study 2   Hosking Tours

Hosking Tours specialise in wildlife photographic holidays aimed at photographers who are specifically interested in photographing the nature and wildlife unique to particular destinations. Tours are organised to a diverse range of destinations worldwide, hosting an assorted variety of animals, birds, flora and fauna, for example Nambia, Kenya, Tanzania, the United States, Australia, the Falkland Islands, the Galapagos Islands and the Italian Alps. Tanzania and Kenya are among the most popular destinations. Most tours last two weeks, except European tours, which tend to be for one week.

Embracing all levels of photographic expertise, the company's customer profile is primarily made up of those people that are retired, with both the disposable income and the time to engage in this type of holiday. The company is marketed through the use of a strong client list and there are high levels of repeat bookings. The company has some participants that have worked their way through the entire range of available tours, and in some instances taken the same tour more than once. One client has travelled with the company to Tanzania six times. The company carries out a mail shot between two and four times a year with brochures and news-sheets advertising updates to their portfolio of holidays. Other, less frequent, forms of advertising include advertisements in specialist magazines, for example *Outdoor Photography* and *Travel Photography*.

As a specialist in the provision of nature and wildlife photographic holidays, Hosking Tours acknowledges the need for good planning and recognizes the ongoing challenges posed by the need to minimize the potentially negative environmental impacts that any form of tourism may generate. Curtailing the number of participants that the company takes on each tour is paramount to their operation. The company considers a group size of nine to be quite large for a photographic tour and more than one guide would often lead this size of group. While the company does not issue a formal code of conduct to its clientele, the expertise and knowledge of the group leaders and guides are an important element in encouraging responsible behaviour among the participants. The particular 'do's and don'ts' pertaining to a destination are reiterated and emphasized while on tour and are important areas covered during the pre-tour meetings that take place prior to departure.

Pre-tour meetings are an integral part of the planning stage of the tours as they give the company an opportunity to cover procedural issues, what to expect at particular destinations and codes of conduct unique to the environment to be toured. Participants are also shown photographs of their forthcoming holiday. Such meetings help to alleviate last-minute stress in the airport and contribute towards the excitement and anticipation stage of the holiday; they are also seen as an excellent opportunity to meet fellow excursionists and develop some elements of social interaction prior to the holiday. Hosking Tours embrace advancements in technology and are experiencing a greater use of digital technology, both in the cameras that they use, and in those that many of their customers use. The pre-tour meetings provide a forum for questions and discussions on such topics as technical requirements and photographic equipment and suitable tour clothing. These meetings are viewed as an excellent opportunity for Hosking Tours to assess individual desires and expectations, particularly in terms of the types of photographs sought.

As well as encouraging high levels of social interaction both pre-tour and on-tour, the company provides opportunities for participants to meet up after their holiday. Being thus organized as a social activity, 'post tour reunions', it offers opportunities for participants to meet again, to reminisce and to network. They also provide the company with a marketing opportunity for future business. Participants bring around 30 slides or prints of their holiday and a slide show is held to view and discuss all the visual memoirs from the trip.

Prices of tours are in the region of £875 for 8 days to Cyprus and £3,416 for a 19 day tour to Galapagos. Prices do not include flights. (www.hosking-tours.co.uk)

Final considerations

The market for specialized photographic tours, while not transparently conveyed, is without doubt a significant one. Such holidays cover a broad spectrum of activities and operate in a variety of destinations renowned for their unique photographic opportunities. Many destinations may be defined as exotic with some environments having fragile eco-systems. Thus the need to curtail group sizes, coupled with the ensuing high operating costs, necessitates a purchase price which appears to be endemic for this type of holiday. Key to the successful management and operation of the tours is to recognize and minimize any potential environmental and socio-cultural impacts that the destinations may incur.

While it is clear that providing unique photographic opportunities is a key aspect of specialist photographic tours, there appears to be limited research into consumer motivations for participating in this type of holiday. Investigating some of the complex reasons why people take photographs on holiday in general may offer some insight in this area.

References

Bourdieu, P. (1990) *Photography, A Middle-brow Art*. Cambridge: Polity Press.

Chalfen, R.M. (1979) Photography's role in tourism. Some unexplored relationships. *Annals of Tourism Research*, 6, 435–447.

Cohen E., Nir, Y. and Almogor, U. (1992) Stranger-local interaction in photography. *Annals of Tourism Research*, 19, 213–233.

Crawshaw, C. and Urry, J. (1997) Tourism and the photographic eye. In C. Rojek, and J. Urry (eds) *Touring Cultures: Transformations of Travel and Theory*. London: Routledge.

Derret, R. (2001) Special interest tourism: starting with the individual. In N. Douglas, N. Douglas, and R. Derett (eds) *Special Interest Tourism*. Australia: Wiley.

Edensor, T. (1998) *Tourists at the Taj: Performance and Meaning at a Symbolic Site*. London, Routledge.

Flusser, V. (2000) *Towards a Philosophy of Photography*. London: Reaktion Books.

Franklin, A. (2003) *Tourism: an Introduction*. London: Sage.

Garlick, S. (2002) Revealing the unseen: tourism, art and photography. *Cultural Studies*, 16(2), 289–305.

Human, B. (1999) Kodachrome icons: photography, place and theft of identity. *International Journal of Contemporary Hospitality Management*, 11(2/3), 80–84.

Joseph Van Os (2003) Photo Safaris, Worldwide Photographic Tours brochure.

Key Note (1999) Camcorders and cameras, September.

Light and Land (2003) Landscape and Wildlife Photographic Tours brochure.
Markwell, K. (1997) Dimensions of photography in a nature-based tour. *Annals of Tourism Research*, 24(1), 131–155.
Mintel (2002) Special Interest Holidays, *Leisure Intelligence*, November.
Mowforth, M. and Munt, I. (1998) *Tourism and Sustainability; new tourism in the Third World*. London: Routledge.
Osborne, P.D. (2000) *Travelling Light, Photography, Travel and Visual Culture*. Manchester University Press.
Redfoot, D.L. (1984) Touristic authenticity, touristic angst, and modern reality. *Qualitative Sociology*, 7(4), Winter.
Schwartz, J.M. (1996) The geography lesson: photographs and the construction of imaginative geographies. *Journal of Historical Geography*, 22(1), 16–45.
Slater, D. (1999) Marketing mass photography. In J. Evans and S. Hall (eds) *Visual Culture: the reader*. London: Sage.
Sontag, S. (1977) *On Photography*. London: Penguin Books.
Sturken, M. and Cartwright, L. (2001) *Practices of Looking: an introduction to visual culture*. Oxford: Oxford University Press.
Teymur, N. (1993) 'Photourism' – or, the social epistemology of photography in tourism'. *Tourism In Focus*, 6, 6, 16.
Todd, S. (2001) Self-concept: a tourism application. *Journal of Consumer Behaviour*, 1(2), 184–196.
Turner, V. and Turner, E. (1978) *Image and Pilgrimage in Christian Culture*. Oxford: Blackwell.
Urry, J (2002[1990]) *The Tourist Gaze* (2nd edn). London: Sage.
Urry, J. (1995) *Consuming Places*. London: Routledge.
Wang, N. (2000) *Tourism and Modernity: A Sociological Analysis*. Oxford: Pergamon.
Wearing, S. and Wearing, B. (2001) Conceptualising the selves of tourism. *Leisure Studies*, 20, 143–159.
Young, L. (2001) Picture this. *Being There*, Tourism Concern, Summer.

Questions

1 Discuss what you consider to be the key operational issues involved in the organization and delivery of specialized photographic holidays.
2 Explore the way in which the taking of holiday photographs may impact on the people and places photographed.

Websites

www.lightandland.co.uk
www.photosafaris.com
www.lakelandphotohols.com

2

Geotourism
Appreciating the deep time of landscapes

Thomas A. Hose

Introduction

To geologists the UK is a 'world by itself' for its:

> ... scenery embodies, at a very small scale, almost all the rock types and landscape features found in countries of considerably greater extent. Its mountains are not of great height nor its rivers of great length, but it is impossible to travel many kilometres without crossing a geological boundary, and it is this irregular juxtaposition of contrasting rocks that gives British scenery its remarkable variety (Whittow, 1992: 1).

Its geodiversity within its small area is unparalleled anywhere else. It bears physical witness to long vanished oceans and seas, long extinct and much-decayed volcanoes, together with ancient and now much worn down mountain chains. Two-thirds of Earth history, some three billion years, is represented within its rocks giving a major advantage in geology's study through the unrivalled access to a broad range of rock types and settings, and one of the most complete and nearly continuous records of life on Earth. This includes some of the earliest and most primitive life forms as well as the most advanced forms such as dinosaurs. Its fossils are the longest and most intensively researched in the world, resulting in a legacy of scientific type and figured material, much dating from the nineteenth century, in museum and university collections. Consequently, much nineteenth century progress in geology was achieved in the UK and numerous of its geosites are 'type areas' for rocks, fossils and minerals, or are standard reference sections for the geological column. Its rocks enclose the ores, fluxes, fuels and building materials that contributed to momentous events in UK and world industrial history. Its geosites range from natural exposures such as caves and cliffs to artificial exposures like quarries, railway and road cuttings. New and internationally significant fossil discoveries are regularly unearthed and this should continue, provided its geosites are protected. It is the justification and promotion of their protection that prompted the 1990s development of geotourism as a form of niche tourism.

The geology-based tourism context

Geotourism, if not named as such (see Jenkins, 1992) has been considered a form of 'special interest tourism', an actively growing tourism market. It has some overlap with 'eco-tourism', 'sustainable tourism' and 'alternative tourism' and potentially much overlap with 'educational travel', 'environmental', 'nature-based' and 'heritage' tourism. The geotourism concept (Hose, 1995) was developed and promoted from the early 1990s onwards. The first attempts to define geotourism were by Hose who was originally working on aspects of interpretative provision at geological (and geomorphological) sites – or 'geosites'; for example:

> The provision of interpretive and service facilities to enable tourists to acquire knowledge and understanding of the geology and geomorphology of a site (including its contribution to the development of the Earth sciences) beyond the level of mere aesthetic appreciation (Hose, 1995: 17).

In Malaysia, 'tourism geology' is a branch of applied geology potentially able to support ecotourism's growth and make geoconservation as important as bioconservation (Komoo, 1997: 2973). Geotourism encompasses the examination and understanding of the physical basis of geosites, together with their interpretative media and promotion – a traditional resource focus. It also encompasses the life, work, publications, notes and artwork, correspondence, diaries, collections, workplaces, residences and even the final resting places of geoscientists – as a strong human interest component. At its heart is the process of recognizing and giving broader meaning, to ensure their protection and conservation, of geosites (Hose, 1997). The term gained UK-wide recognition with the first national conference in Belfast in 1998. Since little specialist equipment is required to examine geosites, people are often attracted to geotourism by the sheer joy of casual collecting. Geotourism at the participant level is 'recreational geology'. It could extend the tourism season in suitable, especially coastal, areas.

An interpretative strategy, such as geotourism, should generate the public pressure required for the promotion and protection of the UK's 'geoheritage'. Such a strategy depends upon identifying and promoting its physical basis, knowing and understanding its users and developing effective interpretative materials. Unfortunately, geology's achievements and societal value are little understood and unappreciated by those outside of the discipline. Consequently, many significant geosites and collections in museums, universities and libraries (where the importance of geology archives as social and historical evidence are often overlooked) – perhaps best referred to as the 'geoheritage' – have been or could soon be lost. There is very limited public awareness of any need to conserve geosites and their associated collections. Hence, the sense of loss if an important geosite was lost would, unlike an orchid-rich meadow or a beech wood, be minimal because community value is not ascribed to them. One of the original reasons for developing geotourism was to promote and fund 'geoconservation': 'The dynamic preservation and maintenance of geosites, together with their associated collections'. It is somewhat interchangeable with 'Earth heritage conservation', 'Earth science conservation', 'geological conservation' and 'geological site conservation'. Geoconservation is about husbandry – much of the value of geosites is in the availability of, and access to, specimens and the appearance of the *in situ* rocks; they benefit from limited disturbance, restricted collecting and removal of rock and soil debris. In providing for, and promoting such geosites and collections to geotourists, caution is required, for there is a difference between informing people about geosites to encourage visits and support for their conservation and sheer exploitation of a finite resource for commercial gain. Fortunately, there is little conflict between geoconservation and tourism promotion. Indeed, there is much to commend geotourism's inclusion within sustainable tourism schemes.

This UK-based account employs 'geosites' for delimited areas of geological or geomorphological interest and recognizes both:

Primary Geosites having geological/geomorphologic features, either naturally or artificially and generally permanently exposed, within a delimited outdoor area that are at least locally significant for their scientific, educational or interpretative value.

And (focuses on):

Secondary Geosites having some feature(s) and/or item(s), within or on a structure or delimited area, of at least local significance to the history, development, presentation or interpretation of geology or geomorphology.

The latter encompasses some 300 museum geology collections, exhibitions, university geology departments and libraries and their collections of original papers, heritage, visitor and tourist centres and their displays, geologists' residences, memorials and commemorative plaques and graves. Often geological collections were created by eminent geologists; they are important in the subject's history. This wealth of material exists because geology is an observational science.

Geotourism and environmental interpretation

Geotourism has marked societal value, for geology contextualizes issues of self and place within the cosmos, together with pressing present-day issues such as global climate change and finite resource management. The presentation of geosites can exemplify such issues. Geosites such as the black shale cliffs on Dorset's coast indicate past cyclic toxic marine events. Geosites such as raised beaches and relict sea cliffs, as seen in Dorset, record geologically recent higher sea-levels. Significantly, for geotourism, it is argued that: 'Science in fact is a cultural exercise and the strong links between geological features and the development of the science, raises the status of sites important in the history of the geology, to a status of cultural importance' (Page, 1998: 206). Hence, the potential to promote geosites for their scientific and socio-cultural significance needs exploring and developing by those concerned with their conservation. Geotourism is essentially a geology-focused development of environmental interpretation: 'The art of explaining the meaning and significance of sites visited by the public' (Badman, 1994: 429). Interpretation should not be confused with either education or short-term knowledge acquisition. Although both involve information exchange the former is based upon revelation; consequently it involves translating the technical language of a natural science into vocabulary and ideas – in a way that is entertaining and interesting – that non-specialists can readily understand. The development of heritage tourism has been a positive agent in interpretation's development, drawing upon a spectrum of USA-pioneered activities aimed at making heritage sites meaningful to visitors through stimulating and arousing their imagination and curiosity; it is aimed at those for whom informal learning about, and appreciation of, the past are important leisure activities. Unfortunately, much heritage tourism provision is characterized by the fictionalization of events by promoting an idealized past. Even at industrial history sites the emphasis is often on rural settings and close-knit working-class communities – somewhat at odds with attempts to conserve the extractive industry heritage with its 'unsightly' spoil tips and slag heaps. Many geosites, as once for industrial history sites, are unwelcome eyesores from a past industrial legacy in the post-modern world – to be remodelled/removed at the earliest opportunity – as communities reinterpret, reinvent and re-present their past. This stems from a lack of recognition that it was the fruits of geological discovery and exploitation that underpinned the world's first industrial economy on which that heritage, now so widely admired, conserved, managed, interpreted and promoted, depended for its very existence. The demise of the coal industry from the late 1980s and the virtual abandonment of metalliferous mining significantly contributed to the dereliction associated with mining areas. Concomitantly, local government and development agency involvement and expenditure on land reclamation and amenity landscaping accelerated; the justification being the removal of the blight of industrial dereliction and the return of the land to agriculture and amenity usage, thus masking and burying the old industrial landscapes even when: '... "conservation-friendly" solutions to the technical problems of conserving faces within landfill schemes do exist, changes to existing landfill designs are viewed with apprehension by the industry because of technical difficulties, and the costs involved in lost tipping space' (Wright, 1993: 18).

There are also threats from coastal and river flood defences along with major road construction, exacerbated by ignorance of planners, politicians and some-times even by thoughtless geologists. Another threat is the unregulated commercial collection, especially by overseas collectors raiding classic sites, of fossils and minerals. However, the legal commercial extraction and sale of specimens has a long history; the major museum collections contain material bought from commercial collectors and dealers. Such fossils are a real tourist attraction and: "Fossils had been collected at sundry localities for sale to visitors in the latter part of the eighteenth century, especially at Lyme Regis and Charmouth" (Woodward, 1907: 115). Geotourism aims to reduce the impact of these threats by combating the ignorance of both the general public and decision-makers, and by re-educating collectors and geologists.

The Dorset and East Devon coast

The Dorset and East Devon coast is a popular holiday destination, especially for visitors from Greater London and south-east England, because of its combination of unspoilt dramatic coastline with excellent beaches, gentle country walks with superb views, picturesque villages and the abundance and diversity of wildlife habitats, coupled with a range of visitor attractions. Dorset's coast alone attracts some 16 million visitors annually; tourism is its largest industry, employing some 37,000 persons. Most tourism arrivals are in the summer months, although there is an increasing out-of-season educational (some 200,000 annual visits) and niche tourism market. Much of the coast and its hinterland are within an Area of Outstanding Natural Beauty, and the West Dorset Heritage Coast and the Purbeck Heritage Coast. There are several biological and geological Sites of Special Scientific Interest (SSSIs), together with major nature reserves including the Chesil Bank and Fleet Nature Reserve and the Purbeck Marine Wildlife Reserve at Kimmeridge Bay. Black Ven, near Lyme Regis, is Europe's largest and most active coastal landslip. The area around Lulworth Cove is one of Europe's classic sites of coastal erosion. Chesil Beach is one of Europe's classic sites of coastal deposition. The UK's and western Europe's only on-shore oil field is at Wytch Farm near Poole. The international significance of the Dorset and east Devon coast to geology and geomorphology, the physical basis of geotourism, was underlined by the initial 1994 proposal for UNESCO World Heritage status: '...for its classic Jurassic-Cretaceous sequences and coastal geomorphology. If we consider that geological World Heritage Sites currently include the Grand Canyon, the Hawaiian volcanoes and Yosemite National Park, then we can begin to see the importance of this stretch of the coastline' (Anon, 1994: 4).

Subsequently, the *Draft Dorset Coast Strategy* (Anon, 1998) envisioned that by the middle of the twenty-first century there would be:

- Continued access to a full range of Dorset's Jurassic geology;
- World Heritage Status secured for the coast's geology;
- Stronger and more robust tourist economies in Weymouth, Lyme Regis and Swanage;
- More environmentally based niche tourism and recreation business;
- Better information and interpretation about the coast;
- Accepted arrangements to promote responsible fossil collecting.

Almost concomitantly, the Jurassic Coast Project was established as a 3-year feasibility study aiming to: '...promote people's understanding and enjoyment of the coast and to deliver economic benefit to areas that have lost jobs through cuts in the defence industry' (Edmonds, 2000: 67). The Project developed with the

realisation that interpretative provision was fragmented across several organisations and sites without any real focus of an underpinning theme or storyline. It was
also intended: '...to develop special interest "niche" tourism that will attract
people who will visit during the out of season "shoulder months" and use local
facilities' (Edmonds, 2000: 67). All of these developments and strategies culminated
in the publication of the UNESCO bid document (Anon, 2000), which included
major claims for the quality of the area's geology, and some limited mention of
its geomorphology, together with promoting the relatively unspoilt nature of
the coastal belt. World heritage recognition was achieved on 13 December 2001.
This has affected the nature and focus of interpretative provision since public
education is a required component of continued World Heritage recognition.
Some 155 kilometres of coast, stretching from Exmouth in East Devon to near
Old Harry Rocks in Dorset and representing about 185 million years of Earth
history, are now the renewed focus of geotourism provision and this is best
exemplified in the area around Lyme Regis.

The Lyme Regis area has been significant in geology's development as a formal
science and its exploitation for commercial gain because of the concentration
of well-preserved, especially large reptile, fossils in the local rocks (see McGowan,
1991). These have led to a flourishing and continuing cottage industry supplying
important public and private collections at home and overseas, as well as the
general tourist gift market, with prepared fossils. For 250 years it has been a centre
of commercial fossil collecting and preparation; it claims to be the British
birthplace of this activity. Lyme Regis and Charmouth were well known in
the nineteenth century for their skilled commercial fossil collectors and preparators.
Mary Anning is especially famous for her work on fossil reptiles. Her modern
successors continue to unearth large ammonites, and spectacular marine reptiles
and offer them for sale locally and at international fossil fairs.

Surprisingly, there is little outdoor interpretative provision on the local geology.
Given the known location of Mary Anning's 'Fossil Depot', it is surprising that
no commemorative plaque adorns any adjacent building, although some mention of
her is made on a town map plaque affixed to road retaining wall. On the site of
the mid-1990s' sea defence and sewerage system are three interpretative
panels installed in 1996. They virtually ignore geology, focusing on local history
and natural history. Visits to the two fossil shops, with much local and some
imported specimens on sale along with a range of geology-focused giftware
and souvenirs, are instructive for fossil collectors. Both produce and retail a variety
of geology-focused publications ranging from postcards to fossil maps and an
account of Mary Anning. Equally interesting are visits to the Philpot Museum
and Dinosaurland. Whereas the Philpot is in a purpose-built (1901) museum
building, Dinosaurland is within a converted eighteenth-century chapel building.

The Philpot Museum, partly built over the site of Mary Anning's 'Fossil Depot',
occupies a prominent seafront position overlooking the very rocks from which
many of the spectacular Victorian large reptilian finds were excavated. The
Museum surprisingly has no geological collections of any significance; its most
prized such asset is an original Mary Anning geology hammer. The Museum also
houses a small collection of personalia associated with geologists who worked
around Lyme Regis in the nineteenth and early twentieth centuries. Its present
graphics-rich display scheme, completed in 1999, replaced a fossil-rich late-1980s'
display; many of the spectacular fossils that were on loan for the latter went to

Dinosaurland. Although the displays were and are focused on geology, geomorphology, the history of geology and local history, the new displays have an increased emphasis on social history, mirroring the general UK decline in museum geology; an entire gallery is devoted to Mary Anning. There are no attempts to reconstruct the past geological environment in the geology gallery – a rather old-fashioned descriptive type. The fabric of the building is the responsibility of the West Dorset District Council and the Museum is operated as a charitable trust. Its shop has little on sale about the local geology, but is strong on general giftware. The Museum is open from April to September; admission is by a moderate charge. Most of its visitors are tourists, with very few geologists, rather than town and local residents.

Dinosaurland opened in 1989, but its content or original material is chiefly non-dinosaur superb quality, and sometimes rare, marine reptiles and ammonites. The displays include numerous high-quality fossils and a series of displays on the history of life. Not all of the fossils on display were sourced from the local area. The quality of the interpretative materials is limited and the execution of graphical and three-dimensional display components is somewhat basic. Alongside the geological material, and reminiscent of the nineteenth-century approach to geology and natural history displays, is a small living collection of birds, reptiles and small mammals. Being a commercial venture the shop is a prominent facility. It is well stocked with a great variety of generally geology-focused items, especially high-quality prepared fossil material. Guided fossil walks are arranged by the attraction.

The Lyme Regis geotourism provision formed part of a major mid-1990s geotourism study (Hose, 2003). This concluded that much of the interpretative materials at the Philpot Museum and Dinosaurland mainly had reading ages of 14 to 18 years and that the text passages were very lengthy – generally unsuitable for the typical casual visitor and parties with children.

The huge popularity of fossil hunting around Lyme Regis is obvious during and outside of the holiday season. However, residents have long considered such activity environmentally detrimental. These concerns were addressed by a 1982 Public Inquiry in Charmouth that concluded the effects of natural erosion were far more significant than anything done by collectors. Proposals to enact byelaws to restrict and in some cases prohibit collecting foundered on the recognition that they would be impossible to either police or enforce. However, a positive conservation approach emerged to provide interpretative facilities to promote safe collecting practices and develop visitors' awareness of the area's geological and wildlife significance; subsequently, the Charmouth Heritage Coast Centre opened in 1985. Additionally, interpretative outdoor panels on geology, topography and natural history were erected along the coast and in the car park adjacent to the Centre. The Centre is open and free to the public from May to September and during the autumn school half-term. Outside of these times, the Centre's full-time warden leads guided walks for pre-booked parties. The Centre is on the first floor of a Victorian stone-built cement factory; underneath are a commercially operated cafe, a geology shop and a general souvenir shop. The Centre is managed as a charitable trust and is funded by grants from various governmental and voluntary sector conservation agencies, donations, fees and retail income. Its first warden was employed in 1986. Its interpretative facilities, mainly installed in 1986 (but partly refurbished in 1999), are a mixture of traditional panels, specimen cases and 'hands-on' facilities. Although predominantly on geology, there is also information on local history, weather and wildlife. An obvious, and much used feature is a 'hands-on' display with examples of local rocks and fossils. The other obvious geology display is a large panorama with associated cases of fossils. There is also a small cold salt-water aquarium. In 1993 an audio-visual theatre was opened showing a populist slide-tape presentation on the local fossils; it attracts about 30% of the Centre's visitors. The Centre has a fairly well-stocked shop and enquiry desk. The warden also provides a free fossil identification service and leads, for a reasonable fee, guided geology walks. About 5% of the Centre's visitors go on the guided walks. From the late 1990s, the Centre's role has centred on general countryside and marine conservation, a diminution of its central role in local geological interpretative provision, just as has happened at the Philpot Museum. The Centre's education work is mainly for primary schools. During the 1990s, it experienced a rapid growth in visitor numbers from some 35,000 to 50,000.

The case study area and the implications for geotourism

These visitors and the Centre's interpretative provision were part of a major geotourism study and audit in the mid-1990s' (Hose, 2003; and see Page et al., 1996), which found that for visitors:

1 Two-thirds were first-time arrivals and many were casual arrivals; that is, their visit was unplanned on the day.
2 About two-thirds arrived in family groups and about one-quarter (mainly older people) arrived alone or in couples.
3 Almost half were aged 30-44 years and almost as many were aged 45-64 years. This, together with the party size data, reflects two main distinct types of visitor:

- families with young children (with parents generally under 40 years of age);
- mature couples;
- additionally, a minor or sub-group is mature couples with children (often their grandchildren).

4 There was an almost equal split between minimum schooling, 'A'-level and tertiary levels of visitors' initial education study. Significantly, and unlike many similar sites, one-third had studied geology to some level; indeed, a fifth were hobby geologists. Clearly, for some a real interest in geology prompted their visit.

Within the Centre, much visitor activity, especially for the children, focused on the handling section. Graphic panels often attracted only cursory attention. Texts within the display elements and associated publications had mainly reading ages of 12 to 16 years (slightly too high for the casual reader) in generally short text blocks. The adjacent outdoor interpretative panels' usage was greatest in the afternoon, when it was cooler, and at high tide. The mean time visitors spent viewing the panels of just over a minute roughly equated to the minimum time required to read and comprehend the basics of the geology panel's contents; but relatively few visitors read the geology panel compared to the other panels.

Visitors on the guided walks tended to be in family groups or parties with primary school age children. The bulk of retail purchases were inexpensive themed souvenirs such as postcards, pens, pencils, pencil sharpeners and erasers. Visitors were reluctant to purchase even inexpensive geological publications; they were much browsed but not purchased, suggesting attention needs to be paid to their graphics, textual style and content.

Overall, the study found that party size and age characteristics identified two target audiences for geotourism provision:

- families with young children;
- mature couples.

The former are likely, because of the constraints imposed by the school calendar, to visit only during the traditional holiday period as part of an extended holiday. However, the latter are potentially, particularly with the increasing availability of short-break holidays, the market for out-of-season geotourism breaks. Both groups benefit from appropriate interpretative provision such as 'hands on' activities and panels, but especially guided walks and the opportunity to 'meet with an expert'. However, when the visitor characteristics are compared with the nature and content of much of the interpretative provision, especially at Lyme Regis, there is an evident mismatch. Clearly greater attention needs to be paid to the design and location of geology-focused panels and publications (see: Hose, 1999; Hose, 2000).

Final considerations

The overall importance of the Lyme Regis area to any account of UK geotourism and geoconservation is its unique place in the development of British geology during the nineteenth century and its continued popularity with geology students and amateur fossil collectors. The way in which geology, and geomorphology, are treated – especially in relation to interpretative provision – at such a prime location is indicative of the general national state and status of geotourism and geoconservation.

Geotourism is a developing form of niche tourism that has yet to reach its full tourism market potential because much of its current provision only partly meets the needs of geotourists. There is a reduction at traditional venues of geology-focused displays and publications in favour of local and social history displays and because of its limited promotion. Geotourism has a potential role in the regeneration of suitable coastal resorts, especially in extending the nature and timing of tourism provision; at such locations, it has limited environmental impact and can be promoted as clearly sustainable tourism because it supports geoconservation.

References

Anon (1994) *The Dorset Coast Today*. Dorchester: Dorset County Council.
Anon (1998) *Draft Dorset Coast Strategy*. Dorchester: Dorset Coast Forum/Dorset County Council.

Anon (2000) *Nomination of the Dorset and East Devon Coast for Inclusion in the World Heritage List.* Dorchester: Dorset County Council.

Badman, T. (1994) Interpreting earth science sites for the public. In D. O'Halloran, C. Green, M. Harley, M. Stanley and J. Knill (eds) *Geological and Landscape Conservation.* London: Geological Society, pp. 429–432.

Edmonds, R.P.H. (2000) Geology and geo-tourism – Dorset RIGS within a county wide strategy. In P.G. Oliver (ed.) *Proceedings of the Second UK RIGS Conference, Worcester, 1999.* Worcester: Worcester University College, pp. 67–70.

Hose, T.A. (1995) Selling the story of Britain's stone, *Environmental Interpretation*, 10(2), 16–17.

Hose, T.A. (1997) Geotourism – selling the earth to Europe. In P.G. Marinos, *et al.* (eds) *Engineering Geology and the Environment.* Rotterdam: A.A. Balkema, pp. 2955–2960.

Hose, T.A. (1999) How was it for you? – Matching geologic site media to audiences. In P.G. Oliver (ed.) *Proceedings of the First UK RIGS Conference.* Worcester: Worcester University College, pp. 117–144.

Hose, T.A. (2000) Rocks, rudists and writings: an examination of populist geosite literature. In A. Addison (ed.) *Proceedings of the Third UK RIGS Annual Conference: Geoconservation in Action.* Worksworth: UKRIGS, pp. 39–62.

Hose, T.A. (2003) Geotourism in England: a two-region case study analysis. Unpublished PHD thesis, University of Birmingham.

Hose, T.A. (2003) The Lyme Regis Geotourism Provison. Unpublished mid-1990s Geotourism Study.

Jenkins, J.M. (1992). Fossickers and rockhounds in northern New South Wales. In B. Weiler and C. M. Hall (eds) *Special Interest Tourism.* London: Belhaven Press, pp. 129–140.

Komoo, I. (1997) Conservation geology: A case for the ecotourism industry of Malaysia. In P.G. Marinos, G.C. Koukis, G.C. Tsiambaos and G.C. Stournas (eds) *Engineering Geology and the Environment.* Rotterdam, Netherlands: Balkema, pp. 2969–2973.

McGowan, C. (1991) Chapter 8 – Not wholly a fish. In *Dinosaurs, Spitfires, and Sea Dragons.* Harvard: Harvard University Press, pp. 185–199.

Page, K.N., Keene, P., Edmonds, R.P.H. and Hose, T.A. (1996) *Research Report No. 176: Earth Heritage Site Interpretation in England: A review of principle techniques with case studies.* Peterborough: English Nature.

Page, K.N. (1998) England's earth heritage resource – an asset for everyone. In J. Hooke (ed.) *Coastal Defence and Earth Science Conservation.* London: Geological Society, pp. 196–209.

Whittow, J. (1992) *Geology and Scenery in Britain.* London: Chapman & Hall.

Woodward, H.B. (1907) *The History of the Geological Society of London.* London: Geological Society.

Wright, R. (1993) Conservation and landfill – a question of timing. *Earth Science Conservation*, 32, 18–19.

Questions

1 Why is the UK, and Lyme Regis in particular, so well placed to develop and promote geotourism?

2 How can geotourism, which might initially appear to be solely an exploitive activity, be justified as a niche form of sustainable tourism?

Further reading

Brunsden, D. (ed.) (2003) *The Official Guide to the Jurassic Coast – Dorset and East Devon's World Heritage Coast: A Walk Through Time.* Wareham: Coastal Publishing.

Hose, T.A. (1998) Selling coastal geology to visitors. In Hook, J. (ed.) *Coastal Defence and Earth Science Conservation.* London: Geological Society, pp. 178–195.

Hose, T.A. (2000) European geotourism – geological interpretation and geoconservation promotion for tourists. In D. Barretino, W.A.P. Wimbledon and E. Gallego (eds) *Geological Heritage: Its Conservation and Management*. Madrid: Sociedad Geologica de Espana/Instituto Technologico GeoMinero de Espana/ProGEO.

Muir, R. (1993) *The Coastlines of Britain*. London: Macmillan.

Weiler, B. and Hall, C.M. (eds) (1992) *Special Interest Tourism*. London: Belhaven Press.

3

Youth tourism
Finally coming of age?

Greg Richards and Julie Wilson

Introduction

Youth travel has long been seen as the poor relation of international tourism, but the growing travel lust and spending power of young people has recently been creating more attention for this market. This chapter focuses on various aspects of youth travel, starting with a brief review of recent studies on the topic before presenting a case study of student travel based on empirical research into long haul international travel by students from eight origin countries. The research indicates that youth tourism is breaking free of former stereotypes, presenting a picture of relatively experienced, adventurous travellers who are keen to experience many facets of the destinations they visit. The chapter closes with a discussion of the various management implications of this growth market.

The niche context

The increased commercial, political and academic interest in young travellers has stimulated a wide range of studies in recent years. Although 'student travel' may be relatively easy to define, there is little agreement concerning the definition of 'youth tourism' (ATI, 1995). Statistical definitions, such as that of the World Tourism Organization (WTO) generally include all travel by young people aged between 15 and 29 years (e.g. WTO, 1991), although a more recent WTO study (2002) used 'less than 25 years' as the cut-off point, while many smaller-scale studies adopt an upper age limit of 26 (Horak and Weber, 2000).

In 1995, the European Travel Commission published a study specifically dedicated to Europe's youth travel market covering 26 countries (ATI, 1995). This study was commissioned in response to a perceived neglect of the market both by the mainstream travel industry and by government authorities. It concluded that the 15 to 26 age group took around 80 million trips and made 100 million border crossings per year, representing a fifth of all international trips and around a quarter of all holiday travel (Horak and Weber, 2000). In a study of outbound travel of German, British and French young people, WTO (2002) stated that outbound youth tourism (age 15 to 25) accounted for 17% of all international trips in these markets in 2000, concluding that more and more young people are travelling abroad on holiday, to visit friends and to study, as well as for business.

This growth has flown in the face of the pessimistic forecasts for a static or even declining market in the mid-1990s. These were based on a fall in European-originating youth travel in the early 1990s combined with a concern that changes in demographic structures would lead to a substantial reduction in the number of young people (see Jefferson, 1991). However, the 1995 ATI report also presented four major growth factors for the market at that time in an 'optimistic scenario' (1995, 40) and indeed these factors have largely held true:

1 Changing perceptions of social class boundaries (which has increased access to various tourism and travel opportunities that were previously only available to higher-class travellers).
2 An increasing percentage of young people in full-time education (including the widening of access to tertiary level education establishments).
3 Levels of youth unemployment were predicted to drop.
4 A growing importance of parental incomes.

Various additional growth factors have emerged more recently that perhaps were not foreseen at that time, such as the rise of budget/low cost airlines, more flexible employment modes, and the growth of the student travel industry. All of these factors have almost certainly contributed to the growth since the mid-1990s, giving an added impulse to youth and student travel worldwide, and also stimulating more research interest in this field.

More recently, a lot of attention has been focused on the growth of 'backpacker' tourism, including the 'gap year' (e.g. Simpson, 2003) and Big Overseas Experience, or 'OE' phenomena (e.g. Bell, 2002) and this has spawned a number of surveys at national level, particularly in Australia and New Zealand (e.g. Bureau of Tourism Research, 2000). There are a growing number of academic studies on backpackers as well, which tend to emphasize the position of backpackers as 'anti-tourists' or nomadic propagators of global youth culture (Richards and Wilson, 2004a). Desforges (1998), for example, looked at global representations and local identities in youth travel, signalling a developing interest in youth and student mobility as a global postmodern phenomenon.

However, more traditional youth markets have also grown, such as 'four s' tourism in beach-oriented destinations (Clarke, 1992); a growth which was acknowledged in claims that a third of youth holidays were beach-oriented (ATI, 1995). But the youth and student market is clearly also diversifying away from traditional beach-oriented experiences; for example, a study by Sellars (1998) observed a growth in young people taking holidays to pursue their interest in alternative and dance music subcultures, emphasizing the importance of niches within the overall youth market. This chapter considers one such important segment: student travel.

Case study: the student travel market

As far as youth tourism is concerned, student travel is probably the most significant single market segment, with growing demand and a global infrastructure of travel suppliers. The diverse range of suppliers in the worldwide student travel market is brought together in the International Student Travel Confederation (ISTC), which has been the umbrella organization for the sector for over half a century.

The ISTC has in recent years stimulated efforts to collect more structured information on the aspirations, motivations and activities of independent student travellers. The most recent of these was the ISTC/ATLAS Independent Traveller Survey, conducted in 2002 (Richards and Wilson, 2003). This survey revealed some of the major trends in this niche market, which are reviewed briefly here.

The data were collected using mailing lists provided by student travel company members of ISTC in Canada, Czech Republic, Hong Kong, Mexico, Slovenia, South Africa, Sweden and the UK. Forty-two different nationalities were represented in the sample of 2,300 respondents, emphasizing the mobility of the international student population (although the majority of respondents were nationals of these eight countries). Over 70% of these respondents were current students, although the fact that many ex-students were included in the survey indicated that many continue to use the services of the student travel industry after they have stopped studying. This is largely due to the replacement of course enrolment requirements by upper age limits, which in most cases are set at 26. Because large numbers of students graduate before they reach this age, they can continue to enjoy 'student' discounts for a period after their studies.

Not surprisingly, the respondents tended to have a high education level, but because they were still studying or at an early stage in their careers, they had relatively low incomes. Over half the respondents were earning less than $5,000 per annum. For many students this forces them to save for long periods prior to travel or to work during their trip. This tendency is confirmed by the rising number of 'working holiday visas' being issued by a number of major student travel destinations, most notably Australia and New Zealand.

In terms of describing their own travel style, student travellers tended not to see themselves as 'tourists', preferring instead to label themselves as 'backpackers' or more frequently as 'travellers'. Interestingly, analysis of travel styles by destination indicates that students were most likely to associate with the 'backpacker' label where the development of the backpacker industry is strongest (for example, within 'enclaves' of dedicated backpacker infrastructure in South East Asia, the Indian sub-continent and Australasia).

The most frequently expressed motivations for travel were to explore other cultures (83%), followed by excitement (74%) and increasing knowledge (69%) – demonstrating the desire to encounter 'different' people and places. A principal component analysis of motivations (including only those respondents that were currently students) indicated that there were four major factors underlying the travel motivations of students. These were: experience seeking, relaxation seeking, friendship/sociability and altruism (Richards and Wilson, 2004b). Those identifying themselves as 'backpackers' tended to be more 'experience seekers' looking for contact with their fellow travellers. Those identifying themselves as 'travellers' had more social motives and were more likely to be visiting friends and relatives during their trip. It was those that identified themselves as 'tourists' that were more likely to be looking for relaxation on their trip.

In spite of their relatively young chronological age, most of the respondents had a fair degree of previous travel experience. The average number of previous trips outside of their own world regions was six, with those aged over 26 averaging eight previous trips. Respondents had also visited many different world regions during these past trips.

The long trips taken by student travellers tended to be aimed at increasing the quantitative extent of travel experience. The average trip tended to include at least two different countries; and for more experienced travellers, the number of countries increased. Those travelling for longer visited more countries.

In terms of the destinations visited by student travellers, the overall distribution was not that different from global tourism in general, with Europe and North America being the leading regions visited on the last big trip taken. However, the destinations that were most popular with those calling themselves 'backpackers' were South East Asia, Australasia and South America. North America was the most popular destination with those calling themselves 'travellers'. Female students were more likely to be travelling in Western Europe, the Middle East and Central/Southern Africa while males were more likely to be travelling in Eastern Europe, North, Central and South America, China/Japan and South East Asia.

The dominance of 'travellers' and 'backpackers' had a clear influence on the choice of accommodation. The most popular forms of accommodation were visiting friends and relatives (41%) and backpacker hostels (32%). Backpacker hostels were particularly used in Australasia and South East Asia. The predominance of cheap or free accommodation is explained by the high average length of the main trip, which was over 60 days. Those calling themselves 'backpackers' travelled for longer (an average of 74 days). The longest duration trips were taken in Australasia (128 days), North America (90 days) and the Indian sub-continent (84 days) and the shortest duration trips were taken in Europe (34 days).

These relatively extensive travel patterns of student travellers contrasted with those of youth travellers in general. According to research conducted for the WTO (2002), youth travellers from the UK, France and Germany stay an average of 8 nights at the destination. Given the relatively long vacation periods still enjoyed by most students, it is not surprising that their travel patterns extend over greater time periods, but with lower per diem expenditure.

Long trips obviously place more emphasis on pre-trip planning. The main information sources used in planning the trip were the Internet (71%) and friends/family (70%). Guidebooks were used by 37% overall but were used far more by slightly older (over 26) travellers, more experienced travellers and those calling themselves 'backpackers'. Less experienced travellers relied more heavily on travel agents for information. In spite of the heavy use the of the Internet for information-gathering though, the majority of students still used travel agents to book their travel (65%), and the overall split between mainstream travel agents and specialist travel agents was more or less equal. However, those calling themselves 'backpackers' were significantly more likely to use specialist travel agencies (42%) and those calling themselves 'tourists' more likely to use mainstream travel agents (51%). With increasing age, they tended to prefer to make their own travel arrangements rather than using travel agencies.

The average travel booking lead time was 6 weeks, rising to 2 months for trips over four months in duration. This lead time was significantly longer for long haul and non-Western destinations. In contrast to the travel element of the journey, few travellers booked any accommodation in advance of their departure.

A 'travel career' (cf. Pearce, 1993) appears to be forming among the students surveyed, as the least experienced travellers were visiting the Westernized areas of Europe and North America but more experienced travellers tend to visit more 'challenging' destinations including South America, China/Japan and the Indian sub-continent. This suggests that many young travellers take their initial long trips in relatively 'easy', familiar or 'safe' destinations before striking out for more adventurous ones.

The relatively long duration tended to depress the average per diem spend to around US$20. However, the total average spend in the destination was high at US$1,200 per trip (not including travel costs). The average total spend was highest in Australasia, South America and South East Asia, and 'backpackers' spent the most overall on their trips (an average total spend of US$2,200) which is explained by their tendency to travel for even longer periods. Previously, youth and student travellers have often been seen as 'time rich, money poor' visitors, who are not as beneficial to the places they visit as other tourists. What this study highlights, however, is the fact that the major trips taken by young people are far from 'budget' holidays in terms of total spending. Relative to their incomes, young travellers spend a lot of money on travel, and will happily save and work to do so.

The most popular activities during the trip were visiting historic sites and monuments (77%), walking and trekking (76%) and more leisurely pursuits such as sitting in cafes/restaurants (72%) and shopping (72%). These activities seem to vary little from those of other tourists, and student backpackers, travellers and tourists had remarkably similar activity patterns, indicating that although the travel styles may be perceived as very different, the activities undertaken in the destination are often very similar. 'Backpackers' tended to do more of everything, which fits with their experience-seeking motivations. Given the long periods spent in the destination, however, there appeared to be intense periods of activity during the trip which were interspersed with periods of 'hanging out'.

The main benefit gained by students from travel was a thirst for more travel, implying that once students start travelling, they find it difficult to stop, underlining the importance of attracting young people early in their 'travel careers' as they are likely to remain avid travellers. Those who undertook more activities also felt they had gained more benefits from their travel.

The main information sources used during the trip were guidebooks (46%), and *Lonely Planet* was the most frequently used guidebook, particularly among those calling themselves 'backpackers', underlining its status as the 'Backpackers' Bible'. E-mail and the Internet were used frequently for keeping in touch 'on the road' (68%).

Management implications

The research indicates that youth and student travellers are experience seekers who travel for long periods in search of culture, adventure and relaxation. They already have a great deal of travel experience and often make repeat visits. Importantly, the total spend on their major trips is higher than for most other markets, even if the daily average spend tends to be lower. The potential is increased even further with the evidence that many young people and students are building a 'travel career': driven by this thirst for more travel, they expand their horizons by choosing increasingly challenging destinations as they become more experienced travellers. This 'development trajectory' indicates the need to develop new products to meet the demands of this market.

However, the youth and student market should not be viewed as a homogeneous group in terms of their style of travel and their motivations. The research in this chapter differentiated many characteristics of youth and student travellers according to how they define their style of travel, as well as other factors. This increases the need to develop products oriented specifically to those who prefer a particular travel style. The travel industry will increasingly need to target niches within the wider youth travel market, such as music tourism, adventure tourism or volunteer tourism.

Perhaps the most important conclusion is that this is a growth market, in that the majority of youth travellers are presently or have previously been students. The continuing rapid growth in student numbers around the globe is a very optimistic prospect. This is because the international student population consists of avid travellers who are prepared to save up to ensure that their trip meets the 'once in a lifetime' requirement, even if the trip does not end up being a one-off (which – judging by the high number of repeat visits – it is clearly not).

Just as in many other niche markets, the use of the Internet will become even more important in future. The big difference in the youth market is the higher level of computer literacy and competence, which should mean that barriers to the use of new information and booking channels should disappear a lot more quickly. Our research indicates that at present the Internet is used mainly for information seeking and communications, but it is likely that Internet reservation systems will have a significant impact in future. The Internet will also become an important platform in providing the increasingly integrated services being sought by young travellers, many of whom are combining holiday, study and work in their long trips. More sophisticated and flexible youth products, which combine travel products with information products, job search, visa services, communications, transport and accommodation opportunities are therefore likely to become more important.

The development of youth niche products is also increasingly likely to revolve around youth travel 'enclaves' (Richards and Wilson, 2004a) where consumers and producers congregate. In many cases, the service providers will be 'lifestyle entrepreneurs' (see Ateljevic and Doorne, 2000) who are building a career on their own travel experiences. Such suppliers are able to get much closer to their customers, and are also able to assume market leadership through product innovation based on their experience of 'life on the road'. In many ways, the shift into lifestyle entrepreneurship is an extension of the 'travel career' (Pearce, 1993) which enables these suppliers to combine their work and leisure activities. These developments may also see a shift in the structure of the industry, as products developed by intermediaries in the destinations become more important than the offer in the tourism-generating countries.

Finally, there are many signs that the youth and student market is undergoing increasing professionalization; for example, the development of new global brands geared to youth travel such as the French hotel chain Accor's *Base Backpackers* brand. This and other such developments indicate that youth and student travel will decreasingly be defined as a distinct tourism niche and increasingly integrated into mainstream markets.

Final considerations

This review indicates that the youth travel market presents considerable opportunities for the future, both in mature destinations and emerging markets. The experience hunger that drives youth tourism is likely to see a growing number of trips, and rising levels of affluence will also drive higher expenditure. Considerable demand potential is likely to emerge from countries such as China and India, where rising student populations and pent-up demand for foreign travel are major factors. In more developed markets, the desire for more distinctive experiences, however difficult to attain, is likely to sustain demand. The fact that young travellers indicate that the main benefit they gain from their travel is a thirst for more travel indicates that growth will continue. The increasing professionalization and flexibility of the youth travel industry should see this market coming of age in the near future.

Acknowledgements

This chapter is based on a research programme developed by the Association for Tourism and Leisure Education (ATLAS) and the International Student Travel Confederation (ISTC). The full study report was previously published as Richards, G. and Wilson, J. (2003). The report and more details of the research can be found on www.atlas-euro.org and www.aboutistc.org. The authors are grateful to ISTC for permission to reproduce elements of the report here.

References

Ateljevic, I. and Doorne, S. (2000) Staying within the fence: lifestyle entrepreneurship in tourism. *Journal of Sustainable Tourism*, 8(5), 378–392.

ATI (Aviation and Tourism International) (1995) *Europe's Youth Travel Market*. Brussels: European Travel Commission (written by S. Wheatcroft and J. Seekings).

Bell, C. (2002) The big 'OE': Young New Zealand travellers as secular pilgrims. *Tourist Studies*, 2(2), 143–158.

Bureau of Tourism Research (2000) *Backpacker Market*. Australia: Tourism Queensland.

Clarke, J.A. (1992) Marketing spotlight on the youth 'Four S's' consumer. *Tourism Management*, 13(3), 321–327.

Desforges, L. (1998) 'Checking out the planet': global representations/local identities and youth travel. In T. Skelton and G. Valentine (eds) *Cool Places: Geographies of Youth Culture*. London: Routledge, pp. 175–192.

Horak, S. and Weber, S. (2000) Youth tourism in Europe: problems and prospects. *Tourism Recreation Research*, 25(3), 37–44.

Jefferson, A. (1991) Demographics, youth and tourism. *Tourism Management*, 12(1), 73–75.

Pearce, P. (1993) Fundamentals of tourist motivation. In D.G. Pearce and R.W. Butler (eds) *Tourism Research, Critiques and Challenges*. London: Routledge, pp. 113–134.

Richards, G. and Wilson, J. (2003) *Today's Youth Tourists: Tomorrow's Global Nomads? New Horizons in Independent Youth and Student Travel*. Amsterdam: International Student Travel Confederation and Arnhem: Association of Tourism and Leisure Education.

Richards, G. and Wilson, J. (2004a, eds) *The Global Nomad: Backpacker Travel in Theory and Practice*. Clevedon: Channel View Publications.

Richards, G. and Wilson, J. (2004b) The global student travel market: travelstyle, motivation and behaviour. *Tourism Review International*.

Sellars, A. (1998) The influence of dance music on the UK youth tourism market. *Tourism Management*, 19(6), 611–615.

Simpson, K. (2003) *Dropping Out or Signing Up? The Professionalisation of Youth Travel*. Paper presented at the Association of American Geographers conference in New Orleans (April).

WTO (1991) *International Conference on Youth Tourism*. New Delhi (India): Final report. 18–21 November 1991, 13 pp.

WTO (2002) *Youth Outbound Travel of the Germans, the British and the French*. Madrid: WTO.

Questions

1 By means of examples, highlight the main characteristics of the youth travel market and assess the costs and benefits that might arise from such a niche segment in the selected destinations.

2 Compare and contrast 'experience-based' youth tourism discussed in this chapter and what has been recently defined as 'clubbing and party tourism' . . . is it not all about young travellers?

Websites

www.goabroad.com
www.istc.org
www.i-to-i.com

4

Dark tourism
The appealing 'dark' side of tourism and more

Peter E. Tarlow

Introduction

As the sun rises over the Dead Sea, hundreds of young men and women shiver in the desert's cold as they listen to their tour guide retell the history of Massada. The guide carefully explains to the visitors the history, how almost 1,000 patriots decided to commit suicide rather than succumb to Roman oppression, and how this place was the last free Jewish community for almost 2,000 years. Often these tourists end the tour repeating the Hebrew words 'Matzada lo yipol shenit' (Massada will not fall again).

At a distance of almost 8,000 miles in San Antonio, another group of visitors is touring Texas' most popular attraction, the Alamo. The guide tells the story of how a group of Texas patriots decided to choose death with freedom rather than live under what they considered to be tyranny.

Some 2,000 miles to the northeast of San Antonio, lies New York City, which is home to some of the greatest cultural and artistic institutions in the world. Yet, despite the city's many attractions and monuments, currently the city's number one attraction is the site of the World Trade Center terrorist attack where more than 3,000 people were murdered, known as *Ground Zero*.

Although almost 2,000 years of history separate the events at Massada from those at the Alamo and over a century and a half separates the Alamo from Ground Zero, these examples share a great deal from a tourism perspective. They recount the history of patriotism and fight for freedom. At Ground Zero there is a sense of innocent blood being shed, of people having died and of death blending with hope to become a place for people to gather.

Returning east we come to Europe's most notorious death camp: Auschwitz. This spot symbolizes the pinnacle of European dark tourism. Here in this small Polish town, the victims are counted by millions. Now history reaches the surreal and mixes with it to become postmodern madness. Just as in Europe's battlegrounds or at its monuments, the past gives way to the present. The visitor may photograph grounds and buildings that have known the agony of death, but modern visitors see only life. Thus, over 50 years from the liberation of Auschwitz's Jewish population, over half a million people come to visit. Some come to pay their respects, others come out of curiosity or because it is the thing to do. The agony of history becomes a tourism attraction once again.

Interestingly enough, even at Auschwitz there is a sense of life-in-process. These centers are places that vibrate with life and seem to attract youth. Massada's summit is filled with young people. School children flock to the Alamo, and at Auschwitz there is the annual 'March of the Living' when thousands of young Jewish tourists from around the world travel from the darkness of the European death camps to the light of Israeli freedom. The aim of the visit to any of these places is to feel the power of faith, and the idea that from death can come hope.

Defining 'dark tourism'

The phenomena described are examples of what is commonly called technically 'thanatourism', more commonly known as 'dark tourism'. In many cases there is no clear definition of this tourism niche. Lennon and Foley (2002) define dark tourism referring to events that have occurred in recent times, which force the visitor to question modernity. Lennon and Foley (2002: 12) see dark tourism as the 'commodification of anxiety and doubt'. Others use a broader definition. Marcel (2003) notes:

> ... when you think about it, people have always been attracted to sites where important or mass deaths have occurred. The early pilgrimages were to sites of religious deaths. The Via Dolorosa, the route followed by Jesus when he was crucified, is only one of many early examples. The Tombs of the Pharaohs in Egypt and the Coliseum in Rome are major tourist attractions. So is the Tower of London, where historically important figures were beheaded. After the Battle of Waterloo in 1815, hotels and restaurants sprang up around the Belgian battlefield and changed the route of the 19th century British Grand Tour forever.

Dark tourism may be identified as 'visitations to places where tragedies or historically noteworthy death has occurred and that continue to impact our lives.' Marcel (2003) goes on to write:

> Thanatourism seems to be the dirty little secret of the tourism industry. It thrives at the Texas School Book Depository and the 'grassy knoll' in Dallas, where you

can buy a coffee mug decorated with cross hair rifle-sights, at Auschwitz and in Holocaust museums around the world, in cemeteries where celebrities are buried, and at the site of Princess Diana's tragic car crash in Paris. Tourists visit places of public executions, like the Place De La Guillotine, sites of mass death like Pompeii and Dachau, places associated with celebrity deaths like Graceland, museums and memorials like the Vietnam War Memorial in Washington, and battlefields like ancient Troy, Gettysburg, Pearl Harbor and Omaha Beach. Does it sound crazy to think of death as a niche market? Then what do you make of the 'Titanic cruises' offered by charter companies, where tourists eat meals identical to those served on the ship, and hear music identical to the music played on the ship, as they travel to the precise spot where the ship lies at the bottom of the ocean.

From this chapter's perspective, thanatourism will refer to those events, which are more than just tragedies in history, but rather touch our lives not merely from the emotional perspective but also impact our politics and social policies.

Mestrovic (1991. 4) notes that '... the most important aspect of modernity is that it causes humankind to suffer from an excess of "mind" at the expense of the "heart": a virulent abstractionism that abhors anything permanent'. Is Mestrovic correct or does dark tourism speak to the other side of Durkheim's concept of anomie? Can there be anything more permanent than death? Is our desire to meet death head-on then a disgrace, as thanatourism forces the permanence of death to confront the ephemeral changes of the living? Or is thanatourism a way in which life renews itself from the horrors of humanity? Postmodernists argue that we live in a world dedicated to fun. Authors such as Bell, Riesman and Rojeck often define modernity as the seeking of fun in the everyday. For example, Rojeck (1993: 133–134) hypothesizes that:

1 The modern quest for authenticity (in leisure travel) and self-realization has come to an end.
2 Due to de-differentiation leisure activity acquires some of the characteristics of work activity.
3 There is a questioning of the state's moral density.
4 Post-leisure and post-tourism celebrate fictive and dramaturgical values.

Thus Rojeck (1993: 134) writes: 'One realizes that what one is consuming is not real, but nonetheless the experience can be pleasurable and exciting even if one recognizes that it is also useless'.

Postmodernists note that the search for fun is often more difficult than it seems at first. Mestrovic (1991: 25) highlights this paradox by saying that 'postmodern vacations are usually stressful, few exotic places are left in the world and most vacation spots promise to deliver the same bland product-fun.' In describing cemetery tours Rojeck (1993: 141) writes:

Bourgeois culture constructed the cemetery as a place of dignity and solemnity. Visitors were expected to show proper respect for the dead. ... However, the actions of Modernity operated to break down the barriers between sacred and profane, the closed world of the cemetery and the outside world of commerce and spectacle. ... Today the most regular visitor to the star cemeteries is in fact the tourist; and the most common accessory they bear with them is not a bunch of flowers, but a camera.

Dark tourism touches many parts of the tourism world. In the US, large cities such as Chicago and smaller cities such as Waxahachee, Texas (home of Bonnie and Clyde) play on their criminal histories. The recent successful US television program, *The Sopranos*, has caused an upsurge in postmodern dark tourism to northern New Jersey. The media's fascination with this subject can be viewed in such films as *Chicago*. The mixture of tourism and film, fact and reality, means that time may no longer be a relevant factor in the definition of dark tourism. Historical memory and fantasy are now mixed and reality may be what is viewed on the screen rather than what is lived. Vernal, Utah's dinosaur park is now a tourism attraction and dinosaurs are now made 'real' due to such films as *Jurassic Park*. Has the dinosaur come to represent the modern unicorn? Is it too a form of dark tourism?

Dark tourism also exists in the upsurge of cemetery tourism that is taking place across the US. From national symbols at Arlington National Cemetery to small town projects called 'find-your-dead-relatives', cemetery tourism currently has become an important micro-niche in the growth of dark tourism. Another example, one of the great symbols of dark tourism, is the National Holocaust Museum on the mall in Washington, DC. This museum continuously ranks as one of the most frequently visited museums in the US capital city. What motivates this American need to face the Holocaust? Why do millions of people from around the US, many of whom were not born during the German acts of genocide, want to visit such places? More interestingly, the Washington Museum has spawned a series of other Holocaust museums around the nation. The National Holocaust Museum or its counterpart in Jerusalem, 'Yad Va'Shem' would seem to contradict the postmodernists cited above. While these national shrines do have the postmodernist prerequisites of museum stores, one is struck by the sanctity of the locations. These museums (or centers) are abnormally quiet, people spend a long time at the exhibits and it is not uncommon for people to leave the museums in tears. In the case of Yad Va'Shem one is struck by the silence of the Judean Hills and the paucity of trees dedicated to the righteous gentiles who were willing to risk their lives to save others. In the US, the National Holocaust Museum has now become a teaching tool for students at the FBI Academy. In both Washington and Jerusalem, there is a sense of seriousness, the right to be sad and angry, to see the world not as an amusement park but as a multifaceted place in which good can be created as well as evil.

Europe may be a model for dark tourism. It is a continent filled with bloody wars, and celebrations of the dead in pantheons and cathedrals. Death dominates much of European tourism, from visits to the graves of poets and kings, to the mass graves of soldiers who died in Europe's many wars. Are the visits of the young and the living a mocking of the dead or a form of respect? While some scholars have called the wearing of shorts or the eating of an ice-cream cone in these places sacrilegious, this form of tourism can be interpreted as symbolic; that in the face of death, tourism sanctifies life. Marcel (2003) argues that 'Unfortunately, in a world where images of crisis and disaster can be instantly broadcast around the world, a strange combination of empathy and excitement can make tragedy sites into tourist attractions'. As a species we come in a great variety of sociological and psychological ranges. Understanding the fact that there is no one size that fits all, this chapter turns to the following:

- What is the role between restorative and reflexive nostalgia in dark tourism?
- Why are we fascinated with places in which people have died?
- What is the role of violence in travel and tourism?
- What groups of people are motivated to visit such sites?
- Is there a major difference between small-town dark tourism and large-scale dark tourism?

Nostalgia

To begin to understand the power of dark tourism we need to connect it to nostalgia. While the word nostalgia in the late twentieth and twenty-first centuries often carries a positive connotation, it originally was a word used to diagnose a military sickness (Boym, 2001: 1). Boym provides us with a great deal of insight into the phenomenon. As Boym (2001: xvi) states in her introduction: 'Nostalgia and progress are like Jekyll and Hyde: Nostalgia is not merely an expression of local longing, but a new understanding of time and space that made the divisions of "local" and "universal" possible'. Boym (2001: 8) also notes that nostalgia is a 'mourning for the impossibility of a mythical return, for the loss of an enchanted world with clear borders and values; it could be a secular expression of a spiritual longing. ... Nostalgia, however, is more than merely a unification of the local and the universal. Nostalgia can have many forms'. Boym (2001) divides nostalgia into restorative and reflexive. Table 4.1 highlights some of the essential differences between these two forms of nostalgia. It shows that restorative nostalgia is action laden while reflexive nostalgia is more of the heart than of the body. The two broad categories, however, do not take into account the traveler who does not seek to reconstruct a now mythical home, but rather seeks to recapture a moment in time.

Table 4.1 Boym's forms of nostalgia

Type of nostalgia	Restorative	Reflexive
Stress	Action of going home	The longing
Push for homecoming	Quickens it	Delays it
Way it thinks of itself	Truth and tradition	Faces modernity
Dealing with absolutes	Protects the absolute truth	Questions absolute truth
Politics	National revivals	How do we inhabit two places at the same time
Emphasis on	Symbols	Details
Memory	National and linear	Social and varied
Plots	Restore national origins and conspiracy theories. A paranoiac reconstruction of 'home' based on rational delusions (p. 41)	Past is dealt with, with irony and humor (p. 49). Mourning mixed play pointing to the future

There is still another form of nostalgia that could be called 'tourism nostalgia': this is the one the traveler seeks to heal from past hurts by traveling back in time. Tourism nostalgia is the blending of 'restorative' and 'reflexive' tourism: it is touching danger without actually being in it. Dark tourism may be a form of virtual nostalgia in which the traveler vicariously visits the tragedy's scene, experiencing the tragedy's place. Tourism nostalgia is a way to dedifferentiate the past from the present, to find danger in the safe. This does not mean that all history is dark tourism, but rather that all dark tourism is history. This problem concerns historical tourism, often called heritage tourism, and real history has been addressed by a number of tourism scholars. For example, Urry (1990: 110) has noted that:

> There is an absolute distinction between authentic history (continuing and therefore dangerous) and heritage (past, dead, and safe). The latter, in short, conceals social and spatial inequalities, masks commercialism and consumerism, and may in fact destroy elements of the building or artifacts supposedly being conserved.

Is this true of dark tourism? In our desire to preserve the tragedies of the past are we creating an artificial world? Few people would want to experience the fog of war first-hand; almost no one would willingly suffer the torment or death of a concentration camp nor run for one's life from the collapsing Twin Towers. Yet while most people would not want to live the experience, many do want, in the simulata of the experience, the model in which they live at home. That is to say, tourists seek the different in the protection of the familiar, they seek the danger of history in the protection of the known.

Tourism nostalgia has still another component: the commercial side. While the soul may seek the spiritual, tourism is business and its job is to attract others to experience what was or what will be. Dark tourism deals with the 'horrors' of the past, which becomes business of today. Thus in places where tragedies have occurred, today there are souvenir stands, politics are taboo and individual memory is replaced by collective memory. Tourism nostalgia, like restorative nostalgia, is both 'a form of deep mourning that performs a labor of grief both through pondering pain and through play that points to the future' (Boym, 2001: 55).

Nostalgic tourism attacks our sense of time. To use Hannah Arendt's phrase, it is a safe confrontation with the "banality of evil" (1977). This is not to say that the visitor to a dark tourism site is a participant in political evil; but the visit rarely goes beyond the banal. As the event from which forms the *raison d'être* for the dark tourism attraction site fades into history, the banal often overtakes the spiritual. In the absence of the spiritual the site becomes simply part of the tour package: 'the thing to do'. Dark tourism becomes a reality made into virtual reality through the prism of history (Table 4.2).

It is in dark tourism that the person's inner space becomes defined by the outer experience. If the dark tourism visitor seeks to blend into the past in a safe and virtual manner, there are cases where terrorists are seeking to blend into the future in the most frightful of ways. In dark tourism, there is a blending of past and future, creator and observer, when perpetrators become producers of the 'attraction' – the niche product, and those who remember the victims become the consumers.

Table 4.2 Virtual tourism vs dark tourism

Phenomenon	Virtual tourism	Dark tourism
Reality based	Simulata	Yes
Site specific	No	Yes
Themed	Yes	Yes
Reality	None	Total
Feeling of being involved in the process	Yes	Surreal sense of involvement
Fabricated	Yes	No

The theoretical context

There is now a great deal of theory concerning tourism. However, this theoretical perspective does not necessarily address dark tourism; in fact, classical tourism/ leisure writers present us with kernels of insight that permit the development of an overall theory of dark tourism.

A way to view dark tourism is from the socio/psychographic model called in tourism science the Plog model, which presents us with a typological continuum (Plog, 1974). At one extreme end of the model are psychocentric travelers, people who tend to be fearful travelers. They seek comforts and protection, and prefer safety to experience. At the other end of the spectrum, Plog places the absolute allocentric traveler, who tends to seek the unique, the daring. He desires adventure rather than safety and creature comforts. Nostalgia can touch anyone along this continuum, but it is safe to say that from a theoretical basis the person who seeks tourism nostalgia is more likely to be found on the psychocentric side of the continuum. This does not mean that those who are of a more allocentric travel orientation will necessarily shun dark tourism sites. It does mean, however, that dark tourism, as a form of history must be presented in a way that permits history to be mixed with adventure, sentimental emotions to be mixed with physical activity.

Dark tourism is a different type of postmodern hyperreality. The Italian author Umberto Eco, one of the great postmodernist social commentators, highlights that 'the real is made fake'. For example, in analyzing the Johnson replica of the Oval Office found at the Johnson Presidential Museum in Austin, Eco (1990: 6–7) writes:

> ... it (the museum's copy of the oval office) suggests that there is a constant in the average American imagination and taste, for which the past must be preserved and celebrated in full-scale authentic copy, a philosophy of immortality as duplication. ... Constructing a full scale model of the Oval Office (using the same materials, the same colors, but with everything more polished, shinier, protected against deterioration) means that for historical information to be absorbed, it has to assume the aspect of reincarnation. ... The 'completely real' becomes 'completely fake'. Absolute unreality is offered as real presence.

Eco paints a portrait in which the fake becomes real and the ersatz becomes the legitimate substitute for the original. In Eco's world a child growing up in

Las Vegas might visit Paris only to be disappointed by the fact that the Paris Arc de Triomphe is not as nice as the one on Las Vegas Boulevard. Dark tourism presents the other side of Eco's coin. Thus in writing about the 'Palace of Living Arts' in Buena Park, Los Angeles, he notes: '... *the palace's philosophy is not, "We are giving you the reproduction so that you will want the original", but rather "We are giving you the reproduction so that you will no longer feel any need for the original"*' (1990: 19). Just as Eco demonstrates different forms of the Middle Ages being presented in a variety of ways so too dark tourism comes in multiple forms, such as:

- *A pretext to understand our own age* with visits to places of tragedy used as the pretext to explain the current political situation. It is a pilgrimage in which the visitor is commanded to remember. The participant is expected not only to learn but also to do, to carry the message forward and to utilize the lessons of the past in the decisions of tomorrow.
- *Romanticism*, which is often found at battlefields or in places of torture, where the visitor can imagine himself as a warrior fighting for a specific cause. An example is the visit to the World War II European battlefields by those who participated in these battles, or by their children.
- *Barbarism,* where the visitor is made to feel superior to the perpetrators of the crime. This form of dark tourism demonstrates how humans can be cruel to each other. The visitor departs feeling compassion for the victims and disgust at the perpetrators. Examples are sites in which the Inquisition occurred in Spain and Portugal or Nazi concentration camps.
- *Part of national identity* producing the message that 'although we suffered we have prevailed'. There is a sense of 'we' and 'they'. The Massada experience is an example, where the visitor comes away with not only a continuum of Jewish history but also a sense of patriotism and pride that despite 2,000 years of persecution, the nation has survived.
- *A sign of decadence*, which gives an idea of how the others mistreated the current ruling group. Europe is filled with such examples. For instance, the ghettos of Europe are examples of how one group of people was forced to live in abject poverty next to incredible opulence and palaces. The visitor to the darkness of Europe's ghettos is struck not only by the cruelties imposed but also by the decadence of those who claimed to have a monopoly on truth.
- *A mystical experience*, with visitors to New York's Ground Zero who speak of a sense of mysticism and awe as they look at the empty hole in which the World Trade Center once stood. Mysticism often grows out of tragedy. This phenomenon is especially true when the visitor has a connection to the spot. Europeans often feel less mystical about slave holding areas in West Africa than do the slaves' descendants.
- *A spiritual experience* in a similar manner, and yet separate from the mystical is the spirituality often felt by visitors to a dark tourism site. While the mystical experience seems to depend on the connection between the visitor and the sufferer, the spiritual experience is wider. It is a trans-group, trans-ethnic experience based more on a common sense of humanity than on commonality of race, ethnicity or nationality or religion.

Throughout all of these forms the careful interpreter of dark tourism will note that four basic emotions interact and play on the visitor's psychological state. These emotions are: a sense of insecurity; a sense of gratitude; feelings of humility; and, surprisingly, feelings of superiority.

Icons and the management of experiences

Unfortunately the world is filled with tragic events, yet not all tragic events become dark tourism attractions. This reality leads us to the realization that dark tourism is as much a part of iconic tourism as it is a part of historical tourism. Indeed dark tourism functions as one of the bridges linking the dark tourism niche to the historical niche in tourism marketing. From the perspective of tourism Sternberg (1999: 4) defines an icon as: 'an object, person, or experience that has acquired added value through the commercial heightening of meaning'. Thus dark tourism can be seen as an economic generator. Though it stresses the historic, spiritual, mystical or national, in reality it never truly develops into an attraction (icon) if it does not transform past tragedies into future economic productivity. Dark tourism then is a product that takes from the past and adds to the economy of the present. Sternberg (1999: 5) notes: 'The driving force in this new economy is not information but image. Now the decisive material is meaning, celebrity underlies wealth, and economic influence emanates from the controllers of content'. In the world of tourism, icons drive economies. Indeed Sternberg emphasizes this point when he states:

> What the tourism industry sells, in short, is an iconic experience – it promotes, packages, and delivers experiential content. . . . Tourism enterprises can function like other makers of iconic products, freely extracting realms of meaning from the universal cultural domain. . . . In tourism more than in other economic sectors, enterprises often have the option to depend neither on stereotyped common-property culture nor cinematic *fabulae* but rather to develop original, perhaps genuine, perhaps even authentic, touristic experiences (1999: 109–110).

In order for this niche to develop, Sternberg proposes the following model. The iconic experience must be staged, arranged, contextualized and thematized.

If the same principle were to be adopted for dark tourism, dark tourism products must first be staged. 'Staging' in Sternberg's vocabulary does not mean falsified. It rather means that the visitor must see the dark tourism icon within its historic context and one must be able to reach it. The skyscrapers that surround Ground Zero in New York, or the stark farmlands around Auschwitz are all examples of staging. Staging also means that the site is now accessible. Ground Zero today is not just a mere hole in the ground, but facilities through which visitors can observe the whole. Massada has both a cable car leading to its summit and a carefully restored Roman path for those seeking a more allocentric dark tourism experience.

The dark tourism experience is never an icon unto itself. How the visitor sees it, what arrangements are made for personal needs, food, medical help, are all part of the dark tourism experience. Does one feel like eating immediately after leaving the gas chambers of Nazi Europe? Is there a need for a place for quiet meditation? How close should public transportation be to the site? While these are essential issues for any icon, because dark tourism commemorates low, tragic or key points in human history, human needs must be arranged in such a way that the essence of the quotidian does not overpower the uniqueness of the spiritual.

The managers of the dark tourism icon must be decided on the icon's contextualization. For example, in the US should Ground Zero be explained within the larger context of the War on Terrorism or within the context of New York's economic struggles? In the case of Auschwitz, is it important to visit the village too, in order to see the villagers as actors in the tragedy or should the Auschwitz experience be kept to the hallowed grounds in which over a million and half people were murdered? How the context is presented not only determines the type of dark tourism but also the type of person the attraction may bring. Finally, the dark tourism icon is thematized. Is the message human cruelty or a particular nation's cruelty? Is the purpose of the dark tourism icon to arouse passions or to create a sense of forgiveness? Do the icon's managers wish the visitor to remember history for its own sake or to use the dark event to create a personal transformation? How these questions are addressed determines the type of theme at each dark tourism icon. Sternberg reminds his reader that '... if composers of touristic experiences do choose multiple themes, they should do so through careful iconic assessment – they should select themes that are compatible, complementary, or purposely contrasting' (1999: 125).

To be an icon requires more than mere profit and economic viability. Icons are seen. There is a clear distinction between the concepts of seeing and hearing. The western world has placed much of its emphasis on seeing rather than hearing. The western attitude toward seeing is perhaps summed up best in the notion of 'seeing is believing'. From brochure development to television ads, the assumption is that what we see is what we believe. This emphasis on seeing has produced what the Italian commentator Sartori (1998) calls '*Homo videns*'. He suggests that *Homo videns* has now replaced through the medium of television *Homo sapiens*. In the world of television, the act of seeing prevails over the act of speaking, and as a consequence the television viewer is more a viewing animal than a symbolic animal. Sartori connects the idea of *Homo videns* with that of the global village. If television can go anywhere, if we are more viewing than symbolic animals, than what is its impact on dark tourism? It is clear to anyone who lived through September 11, 2001 that television has had a major impact on dark tourism. One only had to watch and watch again ad nauseum the falling of the twin towers to know how those images were ingrained within not only the American psyche but that of much of the civilized world. To have been alive on September 11th was to be a viewer. It was to experience the constant repetition of the same images. The global village then made a horrendous event into an iconic event. Almost immediately people wanted (though at first could not) visit the site. It was a place to be, to touch; it was to regain a sense of being a *Homo sapiens* rather than a mere *Homo videns*. Yet as television made us a global village, it also made us forget everything else that was going on that day. One event overtook the world; the local became the international, and we are left to wonder what else happened that day that has now been lost to history.

Final considerations

Tourism professionals have long understood that not every travel and tourism product will appeal to every consumer. Thus, travel and tourism professionals have tried to create products that appeal to specific audiences. One such 'niche' is called dark tourism. Dark tourism is not a new niche market. For example, in the US visitors to New England and New Orleans (Louisiana) have long been fascinated by graveyard visits. Often these tours are connected with specific holidays such as Halloween. Visitors interested in military history have turned battlegrounds around the world into another niche. These sites do not appeal to everyone, but there are clear groups of people who see these locations as tourism draws and travel to these sites for both reasons of curiosity, nostalgia and pilgrimage. This chapter has given a theoretical framework that helps to explain why people chose to travel where others have suffered and died and how this suffering has created a specific niche market.

Television and film can define modern dark tourism. The site of the World Trade Center is visited, while the tragedies of Africa are ignored. Due to the television's selectivity we can say that while all life is precious not all life is remembered. Sartori (1998: 119) notes that the relationship between being a citizen of the world and of a community at the same time is possible. As citizens of television land we can worry about far away causes, while as citizens of our community we tend to worry about what directly impacts our pocketbooks and us. In a similar manner television has provided a place for us to visit in our leisure time. Because we care, we suffer, we visit dark tourism sites, but because in reality we are citizens of another time and place, we are visitors rather than participants. In other words 'Venimus, videmus, abimus' – We come, we see, we leave.

References

Arendt, H. (1977) *Eichmann in Jerusalem: A Report on the Banality of Evil*. New York: Penguin.
Boym, S. (2001) *The Future of Nostalgia*. New York: Basic Books.
Eco, U. (1990) *Travels in Hyperreality*. San Diego: Harvest.
Lennon, J. and Foley, M. (2002) *Dark Tourism*. London: Continuum.
Marcel, J. (2003) Death makes a holiday. *The American Reporter*, May 29, 9(2114).
Mestrovic, S. (1991) *The Coming Fin de Siècle*. London: Routledge.
Plog, S. (1974) Why destination areas rise and fall in popularity. *Cornell Hotel and Restaurant Administration Quarterly*, 14(4), 55–8.
Rojeck, C. (1993) *Ways of Escape*. London: Routledge.
Sartori, G. (1998) *Homo Videns*. Madrid: Taurus.
Sternberg, E. (1999) *The Economy of Icons*. Westport: Praeger.
Urry, J. (1990) *The Tourist Gaze*. London: Sage.

Questions

1 Is there a way of distinguishing dark tourism?
2 Bearing in mind the various forms of dark tourism, can you list and explain which are the four emotions interacting with and playing on the visitor's psychological state?

Websites

http://www.battlefield-tours.com/
http://www.titanic.com/
http://www.remember.org/educate/intro.html
http://alcatraz.san-francisco.ca.us/

5

Genealogy tourism
The Scottish market opportunities

Moira Birtwistle

Introduction

Taylor (2002) defines genealogy as a 'Journey of Discovery' – if you haven't started researching your family tree yet, you are missing out on what must be the world's fastest growing hobby. And it's not about dry, dusty research. It is a journey of discovery that isn't over until you have actually visited your ancestral homeland. Ask anyone who has been 'home' to Scotland. It is a powerful emotion. On the other hand, Keillar (2003) advocates that 'Genealogy is such a depressing study. Neither a science nor an art, devotees ferret away amongst the bones of their ancestors and produce a catalogue of couplings not much more enlightening than the begattings and begettings of the Bible'.

If this observation was universally acclaimed then the development of genealogy as a niche market would not have been a pragmatic decision in Scottish tourism. Yet the tracing of our ancestors has become a major preoccupation — genealogy comes third only to pornography and general entertainment as the most popular subject on the internet (Gilchrist, 2000). Furthermore, anecdotal evidence points to the existence and potential growth of genealogy tourism, alleged to be one of the fastest growing hobbies in the world (scotexchange.net, 2002).

Genealogy is, by definition, the process by which basic information about births, marriages and deaths is linked together to form a family tree. According to Fowler and Fowler (1974) 'genealogy' is 'the account of descent from ancestor by enumeration of intermediate persons; the investigation of the pedigree of a particular person or family'. Most genealogists, however, go further than this and collect information about the way of life of the people concerned, their occupations, stories about them, etc. An old faded family photograph may instigate an investigation into not only identifying the people but finding out where and how they lived – this is 'family history'.

The terms are essentially interchangeable but 'family history' using everyday language perhaps reflects more exactly the 'amateurs' who constitute family history societies worldwide, 'genealogy' more the professionals. The amateur enthusiast will often use the term 'genealogy' to mean ancestral research. For the purposes of this chapter, the terms 'genealogy', 'family history' and 'ancestral research' are synonymous.

Genealogy has previously provided the focus, in 1999, for a targeted British Tourist Authority (BTA) campaign, which encouraged 'descendants of immigrants and transported convicts' to come home for the millennium and trace their roots. The campaign tied in with millennium celebrations at the Public Record Office and several family history projects. Individual Tourist Boards have also organised specific, geographically targeted 'Homecoming' events, e.g. the Orkney Tourist Board's Homecoming Event 1999, the Welsh Tourist Board's 'Homecoming' campaign for 2000.

At a local level, initiatives such as the Isle of Bute's 'Sons and Daughters' project[1] and Ayrshire and Arran Tourism Industry Forum's (A&ATIF) family history project have placed genealogy on the tourist map.

Genealogy developments in Ayrshire and Arran

The *Ayrshire and Arran Tourism Industry Forum* (A&ATIF) is a voluntary organisation bringing together those individuals and organisations with a direct interest in the integrated and sustainable development in the leisure and tourism sector in Ayrshire and Arran. Founded in 1993 (re-branded Ayrshire and Arran Tourism Forum in 2003), the organisation has achieved considerable success through the development work of its project groups. The Family History Project Group, set up in 1999, 18 months prior to the highlighting of genealogy as a tourism niche by the Scottish Executive, provides an excellent example of a working public/private sector initiative (Birtwistle, 2001).

The Family History Project Group was formed as a direct result of a letter from an enthusiastic amateur family historian, in response to a request in an A&ATIF 'Talking Tourism' article in the *Ayr Advertiser* (September 1998), seeking product development ideas. The letter identified the urgent need to educate suppliers of the local tourism product of the potential role of 'family history', as a component in the overall Ayrshire and Arran tourist product. Moreover, the correspondence clearly identified the inherent problems that can arise with defining specialised niches, when suppliers are ill equipped to provide up-to-date and in-depth knowledge on local resources for would-be family historians.

Table 5.1 Objectives and methodology of A&ATIF project group

Objective 1   To assess the current level of knowledge of key tourism providers

Methodology

- A call centre survey of tourism operators in Ayrshire and Arran
- A survey of local taxi drivers (often the first point of contact for visitors to the area)

Objective 2   To quantify the demand for genealogy based tourism in Ayrshire and Arran

Methodology

- An on-line questionnaire piloted on a professional genealogy website
- A face-to-face questionnaire with 'tourists' to Ayrshire and Arran at key gateways

Overall the A&ATIF Family History Project Group concluded that the analysis revealed a general consensus of opinion that there was existing demand and that locally, family history was a recognisable tourist activity. Local suppliers however, were clearly lacking the basic knowledge to respond to questions from genealogy tourists.

Membership of the Project Group was drawn from the private and public sector and included representatives of A&ATIF Executive; local Family History Societies; local libraries; South Ayrshire Council Archives; a professional genealogy company; Enterprise Ayrshire; Ayrshire and Arran Tourist Board; Higher Education and a local freelance historian. The overall aim of the group was:

To promote and encourage family history tourism in Ayrshire and Arran by improving the knowledge about basic family history resources of those involved in the tourism industry in order to enhance the visits of tourists (A&ATIF, 1999).

In Table 5.1, two main objectives are identified and a research methodology outlined.

Three tangible outcomes designed to meet this identified gap in information were produced:

1 Information leaflet on local sources for ancestral research.
2 Training video to equip local suppliers with the knowledge to direct genealogy related questions.
3 A family history website hosted on the Ayrshire-online portal (http://www.ayrshire-online.net/familyhistory).

Significantly, the project, sponsored by Scottish Enterprise Ayrshire (SEA), was highlighted within the Scottish Tourist Board (STB) Genealogy Tourism Strategy and Marketing Plan (2001) as an excellent example of a 'full service approach' linking tourism suppliers and genealogy experts in the development of genealogy training materials for the local tourism supplier. (Following on from this successful initiative, a member of the project group was invited to sit on the STB genealogy working group.)

Genealogy was first identified as a niche market in the Scottish Executive's 'New Strategy for Scottish Tourism' (2000), which outlined and provided the framework for the development of three identified niche markets: golf, genealogy and culture.

In 2001 the STB indicated that worldwide, there are around 28 million people with Scottish ancestry (subsequent research would indicate this to be a gross under-estimate). Early indication of research (Ancestral Tourism Industry Steering Group, 2003), a figure of 50 million was supplied, however the data may again be more of an indication rather than scientifically derived. Notwithstanding the lack of a scientifically sound methodology, the number of Scots descendants worldwide is considerable and may be attributed largely to descendants from the historical out-migration and the emigration patterns of Scottish labour, mainly to Northern USA, Canada, New Zealand, Australia and South Africa.

In Scotland, research indicated that 19% of American visitors stated 'family roots and ancestry' as the main influence on their decision to holiday in Scotland, and that one in ten of these visitors engaged in genealogy study during their stay (STB *Tourism Attitudinal Study*, 1999). Furthermore, the BTA office in New York deals with thousands of enquiries a year from Americans interested in researching their family ties:

> Many of our visitors from America come also in search of their Scottish roots. Twelve million Americans are of Scottish descent. The British Tourist Authority office in New York currently deals with thousands of enquiries a year from Americans interested in researching their family ties (Morrison, 2000).

The Scottish Executive (2000) identified four key elements in the development of this niche:

1 Linking Scots genealogy websites to Ossian.
2 Developing the promotional potential of Scots heritage events overseas.
3 Introducing tactical direct marketing campaigns.
4 Promotion in specialist ex-pat publications.

Responding to this, the STB embarked on a process of research and consultation, leading to the preparation of a Genealogy Tourism Strategy and Marketing Plan. In 2001 the STB clearly stated within their Genealogy Marketing Strategy (2001) that this motivation of family roots would be used as a 'hook' to encourage tourism.

The ancestral tourism initiative

In Scotland in 2001, a working partnership between the three national agencies, Highlands and Islands Enterprise (HIE), Scottish Enterprise (SE) and VisitScotland (formerly STB), was formed to deliver the *Ancestral Tourism Initiative*, in line with the proposals set out by the Scottish Executive's *A New Strategy for Scottish Tourism* (2000).

At the outset it was recognised that there was a need for serious industry ambassadors to provide leadership. An industry Steering Group, chaired by Marco Truffeli (Managing Director of the Edinburgh Town House Company), was established to drive the project forward. Membership of the Steering Group was drawn from key representatives of the public and private sector.[2]

The group's primary role was to drive forward the strategic and operational approach of the project, while playing an ambassadorial role in stimulating industry-wide awareness, thereby enabling the industry 'to buy into' the project. A genealogy promotions manager was appointed by VisitScotland, as clearly promotion would be fundamental to the success of the project.

Extensive research and consultancy undertaken by VisitScotland underpinned the *Ancestral Scotland Initiative*. It provided the evidence and confidence that 'genealogy' was an important stimulus for travel to Scotland. In particular in the markets of North America and Canada, it was discovered that genealogy was a strong motivational factor in travelling to Scotland. Crucially, since electronic marketing had been proven to be the most effective method of reaching this market, a web portal needed to be created (STB, 2001). Moreover since genealogy had been shown to be increasingly an electronically driven hobby,[3] the creation of a single website, which would bring family history and tourism together, was of first priority. Research had revealed that although the worldwide web contained a plethora of Scottish heritage, special interest and genealogy sites, none supplied the essential information required by those contemplating a trip to Scotland in search of their roots (scotexchange.net): the key difference between this web portal and other websites apparently being that the portal would be designed to create an interest in travel to Scotland and not just a general interest in Scotland.

> It is an opportunity to persuade consumers already interested in their Scottish family roots that they will learn much more about who they are if they travel here and stand on home soil, and to inspire them with the range of experiences they can include in such a trip. Only when they are in Scotland can they truly appreciate the culture that they and their ancestors are part of (Sproat, 2002).

The web portal – the first of its kind to link genealogy with the motivation to travel – focuses firmly on convincing 'family history enthusiasts'[4] that they should travel to Scotland to complete their family tree. Additionally, it aims to encourage those people who feel sure they have a connection to Scotland but have no knowledge on how to get started. The website is designed to be simple and user-friendly. A search can be entered for a place name, parish name, or surname (the latter is proving to be the most popular search but was not part of the original specification). The website has a direct link to www.scotlandspeople.gov.uk.[5]

The website was launched live on TV, on 24 January 2002, on the Glen Lee Tall Ship on the River Clyde and simultaneously in New York by supermodel Kirsty Hume. It was subsequently launched in Toronto a day later and in Australia and New Zealand in October/November 2002 (Hamish Clark, from the TV programme *Monarch of the Glen*, launched the site in Australia and New Zealand).

The launch was supported by an extensive marketing campaign to encourage potential genealogy tourists to visit the land of their ancestors, and a series of reciprocal links to other selected Scottish interest and heritage websites was created. Joint promotional opportunities have been intrinsic in supporting this initiative; for example, ancestralscotland.com and VisitBritain in Australia are offering 'Tracing Your Roots' packs for anyone interested in learning more about their Scottish ancestry.[6] Specific opportunities to promote the website have included participation in the Smithsonian annual Folklife Festival in Washington, DC, which in June and July 2003 featured 'Scotland: the People, the Pride and the Passion', a showcase for Scots culture in America.

To complement the investment in the ancestralscotland.com website, SE, HIE and VisitScotland appointed a Project Manager (Blue Toucan) to work with the industry on developing genealogy/tourism products and services. The work would assess market opportunities, review existing products, identify best practice and bring interested businesses and parties together to identify and deliver specific projects. Additionally, the three national partner agencies commissioned market research and an economic impact study.

By October 2003, the delivery of the project could be split into two main phases:

Phase 1   Market appraisal and economic impact study and engagement of the industry and mapping of existing genealogy products.

Phase 2   Delivery of research and product development.

Phase 1
Market appraisal and economic impact study

DTZ Pieda Consulting was commissioned to undertake an appraisal of the market for genealogy/ancestral tourism in Scotland. Primarily the research focused on identifying and contacting all companies with an involvement in genealogy/ancestral tourism. Secondly, in order to quantify the size and nature of the market, the identified companies were asked to quantify, source and expand on the nature of the visits of existing genealogy/ancestral tourists and to comment on potential visits.

Overall the purpose of the research was to ascertain how many people worldwide have direct Scottish ancestry and to determine the current potential value of ancestral tourism to Scotland with forecasts for its likely future value.

The findings of the research are based on 6,000 responses, four times the anticipated response rate, and therefore will provide a more credible and scientific analysis of the market. The research (Ancestral Tourism Industry Steering Group, 2003) indicated that:

- Projected market to be more in the region of 50 mn (but this remains an indicative figure, as was previous estimate of 28 mn)
- Very good dispersal of visitors all year round with a real opportunity to develop off-peak season
- Ancestral tourism can open up new markets for Scotland worldwide
- Very good dispersal of visitors throughout Scotland and rural areas
- Major impact for local communities
- Internet is main form of research prior to visit
- Very high visitor satisfaction during visit
- Nearly 100% of visitors want to return to Scotland
- Very high incidence of repeat visits.

Engagement of the industry and mapping of existing genealogy products
1 Creation of a web-based community

A web-based community was established via scotexchange.net,[7] the Scottish tourism industry's website. This provided the framework for the networking and sharing of ideas and a key tool in generating industry support.

2 Interactive workshops

A series of four interactive workshops were delivered across Scotland: Edinburgh, Inverness, Glasgow and Orkney. The workshops aimed to create innovative and commercially led ancestral tourism product development opportunities to attract visitors to Scotland and to service them effectively when they were here. Additionally, the workshops set about identifying ways to improve industry collaboration and communication on ancestral tourism. The four workshops resulted in the creation of 60 new business or project ideas to be developed in Phase 2.

3 Mapping exercise

A mapping exercise designed to provide an insight into how consumers access the web for Scottish genealogy, identified a wide range of organisations and individuals involved in the promotion and delivery of genealogy information and research. More than 100 websites and 35 independent genealogists and consultants have been identified (Ancestral Tourism Industry Steering Group, 2003). As part of Phase 2 of this project, an area within www.scotexchange.net will be developed to allow businesses to update this list.

Phase 2
Delivery of research and product development

Due to the overwhelming support and interest from industry throughout Phase 1, HIE, SE and VisitScotland have put plans in place to deliver Phase 2.

1 Development of projects

The four workshops resulted in the creation of 60 new business ideas, which are 'owned' by the 150 participants of the four workshops and the industry. Phase 2 will take these ideas forward, through the development of project teams who will be given the support of business advisers to develop the ideas, create a business plan and seek potential funding opportunities.[8]

2 Industry event

The industry event 'Ancestral Tourism – Trading on the family tree' organized by the Ancestral Tourism Industry Steering Group in Hopetown House, South Queensferry, in December 2003, discussed issues such as:

- an overview of the market appraisal and economic impact research findings
- best practice examples identified throughout the project
- prioritising product development opportunities for delivery.

3 Mapping exercise

Continuation of the mapping exercise as outlined in Phase 1. One particular area that the partners of the project would like to develop is an outline of tourism operators who have a direct involvement in genealogy or ancestral tourism. An area within www.scotexchange.net will be developed to allow businesses to update this list.

Implications for management

Four key enablers can be identified that have facilitated the development of this niche:

1 Technology
2 Resources

3 Search for identity
4 Postmodern forms of tourism.

1 *Technology*
The role of the internet has fuelled the growth in 'family history research' and technology can be credited for simplifying DIY genealogy (Gilchrist, 2000). Significantly, the recognition, by the Scottish Executive, of the role of technology and the increasing use of the internet for e-commerce, has offered new opportunities to sell accommodation and other tourism related products.

2 *Resources – internet*
In world terms, Scotland has genealogical records that are genuinely unsurpassed, whereas in comparison, the Irish have created an emigration centre with virtually no records at all (the Irish Census returns were almost completely destroyed in the Civil War in 1921) (Buie, 1998). The growth in family history has been accelerated by the increasing provision of various key online indices (Table 5.2).

As a result of such online resources, the Scottish Diaspora is now traceable, in theory, at the click of a computer mouse and 'it is possible to do much of the basic research in one's living room' (Gilchrist, 2000). In a sense the internet has enabled vicarious *journeys* to homelands and has provided a 'virtual sense of identity' for the researcher. This virtual 'homecoming' may provide a virtual reality experience but as such 'is more likely to provide a spur for the "real" thing' (Brown, 1998: 124).

3 *Search for identity*
It is commonly claimed that access to global information exchange and travel will inevitably lead to a 'placeless' world, yet evidence suggests that both 'can be used to discover and reinforce a sense of community and shared heritage, rooted in shared ancestry and specific territorial homelands' (Meethan, 2002).

This 'sense of belonging' and search for identity is a form of heritage tourism and a cultural component which can be used to forge national identity (a caveat perhaps to be noted is that genealogy should not become an instrument in the hands of politicians). Lennon (2003) recognises the importance of heritage, culture and genealogy, in that along with culture and heritage they offer authenticity and 'real' history that could stimulate belonging and repeat visitation.

The travel to Scotland then is no ordinary journey; it may be a search for identity, to belong, motivated by 'a certain sense of rootlessness' (Basu, 2000). The visit therefore puts the research in context. Futhermore, to many people living overseas, Scotland is considered to be 'home' in some profound sense (Taylor, 2002) and to many 'homecomers', the journey is considered akin to a spiritual experience (Basu, 2000).

4 *Postmodern forms of tourism*
Despite globalisation and the global diffusion of consumer capitalism, individuals continue to exercise strategies of personal identification (Hughes, 1995: 798). In the postmodern society where people, goods and information flow across the borders of nations and cultures with apparent ease, many people are once more looking to their ancestry and 'real' family histories spurred on by the impact of a 'placeless world' (Meethan, 2002).

Table 5.2 Key online sources

http://www.scotlandspeople.gov.uk	Partnership between the General Registrar Office for Scotland (GROS) and Scotland On Line – official online source of parish register, civil register and census records for Scotland – contains almost 37 million names; it is one of the world's largest resources of genealogical information and one of the largest single information resources on the Web.
http://www.scan.org.uk	The Scottish Archive Network (SCAN) is an electronic network and search room linking the catalogues of nearly 50 Scottish archives – opening up Scotland's archives to the world.
http://www.nas.gov.uk	Main archive for sources of the history of Scotland – records spanning the 12th to 21st centuries, touching on virtually every aspect of Scottish life.
http://www.edina.ed.ac.uk	Statistical Accounts of Scotland – in the late 18th and mid-19th century, parish church ministers were required to write a document describing their parishes – fascinating historical documents, rich in detail including, in some cases, comments on the morals and habits of our ancestors!
http://www.scottishdocuments.com	Provides detailed descriptions of all the parishes as described by the local ministers. Free access to a fully searchable index of over 520,000 Scottish wills and testaments dating from 1500 to 1901.
http://www.familysearch.org	The International Genealogical Index (IGI), initially developed for doctrinal purposes by the Church of Jesus Christ of Latter Day Saints (LDS) (commonly known as the Mormons). Database names of more than 640 million people and 8.5 million hits daily.
http://www.scotsorigins.com	Launched in April 1998, provides internet access to more than 25 million index entries from the statutory registers, the Old Parish registers of Scotland (some of them going as far back as mid-16th century and the 1891 census).
http://www.safhs.org.uk	The Scottish Association of Family History Societies are run by local volunteers. Most maintain an index of members' interests which could well lead to long lost 'cousins' being found and perhaps, subsequently visited.

Source: Adapted from *Scottish Ancestral Research: A guide to the wealth of genealogy and family history resources in Edinburgh and Lothians* (2003).

The 'ancestral tourist' is seeking an authentic and a 'real' experience, not therefore belonging to the conceptual mindset associated with postmodern 'simulation' analysis theories supported by Lash and Urry (1994); Eco (1986); Gottdiner (1995). In a sense, the 'ancestral-tourist' displays many of the characteristics attributed to the theoretical mindset supported by Munt (1994) and Poon (1989), which stresses the search for the 'real'. Ancestral tourism in seeking authenticity in the search for a 'real' personal identity, rooted in Scotland's heritage and cultural 'real' past, may be regarded as a form of postmodern heritage tourism. The heritage tourism industry itself has been described largely as a postmodern phenomenon (Walsh, 1992 in Swarbrooke and Horner, 1999: 221).

This search for many ancestral 'tourists' is a very personal journey; an individual search for this 'real' identity. Furthermore, the ancestral 'tourist' will be more individualistic and require highly developed products leading to a form of tourist activity which displays many of the characteristics associated with postmodern tourism: small scale, geographically dispersed, not specifically rural or urban, touching almost all urban and rural areas (Montanari and Williams, 1995: 5) and requiring a more individual and highly developed product (Swarbrooke and Horner, 1999: 221).

Final considerations

Throughout this chapter, the term 'ancestral tourist' is used cautiously. To add to the academic debate regarding the definition of the term 'tourist', research suggests that many 'diaspora tourists' do not consider themselves 'tourists' (Basu, 2000). The motivation for travel stems from questions such as 'who are we?' and 'where do we fit in?', both questions increasingly common in today's world (Palmer, 1999). Moreover, Scotland is no arbitrary destination for a 'holiday' for diaspora visitors (STB, 2001; Basu, 2000).

As noted by Montanari and Williams (1995: 60)

It is important to remember that in the literature of tourism (see Kemper, 1978) the word 'tourism', in its modern usage, was first used in the English language; it in fact has a classical origin. The Latin term 'tornus' derives from the Greek 'τσρνος' which originally referred to a rotating machine but came to mean 'travel around, turn around, go back to the starting place'.

Considering then that the ancestral 'tourist' is going back both spatially and emotionally to their roots, i.e. the starting place, the term 'ancestral tourist' can at least be applied in academic discussion. The recognition and understanding of this emotive typology has had and will have implications for the marketing of this niche. A subtle marketing approach and the implementation of less aggressive promotional methods, which will enable not to exploit ancestral visits, has been and remains fundamental in the management of this niche.

Technology clearly is a central force in the shaping and development of 'ancestral tourism'. It is ironic that one of the key drivers of the globalization process has proved to be an intrinsic and driving force in the search for a local 'identity' and shared ancestry.

The significant Scottish diaspora has a strong unique, global identity. As such, although generally competition in tourism is intense, 'ancestral tourism' is a specialist niche market, similar to pilgrimages, in which competition is noted as limited (Montanari and Williams, 1995: 8).

This niche opportunity recognised by the Scottish Executive and delivered by the key Scottish agencies provides a good example of how the public sector has engaged the private sector in an integrated and planned approach in the development of a niche tourist market. Ancestralscotland.com is where tourism meets the 'real' past. This has enabled Scottish tourism to provide a global key to 'real' Scottish heritage and added a new dimension and challenge for innovative product development.[9]

Notes

1 The 'Bute Sons and Daughters Project' was set up by Bute Enterprises, a local community-based organisation. The online website (http://www.butesonsand-daughters.com) is now well established and aims to develop Bute's genealogy strands, not only in terms of family histories but also local heritage. The project exhibition is based in the Isle of Bute Discovery Centre (the restored Winter Gardens in Rothesay).

2 The Steering Group was given the task of working along with the Project Managers (Blue Toucan) ensuring that the key deliverables developed were in line with a commercially led approach (www.scotexchange.net). Steering group members were drawn from the public and private sector:

- The private sector (including professional genealogists, consultants)
- The National Trust for Scotland (NTS)
- The National Museums of Scotland (NMS)
- General Registrars Office for Scotland (GROS)
- The Conchra Charitable Trust
- HIE
- SE
- VisitScotland
- Area Tourist Board Network
- Blue Toucan (Ancestral Tourism Project Manager)

3 Anecdotal evidence suggests that in the last 5 years, people paying to access the web has increased by 500%, reinforcing the fact that being Scottish is in vogue.

4 Three potential markets had been identified by VisitScotland: Amateur Enthusiasts, Scots Aficionados and Homecomers. The challenge facing Scottish tourism was to develop a niche marketing strategy, which would achieve additional visits and revenue by capitalising on the growing interest in genealogy and Scots heritage. Resources therefore must be carefully targeted to convert the 'contemplators' thereby increasing the length of their stay and/or geographical breadth of their travel (scotexchange.net, 2002).

5 http://www.scotlandspeople.gov.uk charges a small fee for downloading information and copies of birth certificates. It has just added all the data from the 1902 Census in Scotland to its comprehensive database.

6 Ancestral Scotland in Australia – 'Tracing your Ancestors Pack' includes:

- Inside Britain Holiday Planner
- Ancestral Scotland Guide
- Tracing Your Ancestors Fact Sheet
- Britain Map
- Explore Holidays Special Scotland Offer (http://www.ancestralscotland.com/news/features.asp?id=24)

7 Scotexchange.net provides practical, up-to-date and relevant market information for the Scottish tourism industry. The site was developed by the Scottish Tourist Board in partnership with Scottish Enterprise and the Highlands and Islands Enterprise, fulfilling a commitment made in the Scottish Executive's New Strategy for Scottish Tourism, published in February 2000.

8 Eleven key areas have been identified for project development:

- Marketing and Incentives Branding
- Emotions
- Corporate Sponsorship Opportunities
- Packages
- Information Provision
- New and Mobile Technologies
- Visitor Experience
- Events and Festivals
- Quality Assurance
- Awareness Raising and Education
- Other

(Blue Toucan, July 2003)

9 A Scottish Family History Research Service is to be set up with a grant from the Executive of £1.6 million. The service, to be fully operational in 2006, will create a 'one-stop-shop' for genealogy research by bringing together internet services provided separately by project partners the General Register Office for Scotland, National Archives of Scotland and Court of the Lord Lyon. There will be a family history 'campus' based around the General Register House and New Register House buildings. A part of the project will encourage local authorities to set up similar one-stop-shops in their areas (Henry, 2002).

References

A&ATIF (1999) Family History Project Group. Minutes of Meetings.
Ancestralscotland.com (2003) http://www.ancestralscotland.com/genealogy/information.asp
Basu, P. (2000) *Genealogy and Heritage Tourism in the Scottish Highlands and Islands*. A report prepared for Moray, Badenoch and Strathspey Enterprise.
Birtwistle, M. (2001) Genealogy a niche market opportunity: Developments in Ayrshire and Arran. In M. Mitchell and I. Kirkpatrick (eds) *New Directions in Managing Rural Tourism and Leisure*. The Scottish Agricultural College, Auchincruive, Conference Proceedings 5–8 September 2001.
Brown, F. (1998) *Tourism Reassessed. Blight or Blessing?* Oxford: Butterworth-Heinemann.
BTA Campaign (1999) *The Times*, 15 February 1998.
Buie, E. (1998) Man with a mission, *The Glasgow Herald*, 2 March 1998.
Eco, U. (1986) *Travels in Hyper-Reality*. London: Picador.
Fowler, H.W. and Fowler, F.G. (eds) (1974) *The Concise Oxford Dictionary of Current English*. Oxford: Oxford University Press.
Gilchrist, J. (2000) Roots systems. *The Scotsman*, Saturday 12 February 2000.
Gottdiner, M. (1995) *Postmodern Semeiotics: Material Culture and the Forms of Postmodern Life*. Cambridge: Blackwell.

Henry, H. http:www.scotland.gov.uk/pages/news/2002/12/SEJD166.aspx

Hughes, G. (1995) Authenticity in Tourism. *Annals of Tourism Research*, 22(4), 781–803.

Keillar, I. (2003) Book review, *History Scotland*, September/October 2003, Edinburgh, p. 58.

Kemper, F.J. (1978) *Probleme der Geographie der Freizeiht*, Bonn: Ferd. Dummlers Verlag.

Lash, S. and Urry, J. (1994) *Economies of Sign and Space*. London: Sage.

Lennon, J. (2003) *Niche Markets*. Edinburgh: Holyrood, p. 11.

Mccthan, K. (2002) Tourism, 'roots' and the internet. Paper presented to the *Wales 2002 Tourism Research Conference*, University of Wales Institute Cardiff, 4 7 September.

Montanari, A. (1995) The Mediterranean region: Europe's summer leisure space. In A. Montanari and A.M. Williams (eds) (1995) *European Tourism. Regions, Spaces and Restructuring*. John Wiley & Sons: Chichester, pp. 41–65.

Montanari, A. and Williams, A.M. (1995) Introduction: Tourism and economic restructuring in Europe. In A. Montanari and A.M. Williams (eds) (1995) *European Tourism. Regions, Spaces and Restructuring*. Chichester: John Wiley & Sons, pp. 1–15.

Morrison, A. (2000) *Golf and Genealogy to Spearhead Drive for us Tourists*. http://www.scotland.go.uk/news/2000/04/se1024.asp

Munt, I. (1994) The 'other' postmodern tourism: Culture, travel and the new middle class. *Theory, Culture and Society*, 11, 101–123.

Palmer, C. (1999), Tourism and the symbols of identity. *Tourism Management*, 20, 313–321.

Poon, A. (1989) Competitive strategies for a new tourism. In C. Cooper, (ed.) *Progress in Tourism, Recreation and Hospitality Management* (Vol. 1), London: Belhaven.

Scotexchange.net (2002) *Know Your Market*. http://www.scotexchange.net/know_your_market/genealogy_-_niche_-_genealogy.htm

Scottish Enterprise Edinburgh and Lothian and The City of Edinburgh Council (2003) *Scottish Ancestral Research: A guide to the wealth of genealogy and family history resources in Edinburgh and Lothians*. Scottish Enterprise Edinburgh and Lothian and The City of Edinburgh Council, Edinburgh.

Scottish Executive (2000) *A New Strategy for Scottish Tourism*. Edinburgh.

Scottish Tourist Board (1999) *Tourism Attitudinal Study*. STB.

Scottish Tourist Board (2001) *Genealogy Tourism Strategy and Marketing Plan*. STB.

Sproat, M. (2001) *Genealogy Tourism Strategy and Marketing Plan*. STB.

Sproat, M. (2002) *Scottish Roots Dig into the Past*. www.scotland.gov/pages/news/extras/00005600.aspx

Swarbrooke, J. and Horner, S. (1999) *Consumer Behaviour in Tourism*. Oxford: Butterworth –Heinemann, p. 221.

Taylor, C. (2002) *Genealogy: No Ordinary Journey*. Scotland Vacation Planner 2003. Great Britain: VisitScotland and British Tourist Authority, pp. 68–71.

Walsh, K. (1992) *The Representations of the Past: Museums and Heritage in the Postmodern World*. London: Routledge.

Further reading

Ancestral Tourism Industry Steering Group (2003) 'Ancestral Tourism – Trading on the family tree', Hopetown House, South Queensberry.

Basu, P. (2001) Hunting down home: Reflections on homeland and the search for identity in the Scottish diaspora. In Bender, B. (2001) *Contested Landscapes: Movement Exile and Place*. Oxford: Berg.

Cohen, R. (1997) *Global Diasporas: An Introduction*. London: Routledge.

Pretes, M. (1995) Postmodern Tourism. The Santa Claus industry. *Annals of Tourism Research*, 22(1), 1–15.

Sharpley, R. (1996) Tourism and consumer culture in postmodern society. In M. Robinson, N. Evans and P. Callaghan (eds) *Proceedings of the Tourism and Cuture: Towards the 21st Century Conference*, Centre for Travel and Tourism/Business Education Publishers, Sunderland, pp. 203–215.

Tomlinson, J. (1999) *Globalization and Culture*. Cambridge: Polity Press.

Questions

1 Discuss whether technology is leading 'ancestral tourism' or vice versa.
2 Develop an alternative to the term 'ancestral tourist' that may be meaningfully applied to this niche.

Websites

http://www.ancestraltourism.com
http://www.butesonsanddaughters.com
http://www.rootshebrides.com/
http://scotsorigins.com
http://scotexchange.net/ancestral/knowyourmarket/genealogy

6

Gastronomic tourism
Comparing food and wine tourism experiences

C. Michael Hall and Richard Mitchell

Introduction

Since the 1960s, interest in wine and food – as illustrated through cooking programmes on television and radio and sales of cookbooks – has become a significant component of popular culture in the developed world. Indeed, the consumption of wine and food is an important part of contemporary lifestyles, often indicating social status and the extent of cultural capital. The changed consumption of wine and food in western society is also marked by an increase in eating out or purchasing takeaways, this occurring at a time when not only are there more cookbooks and cooking shows on television than ever before, but also fewer and fewer people actually know how to cook. As a significant component of contemporary lifestyles it should therefore be of little surprise that specific forms of wine and food consumption have also become an important part of tourism (Hall and Mitchell, 2000). This chapter will use a case study from New Zealand to highlight key characteristics of the gastronomic tourism niche.

Defining the niche

Clearly we all have to eat, whether at home or at holiday. However, food and wine has historically tended to be in the background of the tourist experience as part of the overall hospitality service that is provided for travellers. Yet, increasingly, wine and food has become a focal point for travel decision-making and the hallmark attraction of a number of destinations around the world. This chapter will provide an examination of the wine and food tourism niche, which is often described as gourmet or gastronomic tourism, providing a definition of the subject. It will then go on to examine gastronomic tourism from demand and supply perspectives. A study of winery visitation and post consumer behaviour in New Zealand will be presented. The chapter also serves to illustrate the potential of gastronomic tourism as a tool for rural regional development.

Food tourism is defined by Hall and Mitchell (2001: 308) as 'visitation to primary and secondary food producers, food festivals, restaurants and specific locations for which food tasting and/or experiencing the attributes of specialist food production region are the primary motivating factor for travel'. Wine tourism is a subset of food tourism, being defined as visitation to vineyards, wineries, wine festivals and wine shows, for which grape wine tasting and/or experiencing the attributes of a grape wine region are the prime motivating factors for visitors (Hall, 1996). Such definitions do not mean that any trip to a restaurant is food tourism; rather the desire to experience a particular type of food or the produce of a specific region or even to taste the dishes of a particular chef must be the major motivation for such travel. Indeed, such is the need for food to be a primary factor in influencing travel behaviour and decision-making that as a form of special interest travel, food tourism may possibly be regarded as an examples of culinary, gastronomic, gourmet or cuisine tourism that reflects consumers for whom interest in food and wine is a form of 'serious leisure' (Hall and Mitchell, 2001; Hall *et al.*, 2003; Mitchell and Hall, 2003) (Figure 6.1).

Although there is substantial overlap between these concepts, subtle differences in interpretation do exist. Gourmet tourism usually occurs in terms of visits to expensive and/or highly rated restaurants, wineries and festivals. There is a

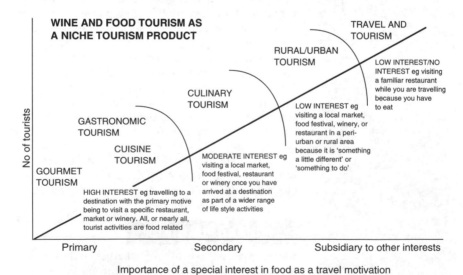

Importance of a special interest in food as a travel motivation

Figure 6.1 Food tourism as niche and special interest tourism. *Source*: After Hall & Sharples, 2003.

tendency for such products to be expensive and exclusive. Gastronomic or culinary tourism suggests a wider interest in food and wine, that may include expensive products, but which is also typically related to interest in the broader dimensions of wine and food and the cultures and landscapes that produce them. Cuisine tourism is similar in scope but instead reflects special interests in specific types of cuisine, whether national or regional. In all three categories, visits to adjunct products such as cooking schools or specialist tours (whether accompanied or self-guided) is important. Such definitional distinctions are also significant because they also alert the reader to the potential dimensions of the food and wine tourism market. However, for all these categories described so far as part of food tourism, food and wine will rank as the main or a major travel motivator. Although food and wine are also significant elements of what is usually described as rural or urban tourism, they are not major motivations for travel; instead food and wine (or beer or whisky) become a part of the overall attractiveness of a particular location and the rural or urban tourism experience. Nevertheless, the sales of food to such tourists may also be significant from the perspective of individual firms and regions as whole.

The emergence of food and wine tourism

A lay perspective on food and wine tourism might suggest that food and drinks have always been a part of the tourism experience. Indeed, that is true, but accounts suggest that it was not until the early to mid-nineteenth century, with the invention of the restaurant and the commodification of cuisines into regional and national categories and as a result of the medium of cookbooks and codification of cooking styles, that food and wine became a travel product in its own right. However, the number of travellers who were food and wine tourists at this time was extremely small, not only because of lifestyle interest but also because of the time and monetary costs of mobility. However, improvements in technology allowed not only people to travel further in a shorter period of time but also allowed foodstuffs to do the same. It is therefore perhaps of no great surprise that the designation of the first wine trails and roads in Germany in the late 1920s coincided with the growth of automobile ownership and the development of autobahn out from the larger cities. Reflexive interest in food also began to grow in the immediate post-Second World War period as not only did the range of foodstuffs available to households in western countries also grow rapidly because of the end of rationing and further improvements in transport technology but, so of course did the movement of people.

One of the key understandings of the tourism-food and tourism-wine relationships is that when people travel they take their 'tastebuds and stomachs' with them and, when they return home, some of the new acquired tastes may then influence their food consumption in terms of choice of restaurant and selection of what is purchased to eat at home. Arguably, demand for the wide range of cuisines to be found in restaurants in the developed world is as much a function of travel and interest in 'the other' as it is the mobility of migrant or ethnic populations. The rise of celebrity chefs and celebrity restaurants that has occurred since the late 1970s has served to reinforce not only the potential attraction of such restaurants, but also the role of the media with respect to food and drinks in making cuisine a major element of contemporary western lifestyle. Nowadays, the 'kind' of food and wine consumed and the 'location' where it is consumed are indicators of a lifestyle as much as the holiday destination and the activities undertaken. The transition of food and drinks, from a necessity to a status commodity, has extremely important implications for the firms, places and people that produce food and wine tourism.

Food and wine tourism production

Although food and wine tourism existed on a small scale, through for example wine trails in parts of Europe, it was not really until the 1970s that it started to develop to any scale. As noted above, part of the reason for this was greater personal mobility and changes in consumer tastes, but, just as important, was the beginning of agricultural restructuring in the developed world that is continuing to the present day. As a result of changes to international trade agreements and the move toward tariff removal and reductions in agricultural subsidies many producers had to find new ways of doing business. Some left the land; however a number also started to diversify into new products, for example, new wine production as in Australia, Canada, New Zealand and South America; or the growing of new livestock or crops to take advantage of new export opportunities, e.g. deer farming in New Zealand, avocado farming in Australia. Another response to agricultural restructuring was to add value to existing production, often by selling direct to customers, e.g. the farmers' market boom in North America began in the 1970s, arriving in Australia and the United Kingdom in the mid-1990s. A further response was to focus on artisan production of small-scale high-value products, such as specialist cheeses, which could be sold direct to restaurants or consumers for a premium. A critical element in all of these responses was the role of direct customer contact as a means of increasing return on production. Although many customers often would not see themselves as tourists, to the tourism researcher they indeed are, often day-visitors, but also including weekenders within the peri-urban zone, while the growth in international holidays and international business and transport networks also provided opportunities for the internationalisation of even small food firms.

From the production perspective, a number of advantages of food tourism can therefore be identified (Hall *et al.*, 2003), particularly for small producers.

- *Create relationships with customers.* The opportunity to meet staff and to see 'behind the scenes' can lead to positive relationships with consumers which may lead to both direct sales and indirect sales through positive 'word of mouth' advertising.
- *Increased margins* through direct sales to the consumer, where the absence of distributor costs is not carried over entirely to the consumer.
- *Increased consumer exposure* to product and increased opportunities to sample product than through normal retail outlets.
- *Build brand awareness and loyalty* through establishing links between the producer and consumer, and purchase of company branded merchandise.
- An *additional sales outlet*, or for smaller producers who cannot guarantee volume or consistency of supply, perhaps the only feasible sales outlet.
- *Marketing intelligence* on products and customers. Producers can gain instant and valuable feedback on the consumer reaction to their existing products, and are able to trial new additions to their product range. Visitors can be added to a

mailing list which can be developed as a customer database to both target and inform customers.

- *Educational opportunities*. Visits help create awareness and appreciation of specific types of foods and food as a whole; the knowledge and interest generated by this can be expected to result in increased consumption.

However, this is not to argue that tourism operations may be right for all firms. Potential drawbacks may include demands on scarce capital, opportunity costs, seasonality, inappropriate location or product, and increased costs and management time required to serve consumers direct. The wider region within which firms are located can also benefit from food tourism development. Apart from the more obvious benefits such as employment and income generation, regions may also benefit because of

- Association with a *quality product*.
- Reinforcement of *authentic* tourist experiences allows visitors to see beyond the shop front and establish strong relationships with a destination, often in relation to the heritage dimensions of particular foods.
- Food products are an *attraction*. Existence of product suppliers, such as markets and wineries and producers, as well as the landscape within which they are located, provides a motivation to visit an area, stay in accommodation and eat at restaurants. The development of new products may also help extend length of stay.

Indeed, such is the potential interrelationship between food, wine and tourism at the regional level, because of their often place-branded nature, that there is increasing emphasis being given to the protection of the intellectual property of place, e.g. the right to use place names such as Champagne. Nevertheless, given the increasing importance attached to gastronomy as a mechanism for regional development it should therefore not be surprising that governments and development agencies around the developed world are now increasingly seeking to intervene to assist in the development of food and wine tourism, particularly given the perceived growth in consumer interest.

Food and wine tourism demand

It is widely recognised that tourists provide a significant proportion of the market for restaurants and cafés around the world (Mitchell and Hall, 2003). For example, dining or eating out is usually one of the most commonly cited activities for international visitors. Nevertheless, as noted by the Economic Planning Group of Canada (EPGC) (2001: 10) 'there appears to be little market research on culinary tourism'. In response, the EPGC developed a 'Cuisine and Wine Interest Index' as part of a travel activities and motivation survey of Americans and Canadians. The Index was developed from a number of cuisine related activities undertaken in the previous two years, including:

- Pursuit of vacation experiences relating to cuisine and wine.
- Participation in restaurant dining and local outdoor cafes.
- Touring a region's wineries where you stay one or more nights.

- Going to wineries for a day visit and tastings.
- Interest in wine regions and attractions.

Factor analysis was then used to classify respondents according to their level of interest. According to the study results in Canada high interest respondents accounted for 14.2% of respondents (extrapolated to 2.5 million individuals), while another 18.8% (3.37 million) had a moderate interest. In the United States high interest accounted for 19.6% (30.65 million) and a further 18.8% exhibited a moderate interest. Interest was strongest in the Pacific/Hawaii states of California, Hawaii, Oregon, Washington, Alaska and the Southern Atlantic states of Florida, Georgia, North Carolina, South Carolina. In both Canada and the USA higher levels of interest were observed amongst the more affluent and better educated sectors of the marketplace, particularly couples without children (EPGC, 2001).

One area in which some marketing research has been conducted is with respect to farmers and produce markets and farm outlets. Research by the UK National Association of Farmers' Markets suggests that the typical customer falls into the AB (upper/middle class) or C1 (lower middle class) socio-economic group – working people with high disposable incomes, 'the kind who know a good cut of Dexter beef when they see one' (Purvis, 2002). In the United States, demographic surveys at farmers' markets have indicated that patrons are predominantly white females with above average incomes and education (Mitchell and Hall, 2003).

One of the more in-depth studies of the local food tourist market was undertaken by Enteleca Research and Consultancy (ERC) (2000) in a study of four regions in England (the South West, Cumbria, Yorkshire and the Heart of England). Overall 72% of people visiting the four regions took an interest in local foods during their visit. However, as suggested by Figure 6.1 the vast majority were not actively seeking local food out but were happy to try it when they came across it. According to ERC (2000) only 6–8% of UK holidaymakers and visitors (day visitors as high as 11%) and 3% of international visitors could be described as gastronomy tourists – seeking local food and drink is a particular reason for choosing their holiday destination. However, 30–33% of UK holidaymakers and visitors were also described as interested purchasers – people who believe that food in general can contribute to their enjoyment of their holiday and they purchase/eat local foods when the opportunity arises. Nevertheless, such snapshot market profiling gives only a partial picture of the potential value of gastronomic tourism as a niche tourism market and product opportunity. The following case study of winery visitors in New Zealand instead examines not only different dimensions of the wine tourism experience but how they may change over different stages of the travel experience and the potential implications that this may have for longer-term consumption of the product.

Case study: winery visitation and post-visit behaviour in New Zealand

The tourism experience can be defined as consisting of five stages (see also Mitchell *et al.*, 2000): pre-visit, travel-to, on-site, travel-from and post-visit. However, few empirical studies of tourism study more than one stage of the experience. Nevertheless, as Mitchell *et al.* (2000: 132) note, wine tourism 'provides an excellent opportunity to study the on-site tourist experience within a wider temporal (pre- and post-visit) and spatial (the experience at home and of the wider regional tourism) context'. In particular, wine is 'a tangible, transportable and durable product that can be experienced in a number of locations before, during and after the on-site winery experience (which tends to be less tangible, transportable and durable)'. Table 6.1 demonstrates this by providing a list of wine experiences and business opportunities across all five phases of the tourist experience. Several authors have also noted the significance of winery visitation for wine distribution, customer satisfaction and positive brand and image development (e.g. Charters and Ali-Knight, 2002; Hall *et al.*, 2000; Houghton, 2002; King and Morris, 1999, n.d.; Mitchell *et al.*, 2000; Morris and King, 1997; O'Neill and Charters, 2000) at both the individual winery and regional level. Recognition of the significance of winery visitation is not limited to academic study, with Mark Mathewson (cited in Hall *et al.*, 2000: 12), of Kendall-Jackson (a major Sonoma Valley wine producer), stating that while tourism may not be a major outlet for all wineries for operations such as Kendall-Jackson 'the benefit lies in the opportunity we have to make a lasting impression on a consumer. It is my belief that the positive [wine tourism] experiences in our retail room affects purchase behaviour in the marketplace'.

Methods

The 1999 New Zealand Winery Visitors Survey surveyed winery visitors on-site at 33 New Zealand wineries (hand-out mail-back) and then a follow-up survey was mailed out 6 to 8 months post-visit. From an initial sample of 1,090, 636 follow-up surveys were distributed to those that had indicated a willingness to take part. Some 358 usable surveys were returned, giving a response rate of 56.3% and a sub-sample of 32.8% of the original sample. Included in the follow-up survey were elements of on-going purchase and consumption of wine, as well as more experiential elements such as recollection of the visit and word-of-mouth behaviour and enduring levels of satisfaction. Data were entered into a duplicate copy of the original SPSS (Ver. 11) database so that all information from the Phase One questionnaire was able to be analysed for the Phase Two sample. This was done to enable a comparison of the sample characteristics (Table 6.2) and behaviours (both on-site and post-visit) to be compared for the Phase Two sub-sample, as well as to minimise the duplication of data collection and data entry. Both the Phase One and Phase Two samples have very similar characteristics, with only a very small number of differences observed between the main demographic, psychographic and supply side variables.

Recollections of the visit

Both the Phase One and Phase Two questionnaires asked respondents to provide a list of positive (most enjoyable aspects) and negative (suggested improvements) elements of their visit. In Phase Two, as in Phase One, the vast majority of respondents provided a list of positive elements (336 of 358 respondents providing 695 items), while less than 45% provided negative elements (157 of 358 providing 204 suggestions). Interestingly, however, the Phase Two sub-sample saw a dramatic increase in the number of respondents providing

Table 6.1 Wine tourism and the stages of the travel experience and associated marketing activities

Stage of travel experience	Wine experience	Marketing opportunities
Pre-visit (Anticipation)	Wine from destination/winery at home, restaurant or wine club.	Distribution in main origin areas for regional tourism.
	Previous experience at winery/wine region.	Positive on-site experiences (past).
	Previous experience of other wineries.	Promotional material that uses place attributes as well as wine attributes.
	Promotional material and advertising for winery/ wine region.	
Travel to	Wine en route (e.g. at restaurant or on airline).	Wine on airlines or major stopping points en route.
	Airline promotional video/ in-flight magazine article of destination that includes wine.	Promotional video and magazine articles.
Destination/ On-site visit	Winery experience:	Positive winery experience.
	- Tasting	
	- Education/interpretation	
	- Service	
	- Setting	
	- Activities (e.g. tours)	
	- Food	
	Wine at hotel, restaurant or café in region.	Wine in local hotels, restaurants and cafés.
Travel from	Wine en route home (e.g. at restaurant or on airline).	Wine on airlines or major stopping points en route.
Post-visit (reminiscence)	Wine from destination/ winery at home, restaurant or wine club.	Distribution in main origin areas for regional tourism
	Previous experience at winery/ wine region.	Positive on-site experiences (past).
	Previous experience of other wineries.	Promotional material that use place attributes as well as wine attributes.
	Promotional material and advertising for winery/wine region.	
	Photos and souvenirs.	Souvenirs, including videos, DVDs and books.
	Wine purchased at cellar door.	
	Mail order/newsletter	Mail order/newsletter.
	Interactive website	Interactive website

Source: After Mitchel *et al*. (2000) and Mitchell and Hall (2003).

suggested improvements, rising from just 36 respondents at Phase One to 157 respondents at Phase Two. Overall this suggests that the winery experience was overwhelmingly positive and that the positive nature of the experience is relatively enduring (also reflected in very high satisfaction ratings, see below).

Table 6.2 Differences between the proportions of the two samples

Variable	Phase 1 (% of sample)	Phase 2 (% of sample)	SSD
Region	(*n* = 1,090)	(*n* = 358)	
Auckland	9.4	10.3	n/a
Bay of Plenty	4.8	5.3	n/a
Hawkes Bay	14.0	15.1	✓
Northland	2.5	2.0	n/a
Wairarapa	6.0	6.1	n/a
Central Otago	32.4	34.9	✓
Marlborough	20.3	17.9	×
Nelson	10.0	8.1	n/a
Canterbury	0.7	0.3	n/a
Origin	(*n* = 1,043)	(*n* = 349)	
Local	19.0	20.6	×
Non-local	65.7	67.3	×
International	15.3	12.0	×
Income	(*n* = 1,000)	(*n* = 336)	
Lower	20.0	19.0	×
Middle	50.1	47.9	×
Upper	11.6	16.1	×
High	18.3	17.0	×
Education	(*n* = 1,057)	(*n* = 353)	
High school	18.4	17.6	×
Trade	20.7	20.4	×
Some university	15.9	16.4	×
Undergraduate	14.1	14.7	×
Postgraduate	30.8	30.9	×
Winery Category	(*n* = 1,090)	(*n* = 358)	
Category I	74.9	74.6	×
Category II	11.4	12.6	×
Category III	13.8	12.8	×
Gender	(*n* = 1,076)	(*n* = 349)	
Male	45.7	50.3	×
Female	53.6	49.7	×
10-Year Age Group	(*n* = 1,079)	(*n* = 358)	
18–29	18.4	17.9	×
30s	26.8	25.7	×
40s	22.8	24.3	×
50s	20.1	20.1	×
60+	12.0	12.0	×
Generation	(*n* = 1,079)	(*n* = 358)	
Generation X & Y†	45.1	43.6	×
Baby boomers	35.3	39.4	×
Matures & seniors†	19.6	17.0	×
Wine Knowledge	(*n* = 1,082)	(*n* = 354)	
No or basic	40.9	35.6	×
Intermediate	51.5	54.5	×
Advanced	7.6	9.9	n/a

✓ = a statistically significant difference identified between the proportions of the two samples at the 95% level. × = no statistically significant difference identified at the 95% level. n/a = no test for statistically significant difference was possible as both proportions must be above 10%. † = variables combined to ensure that a test for statistically significant difference was possible (i.e. all proportions were greater than 10%). *Lower Income* = < $30,000 per annum, *Middle Income* = $30,000--$59,999, *Upper Income* = $60,000-$79,999, *High Income* = > $80,000.

Positive recollections: most enjoyable aspects

Figure 6.2 demonstrates that several positive aspects (namely the wine and tasting, food, socialising and price) were mentioned by a similar proportion of respondents from the overall sample and the Phase Two sub-sample (both in terms of their Phase One and Phase Two responses). This suggests that these items do not attain any greater or lesser significance as time progresses post-visit. However, aspects of the service and staff and learning about wine are cited by a smaller proportion of respondents in the post-visit phase of the survey. Despite this, aspects of the service and staff still remain as the most frequently cited positive aspects of the visit, but in relative terms the wine attains greater significance. Perhaps more significantly, the setting of the winery experience attained a greater significance in the post-visit phase of the survey. In particular the proportion of respondents mentioning aspects of the setting increased by around 50% to be almost a third of respondents, placing it well ahead of learning about wine post-visit. While atmosphere and ambience also increases in proportion and ranking, this would seem to be less significant as comments relating to atmosphere tend to be quite generic and therefore may have been a default response (e.g. 'just a lovely day' 'very relaxing atmosphere', etc.)

Negative recollections: suggested improvements

Setting appears to take on even more significance when the negative recollections of the visit are taken into consideration, with Figure 6.3 showing a rise in the proportion of respondents making suggested improvements to facilities post-visit. A lack of food (cafés and restaurants) at wineries also remained an important issue for around 20% of responses and reflects the relatively under-developed state of wine tourism in several regions in 1999. The wine itself, the wine tasting and learning about wine were half as

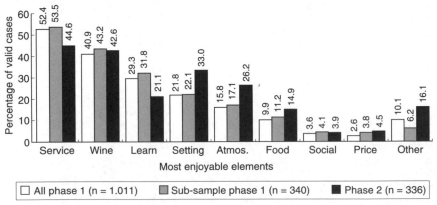

Figure 6.2 Positive recollections of the visit (immediately and post-visit). *Service* = service and staff, *Wine* = Wine and tasting, *Learn* = learning about wine including tours, *Setting* = includes the cellar door, vineyard and the surrounding scenery, *Atmos.* = atmosphere and ambience, *Social* = socialising with others, *Price* = good price for wine or tasting or value for money.

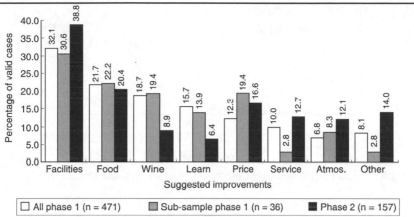

Figure 6.3 Negative recollections of the visit (immediately and post-visit).
Facilities = includes improvements to the cellar door, outdoor areas, access and equipment, *Wine* = Wine and tasting, *Learn* = learning about wine including tours, *Price* = good price for wine or tasting or value for money. *Service* = service and staff, *Atmos.* = atmosphere and ambience.

likely to be cited as areas requiring improvement, perhaps suggesting that a negative wine experience was not as enduring as other negative aspects of the winery visit.

Enduring satisfaction

Levels of satisfaction with both the wine and winery experience were measured via an 11-point Likert scale (where 0 is *Totally Dissatisfied* and 10 is *Totally Satisfied*). Ratings for both wine and the winery experience were relatively high for Phase Two, as they were in Phase One. Figure 6.4 demonstrates that, as with satisfaction measured on-site (see Mitchell and Hall, 2001), around one in four respondents remained totally satisfied with their experience (29.3%) and the wine (24.4%), while less than 4% of respondents scored their experience (3.7%) or wine (3.9%) less than average. Once again, similar ratings of experience and wine satisfaction were recorded.

A Pearson's correlation coefficient of 0.538 (0.01 significance level) between Phase One and Phase Two satisfaction with wine and 0.574 (0.01 significance level) between Phase One and Phase Two satisfaction with winery experience suggests a moderate level of enduring satisfaction. This is further demonstrated by Figures 6.5 and 6.6, which show that around 65% to 70% of respondents made little or no change to their original score (i.e. their post-visit rating was within one point of their original rating). Meanwhile, ratings higher and lower than their original were provided by similar proportions of respondents (i.e. around 15% in each instance). This suggests that satisfaction with the winery visit (including the wine tasted) does not alter much over time and this confirms much of what has been suspected about the significance of the winery visit in terms of positive brand association but, until now, has not been empirically tested.

The only statistically significant difference identified between different segments of the winery visitation market identified was between males' and females' satisfaction with the winery experience, with males being almost twice as likely as females to have a diminishing level of satisfaction with their experience. Conversely females were more

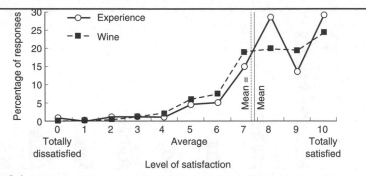

Figure 6.4 Enduring satisfaction with winery experience ($n = 348$) and wine ($n = 332$).

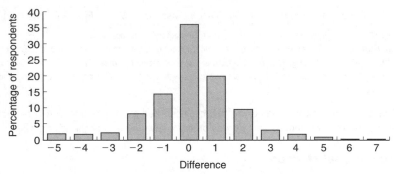

Figure 6.5 Difference between on-site and post-visit satisfaction with wine.

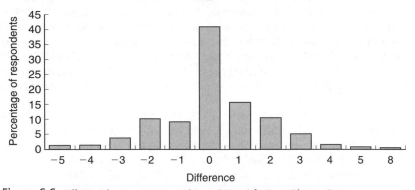

Figure 6.6 Difference between on-site and post-visit satisfaction with experience.

likely to report no change or an increase in satisfaction over time. While these on-site differences related to satisfaction with wine (with women rating it higher than males) and the post-visit behaviour relates to experience, this does follow Mitchell and Hall's (2001: 72) suggestion that the gender specific attitudes to the winery may be 'borne out in the longer term, with positive assessments by women leading to greater customer loyalty'. In this case, customer loyalty is borne out in a more enduring favourable attitude towards the winery and the experience it provides than their male counterparts. Therefore it might be expected that this will also translate into positive post-visit purchasing behaviour by females, and it might also be expected that this gender difference will flow through to recommendations made to others.

Recommendations to others (word-of-mouth behaviour)

High levels of satisfaction and few suggested improvements would suggest that respondents might be likely to make recommendations to other parties relating to the winery or the region. Indeed, the vast majority of respondents reported that they had made some form of recommendation to another party following their winery visit, with just 7% of respondents stating that they did not make any recommendation at all. A visit to the winery of survey was the most frequently made recommendation, with recommendations of the wine and wine region also being made by more than half of all respondents.

The question also arises as to which segments might provide the greatest level of opinion leadership, a term describing those most likely to make recommendations for a particular product category (Schiffman and Kanuk, 1987). Very few statistically significant differences were identified between segments, with only winery category and wine knowledge showing any differences. Those visiting Category III wineries (i.e. those producing greater than 200,000 litres per year), were less likely to recommend a visit to the winery than those visiting small and medium sized wineries. There are several possible reasons for this that are likely to include aspects of the market itself and the nature of the experiences provided by the different categories of the wineries. For example, it could be that smaller wineries are more likely to offer more intimate experiences related to lifestyle behaviours (i.e. indulgence, relaxation and café lifestyle) and these experiences help individuals define who they are and, as such, they receive a form of self-assurance from making such recommendations (i.e. a form of self-involvement), whereas larger wineries, where larger numbers of visitors are involved, might be perceived as a less personal or intimate experience, therefore providing less appeal in terms of the self-definition necessary for those motivated by self-involvement (i.e. they might have 'snob-value').

Implications for management

There are several implications of these findings of the above case study for gastronomic tourism in general, and for wineries in particular. These findings have confirmed that, in terms of the enduring positive qualities of the experience, service and staffing issues are critically important, but that the significance of this may decline in relative significance over time, while other aspects (notably the setting and atmosphere) appear to take on greater significance. This means that in gastronomic tourism, visitation to the site of production is a key component of consumer behaviour, e.g. food markets, farm-gate sales, food factories and providers need to take care in the planning and management of the servicescape of businesses. For wineries, for example, this most definitely includes the vineyard and winery itself, as well as the cellar door facilities, which appear also to take on more significance in terms of negative recollections of the experience. Not surprisingly, the wine itself remains a core component of the winery experience and, in fact, the negative aspects of the visit relating to the wine diminish with time. Therefore, businesses not only have to provide a good product and high levels of service, but they must pay particular attention to the setting within which the experience occurs. The identification of reasonably strong levels of enduring satisfaction further reinforces the need for product and service delivery to be included in the planning, development and management of direct sales venues, such as the cellar door, particularly given the impact of enduring satisfaction on purchasing behaviour and word-of-mouth.

It is also interesting to note that the gender differences identified by Mitchell and Hall (2001) continue through to enduring satisfaction, where they suggested that the development of marketing and service strategies on the basis of typologies of the 'typical winery visitor' is fraught with difficulties. The current findings suggest that it is now even more important to further understand the differences between male and female consumers, their attitudes and behaviours.

Final considerations

Gastronomic tourism is a rapidly growing area of niche tourism. However, as this chapter has demonstrated, there are a number of different elements of supply and demand that lead to a complex business environment. Nevertheless, changes in consumption mean that food and drinks, rather than being just regarded as fuel, are now elements of lifestyle creating substantial opportunities for producers.

Several examples of the advantages that gastronomic tourism can provide for producers have also been identified. However, as the case study has demonstrated, for food tourism to be a success it is vital that a positive relationship is established with customers not only through the delivery of good food products but that attention also be given to the wider service scape in which it occurs. For tourism at a regional level such an observation is also important because it reinforces the relationship between the environment in which food is produced and the development of destination image and brand. Finally, though, the chapter also cautioned that for some producers food tourism may not be the best form of business strategy.

Undoubtedly, gastronomy has come to the forefront of the tourism experience and of tourism research in recent years. It has also developed its own niche characteristics that have proven attractive to firms, particularly in rural areas. From the perspective of many consumers, food is also a significant motivation in tourism lifestyles. Finally, as the case study in this chapter has demonstrated, the sensuous nature of gastronomy can provide substantial opportunities for visitor recollection of the tourism experience for many years after the initial visit. There are few other forms of tourism, if any, in which travel memories can be so easily revisited – just by opening a bottle of wine or tasting a slice of cheese.

References

Charters, S. and Ali Knight, J. (2002) Who is the wine tourist? *Tourism Management*, 23, 311–319.

Economic Planning Group of Canada (EPG) (2001) *Wine and Culinary Tourism in Ontario – Executive Summary*. Toronto: EPG.

Enteleca Research and Consultancy (2000) *Tourist's Attitudes Towards Regional and Local Food*. London: Ministry of Agriculture, Fisheries and Food, and The Countryside Agency.

Hall, C.M. (1996) Wine tourism in New Zealand. In G. Kearsley (ed.) *Tourism Down Under II, Conference Proceedings*. Dunedin: Centre for Tourism, University of Otago, pp. 109–119.

Hall, C.M. and Mitchell, R. (2000) We are what we eat: food, tourism and globalisation. *Tourism, Culture and Communication*, 2, 29–37.

Hall, C.M. and Mitchell, R. (2001) Wine and food tourism. In N. Douglas, N. Douglas and R. Derrett (eds) *Special Interest Tourism: Context and Cases*. Brisbane, Australia: John Wiley & Sons, pp. 307–329.

Hall, C.M., Sharples, E. and Smith, A. (2003) The experience of consumption or the consumption of experiences?: Challenges and issues in food tourism. In C.M. Hall, E. Sharples, R. Mitchell, B. Cambourne and N. Macionis (eds) *Food Tourism Around the World: Development, Management and Markets*. Oxford: Butterworth-Heinemann, pp. 314–336.

Hall, C.M., Johnson, G.R., Cambourne, B., Macionis, N., Mitchell, R.D. and Sharples, E. (2000) Wine tourism: an introduction. In C.M. Hall, E. Sharples, B. Cambourne, and N. Macionis (eds) *Wine and Tourism Around the World*. Oxford: Butterworth Heinemann, pp. 1–23

Houghton, M. (2002) Wine festivals: their effectiveness as a promotional strategy for wineries (a case study of the Rutherglen region). Unpublished Masters Thesis, La Trobe University, Victoria, Australia.

King, C. and Morris, R. (1999) Wine tourism: costs and returns. In R. Dowling and J. Carlsen (eds) *Wine Tourism: Perfect Partners. Proceedings of the First Australian Wine Tourism Conference, Margaret River, Western Australia, May* 1998. Canberra: Bureau of Tourism Research, pp. 233 45

King, C and Morris, R. (n.d.) The flow on effects of winery cellar door visits. Unpublished report, Bunbury: Edith Cowan University.

Mitchell, R.D, Hall, C.M. and McIntosh, A.J. (2000) Wine tourism and consumer behaviour. In C.M. Hall, E. Sharples, B. Cambourne, and N. Macionis, (eds) *Wine Tourism Around the World*. Oxford: Butterworth Heinemann, pp. 115–135.

Mitchell, R.D. and Hall, C.M. (2001) The influence of gender and region on the New Zealand winery visit. *Tourism Recreation Research*, 26(2), 63–75.

Mitchell, R. and Hall, C.M. (2003) Consuming tourists: food tourism consumer behaviour. In C.M. Hall, E. Sharples, R. Mitchell, B. Cambourne, and N. Macionis (eds) *Food Tourism Around the World: Development, Management and Markets*. Oxford: Butterworth-Heinemann, Oxford, pp. 60–81.

Morris, R. and King, C. (1997) Cooperative marketing for small business growth and regional economic development: a case study in wine tourism. In S. Kunkel and M. Meeks (eds) *The Engine of Global Economic Development, 42nd World Conference International Council for Small Business, San Francisco, June* 1997, *Conference Proceedings*. http://www.icsb.org/conferences/w97/papers/FullPapers/index.htm [accessed 7 August 2000].

O'Neill, M. and Charters, S. (2000) Delighting the customer – how good is the cellar door experience? *International Wine Marketing Supplement*, 1(1), 11–16.

Purvis, A. (2002) So what's your beef? *The Observer*, 14 April. (http://www.observer.co.uk/foodmonthly/story/0,9950,681828,00.html)

Schiffman, L.G. and Kanuk, L.L. (1987) *Consumer Behavior* (3rd edn). London: Prentice-Hall.

Further reading

See the special edition of *Journal of Travel and Tourism Marketing*, 14(3/4), 2003 on wine and food tourism marketing.

Hall, C.M., Sharples, E., Mitchell, R., Cambourne, B. and Macionis, N. (eds) (2003) *Food Tourism Around the World: Development, Management and Markets*. Oxford: Butterworth-Heinemann.

Hall, C.M., Sharples, E., Cambourne, B. and Macionis, N. (eds) (2000). *Wine Tourism Around the World: Development, Management and Markets*. Oxford: Butterworth-Heinemann.

Mitchell, R.D. and Hall, C.M. (2001) The influence of gender and region on the New Zealand winery visit. *Tourism Recreation Research*, 26(2), 63–75.

Questions

1 What are the advantages and disadvantages for small food producers of using tourism as a business strategy?
2 How might the benefits of post-visit behaviour be maximised for firms in food tourism?

Websites

International Culinary Tourism Association
www.culinarytourism.org/index.php
New Zealand Wine Growers
www.nzwine.com

7

Transport tourism
Travelling through heritage and contemporary recreation

Derek Hall

Within both 'Western' economies and 'transitional' societies post-industrial interest in heritage has encouraged a repositioning of the role of transport as an attraction. One aspect of this is a broadening of visitor markets in respect of gender, age and seasonality, to evolve products whose market appeal transcends that of the niche but does not (yet) possess the full characteristics of the mass.

Within such a dynamic context, this chapter aims briefly to:

- exemplify the 'niche' context of transport tourism
- discuss and evaluate the nature of transport enthusiasm and its role as niche tourism
- identify ways in which transport heritage tourism has broadened its market appeal.

The chapter concludes that transport, as both a heritage and a contemporary niche attraction, has been undervalued by tourism and leisure promoters. However, it is increasingly being recognized that transport has significant potential both in its own right and in combination with other locally or regionally based attractions.

Transport tourism: niche, mass or ?

Until relatively recently, transport for tourism was viewed as a means to an end, rather than a self-contained experience in its own right. It was conceptualized as a consumer-service rather than as a producer-service (Debbage and Daniels, 1998). Yet, not only is transport important as an essential underpinning for tourism, and helps to place tourism within a wider societal and environmental context, it can also be a focus of interest both because of its functions and also because of its intrinsic attributes. There are several dimensions to the relationship between transport and tourism (Hall, 1999), although only a few of these may render transport as a 'niche' tourism attraction.

The transport experience can be the primary if not the exclusive tourism experience, embracing qualities of heritage, nostalgia, education, uniqueness, added-value and entertainment. The commodification of transport and of travel experiences has generated new niche products, such as hot air ballooning or snowmobiling. There are perhaps three categories to be explored here: unique transport experiences, added-value experience within transport services, and the intrinsic attraction of transport itself.

First, certain forms of transport offer a unique transport experience based on the nature of the transport and the location it is set in, thereby contributing to the spirit of place. Diverse examples include Venetian gondolas plying the Grand Canal, San Francisco cable cars climbing Nob Hill, or Poland's Ostróda-Elblag Canal, providing cruises which involve the unique experience of the vessel being hauled overland on skipways to overcome an elevation difference between waterways (Furgala-Selezniow et al., 2003; Ostróda-Elblag Navigation, 2003). Such transport modes may be intended to be, or have become, a predominantly recreational attraction and experience rather than a practical means of getting from one place to another: being in or on the particular transport mode in its geographical setting is the primary experience. Second, added-value experience within transport services can embrace one-off prestige experiences such as travel in one direction on the opulently restored Orient Express (Orient Express, 2003).

Such commodification fuels the desire to experience transport and results in demand for visitor experiences rather than merely the products and services that support them. The concept of the experience economy, as articulated by Pine and Gilmore (1998); Gilmore and Pine (1999), is based upon an understanding that visitors need experiences with which they and the provider can engage and thereby both derive added value. Three similar transport-based case studies can exemplify this, incorporating two cultural heritage experiences from Central and Eastern Europe and one from North America (Table 7.1). In each case, an externally derived experience is superimposed upon three sets of 'internal' experiences: those of travel through an engaging landscape viewed from the transport mode, travel in or on heritage/nostalgia transport, and experience of service within that transport.

These examples suggest that a transport product and service combined can be sold at a premium when staged as an experience. Excitement and interaction particularly derive from 'captives' being assigned roles to play within their experience, which is taken one stage beyond evoking nostalgia by travelling on famous trains with historic associations (Page, 1975), or the desire to return to a personal past (Dann, 1994: 779).

Third, transport acts as a focus for the significant recreational sub-group whose interest and source of travelling is actual transport forms. Attendances at transport museums, rallies and excursions, and memberships of transport enthusiasts'

Table 7.1 Transport and cultural heritage tourism: added-value experience

Experience dimension	Exemplification		
	Pirin, Bulgaria	MÁV, Hungary	Grand Canyon Railway, USA
Transport Landscape Service experience	Horse and cart Bulgarian countryside Guided tour, stops, picnic lunch	Restored steam-hauled train Hungarian countryside Buffet coach, music, souvenirs, special car for children, competitions, photo stops, footplate experiences	Restored steam-hauled train 130 mile round-trip to the Grand Canyon Five classes of service are available with quality gastronomy. Strolling musicians entertain passengers with classic Western songs to recreate train travel as it was at the turn-of-the-century.
External experience	Met en route by bandits, 'kidnapped' and taken to an outlaws' hut where participants share a meal of locally hunted and freshly cooked game around a camp fire.	Held up by Gypsies and taken in horse carriages to a wedding where all passengers engage with the wedding guests through song and dance at the wedding reception.	Western characters stage a train robbery on the return trip to Williams.
Other detail	The Pirin Tourism Forum, established in 1997, is a regional tourist board, aiming at the development of sustainable tourism in Southwest Bulgaria, a member of the National Tourism Council and the Bulgarian Association for Alternative Tourism (BAAT).	An arm of the Hungarian state railways, MÁV Nostalgia, markets steam and diesel hauled excursions of restored luxury coaches to key locations within the country. Flagship of the fleet is the 'Royal Hungarian Express', formerly the presidential train, luxuriously appointed, with sleeping and dining cars and a piano bar car. It is promoted as being available from Budapest to any destination in Europe.	Recently added to the US National Register of Historic Places. Closed to normal service in 1968 and reopened with restored rolling stock between Williams (Arizona) and the Grand Canyon in 1989. The GC Railway is a tourism attraction in itself but it takes travellers to one of the world's largest natural tourism attractions, with a three and a half hour layover at the Grand Canyon. Williams' railway depot, historical buildings and museum provide a static attraction.

Sources: GCRR (2003); MÁV Nostalgia (2000); Pirin Tourism Forum (2000); Roberts and Hall (2001: 148–149).

organizations, emphasize that transport enthusiasts represent a significant leisure sub-culture and substantial niche market. In the UK, for example, more than 170 bus and/or tram rallies and special events are held annually (Anon, 2003). A voluminous literature exists aimed at all levels of transport enthusiasts and specialists, and is becoming increasingly international in scope, not least through the burgeoning of enthusiasts' websites (e.g. Indian Steam Railway Society, 2003; SteamRanger, 2003), organized visits programmes (Table 7.2) and merchandising (e.g. IGE, 2003). As indicated in Table 7.2, LCGB, arguably the UK's leading rail enthusiasts' society, collaborates with its equivalents as well as with transport engineering and historical organizations around the world, emphasizing the globalized network of such interest groups. Table 7.2 also draws the reader into the enthusiast's lexicon of locomotive designations, specialist activities and meaningful locations.

However, the insidious effect of, and responses to (perceived) global terrorism have impacted upon transport enthusiasm. A meeting of US security officials in Washington in March 2003 reportedly classified 'people sitting on train platforms who appear to be monitoring the timing of arrivals and departures' as suspicious behaviour (Wilson, 2003). In the UK, Network Rail, the company currently running the rail network, has taken this seriously, apparently regarding railway enthusiasts to be potential terrorists, and instructing those standing on platforms at its 16 major stations to move to the station concourse or leave. Some enthusiasts have complained about having film removed from their cameras.

The heightened security since 9/11 has otherwise inhibited the activities of aircraft enthusiasts, with many airport observation balconies remaining closed. Indeed, aviation enthusiasts are even more likely to have their motives misunderstood than other transport enthusiasts, and reports of their arrest are not infrequent. For example, the conviction of 12 British and two Dutch plane spotters on espionage charges by a Greek court in 2002 reflects certain countries' (in)security services' ignorance of the nature and purpose of transport enthusiasm, and of the extent to which detailed information on, for example, military aircraft, airfields, ships and other military transport, is widely available in the public domain (BBC, 2002a, 2002b).

Embracing wider arguments over the relationship between virtual reality travel and the real thing, the use of webcams for encouraging vicarious transport tourism experience raises some interesting questions. For example, the Llangollen Railway, a heritage attraction in Wales, has installed internet cameras linked by satellite to transmit images such that 'railway enthusiasts across the world are being given the opportunity to carry out their favourite hobby from the safety of their own armchair' (BBC, 2002c). In this pay-per-view scheme one camera records output from the locomotive shed while the other offers a view over the main railway track. Since 1430, steam locomotives can be viewed being cleaned and prepared, presenting what MacCannell (1974: 589) would interpret as back stage reproduction of otherwise forbidden spaces. Other railways are being encouraged to collaborate with the venture. But for many this application of information and communications technology cannot supplant the sensory stimulation of the all-embracing sights, sounds, smells and tactile experiences – heat from the engine, grit in the eye, the

Table 7.2 The Locomotive Club of Great Britain (LCGB) 2004 Visits Programme

Tour title and month	Brief tour details
1. IGE Slovakia Steam in the Snow: February	A repeat tour organized by IGE (InteressenGemeinschaft Eisenbahn).
2. Eritrea – Steam Charters: February	Organized in conjunction with DGEG (Deutsche Gesellschaft für Eisenbahngeschichte): LCGB's third visit to Eritrea.
3. USA – West Coast Action: March	A repeat visit to Los Angeles, San Diego, San Francisco, travelling on ordinary trains, LRT and trolleybuses.
4. Sri Lanka – Viceroy Steam: April	Travel on the chartered Viceroy set into the hill country and along the coast, to Kandy, Badulla and Galle. Shed and workshop visits and many photographic opportunities on the special trains.
5. France – Narrow Gauge Steam: April	A minibus tour to the area south of Paris to visit the Tacot de Lacs line and the tourist operation at Pithivier. Both lines will be laying on special photographic charters, passenger and freight trains.
6. Spain – Museum Visits: April–May	Two tours running back to back. The first weekend will be Madrid and the area to the north as far as Ponferrada. Then a high-speed train to Sevilla to feature the Rio Tinto area.
7. The Netherlands – Dordt in Stoom: May	Every 2 years there is a big steam festival in Dordrecht: boats, traction engines, railway locomotives.
8. Germany – Dresden Dampffest: May	A repeat Dampffest (steam festival) which will benefit from many of the lines around Dresden having been rebuilt after the floods of 2002.
9. Russia – Moscow, Gorki, Kolomna: June	Several days in Moscow, visiting main line stations, depots and preserved locomotives. Also Scherbinka Test Plant with charter trains there. The Dzherelo Hotel Train takes the tour from Moscow via Vladimir to Gorki, Murom and Kolomna. Shed, museum and Kolomna diesel locomotive factory visits. At night the train will be diesel or electrically hauled but on suitable lines steam locomotives of classes LV, Su, L and Er will be used, with photo stops and runpasts.
10. Japan – General Interest: August	Museum lines using steam locomotives as well as the contemporary scene
11. Germany – Berlin Innotrans: September	Innotrans is a transport technology trade fair held every 2 years in Berlin. It is intended to spend about a week in the Berlin area, also visiting sheds, museums and other places of interest.
12. France PVC Steam: September/October	A tour to the south of France using one section of the PVC 231G558 and further on probably an oil burning 141R, from Dijon, Lyon to Marseille. The Vivarais line might be included if the train uses the freight side of the Rhone valley.
13. Germany – Plandampf: October	Rheinland-Pfalz is expected to run another Plandampf event. Plandampf is the concept of getting sufficient enthusiasts to pay to use preserved steam locomotives to haul scheduled passenger and/or goods trains over a long weekend. This idea started in Germany in October 1990, and has seen a large number of highly successful events.
14. South East Asia – Thailand/Cambodia/Borneo: December	A steam special runs from Bangkok to the ancient capital of Ayutthaya on 5th December, the King's birthday. A charter to the River Kwai might be possible. In North Borneo, a charter with a Vulcan Foundry loco to Beaufort (and possibly further up the Pades Gorge to Tenom, but this might be with a diesel). In Cambodia 2–3 days minimum would be spent in the country chartering the metre-gauge wood-burning French Pacific 231.501 on lines around Phnom Penh. Also visit the temple complex at Angkor Wat.

sensation of deep-sprung upholstery – derived from travelling on or engaging with steam railways.

Management implications: transport, collaboration networks and place promotion

The transport enthusiast leisure sub-culture tended to be perceived as representing a male-dominated specialist, esoteric, often far from fashionable, interest. But as tourism development in the 1970s and 1980s drew increasingly on heritage and nostalgia, so existing transport attractions responded, albeit somewhat slowly, with innovations to appeal to broader market segments, while new transport and heritage attractions introduced products to encourage further segmentation. Repositioned transport attractions such as 'heritage' steam railways, incorporated into local and regional networks and place-promotion collaboration, developed family-oriented marketing (Table 7.3). Such 'preservationism' may be seen as part of a collective nostalgia for the (usually masculinized) skills, symbols and certainties of our recent industrial past (Urry, 1995: 124). Yet Halsall (2001) argues that the social and cultural identity which has become attached to heritage railways is stronger than mere nostalgia. Thus in the UK, for example, some 140 restored railways (Butcher, 2002) now promote themselves with a strong emphasis on heritage, place and interactive experience involving both entertainment and education.

With reference to the last entry in Table 7.3, the attraction of transport (infrastructure) and its associated locations (re-)generated by popular culture can enforce the concept of a fictional heritage place (Couldry, 1998). For heritage railways, providing a 'front stage' set for filming has the multiple value of generating income from the film company for use of the location, providing out of season employment for rolling stock, and generating more custom through recognition in and association with particular films. Perhaps the UK model for this was the Keighley and Worth Valley Railway, situated in 'Brontë Country' (West Yorkshire), which featured heavily in the sentimental 1970 film *The Railway Children*. The Kent and East Sussex Railway claims to have appeared in more than 30 film and television productions (Tenterden Railway Company, 2003).

There are perhaps two critical management implications arising from these trends. First, attractions need to be continually improving the quality and range of visitor experience and evolving their promotion and marketing in order to be suitably positioned to appeal to continually fragmenting and fusing market segments.

Second, networking to reinforce collaboration based on propinquity and function is now essential. Transport attractions need to complement, and be promoted alongside other attractions in their region as part of 'place promotion' (Kotler *et al.*, 1993), and as a means of becoming embedded within perceived attraction clusters and circuits in order to better attract family-based markets. Further, transport attractions also need to maintain close collaborative links both nationally and internationally with other transport attractions in order to reach the now globalized 'niche' transport enthusiast market. A major challenge for policy makers and resource managers is to render both attractions and their markets sustainable.

Table 7.3 Widening the appeal of preserved steam railways

Objective	Activity
Conservation 'Preservationism'	Elements of traditional appeal to railway enthusiasts, such as restored rolling stock, stations, buildings, the wearing of historic uniforms and the pursuit of defunct practices, have been more closely associated with nostalgia and the opportunity for family interaction.
Broadening gender appeal	Retailing facilities to offer shopping experiences aimed at appealing to a wider gender market.
Attracting families of different age ranges	Combining with a different yet complementary experience, such as a farm park (e.g. Almond Valley Heritage Centre), or garden centre (e.g. Bressingham's 'Steam and Gardens'), to provide, in combination, a full day's experience appealing to family groups. Family-oriented special activity weekends, such as the Brecon Mountain Railway's family history weekend and Halloween special weekend.
Attracting families with children for entertainment	*Thomas the Tank Engine* days, weekends and weeks, and other special entertainment events aimed at children, especially during school holidays. The Mid-Hants Railway has several illustrated web pages devoted to *Thomas* events (derived from the children's fiction of the Rev. W. Audrey).
Attracting families with children for education	Educational activities aimed at children who may otherwise have little experience of this form of transport, e.g. the Young SteamRangers club (SteamRanger is the operating arm of the Australian Railway Historical Society in South Australia).
Extending the operating day	Evening attractions, such as August Saturday music evenings (Gwili Steam Railway).
Season-extending activities	Running 'Santa specials' – during which a Santa Claus makes his way through the train (perhaps helped by his team of pixies, as on the Keighley and Worth Valley Railway), visiting all children on the train to give them a present. 'Mince pie specials', offering on-train seasonal fare to extend the season through the darkest days of the northern hemisphere mid-winter from Christmas into the new year. In winter and spring in South Australia, SteamRanger promotes its coastal trains as a whale watching experience.
Targeting non-family niche markets	Valentine special evenings, appealing to younger couples, 'War on the Line' events, folk festivals.
Hosting private special events	Offering train hire for private special events such as weddings and anniversaries.
Provision of professional training facilities	At a time when the skills involved in driving steam engines are held by relatively few people, a number of steam railways offer professional 'footplate' training facilities.
Acting as film locations	Period rolling stock, station architecture and railway uniforms provide historic film set locations.
Networking with other attractions as an embedded element of place or region promotion	Multi-visit tickets and discounts. Joint promotion and marketing material. Linked websites. Other attractions actually on the route of and linked by the railway. The Polish museum railway Wenecja is promoted as a spatially linking component of an attractions cluster which includes local lakes, an open air archaeological museum, a fourteenth-century castle, and the presentation of local myths and legends.

Sources: Almond Valley Heritage Trust (2003); BSPC (2003); Douglas (2001); Gwili Steam Railway (2003); Jokioinen Railway Museum (2003); Keighley and Worth Valley Railway (2003); Mid-Hants Railway (2003); Rosiak and Szarski (1995); SteamRanger (2003); Tenterden Railway Company (2003).

Final considerations

Transport as both a tourism facilitator and tourism object performs a number of roles which continue to change and evolve as markets segment or fuse. This chapter has briefly discussed some of these roles and the associated components of change.

Overall, transport is an essential concomitant of tourism, and as such has a ubiquitous role. Yet there are several market segments to which transport appeals, either as an object of gaze or of added-value experience. And finally certain transport attractions, and notably heritage steam railways, drawing upon the global interest in cultural heritage, have repositioned themselves by virtue of broadening their target markets.

Just as in more developed tourist economies, emerging tourist regions such as Central and Eastern Europe and less developed countries have recognized the potential of transport-related attractions (e.g. Rosiak and Szarski, 1995; Ronedo, 1998), particularly when complementing cultural and/or heritage themes. Further, 'non-Western' attractions may also be enhanced by the appeal of 'the other' – offering significantly different cultural and technological experiences compared to those of 'Western' attractions. These have significant potential as evolving niches.

Transport as both a heritage and a contemporary niche attraction has been largely undervalued by tourism and leisure promoters. However, it is now recognized that transport has significant tourism potential both in its own right and in combination with other locally or regionally based attractions.

References

Almond Valley Heritage Trust (2003) *Welcome to Almond Valley*. Edinburgh: Almond Valley Heritage Trust < http://www.almondvalley.co.uk >.

Anon (2003) 2003 rally calendar and museum guide. *Buses*, 55(577), supplement i–xii.

BBC (2002a) Greek court convicts plane spotters. *BBC News Online*, 26 April < http://news.bbc.co.uk/1/hi/uk/1953132.stm >.

BBC (2002b) I'm Greek and, yes, I spot planes. *BBC News Online*, 25 April < http://news.bbc.co.uk/1/hi/uk/1949027.stm >.

BBC (2002c) Trainspotters webcam on track. *BBC News Online*, 18 October < http://news.bbc.co.uk/1/hi/wales/2334031.stm >.

BSPC (Bressingham Steam Preservation Company) (2003) *Bressingham Steam and Gardens*. Bressingham: BSPC < http://www.bressingham.co.uk >.

Butcher, A.C. (ed.) (2002) *Railways Restored* (23rd edn). Hersham: Ian Allan Publishing.

Couldry, N. (1998) The view from inside the simulacrum: visitors tales from the set of Coronation Street. *Leisure Studies*, 17(2), 94–107.

Dann, G.M.S. (1994) Travel by train: keeping nostalgia on track. In A.V. Seaton (ed.) *Tourism: the State of the Art*. Chichester and New York: John Wiley & Sons, pp. 775–782.

Debbage, K.G. and Daniels, P. (1998) The tourist industry and economic geography: missed opportunities? In D. Ioannides and K.G. Debbage (eds) *The Economic Geography of the Tourist Industry*. London: Routledge, pp. 17–30.

Douglas, Y. (2001) *Steam Railways: Britain's Preservation Railways and Museums*. Navigator Guides, Melton Constable.

Furgala-Selezniow, G., Turkowski, K., Nowak, A., Skrzypczak, A. and Mamcarz, A. (2003) The Ostroda-Elblag Canal – its past and future in aquatic tourism. In T. Härkönen (ed.) *International Lake Tourism Conference 2–5 July*. Savonlinna: Savonlinna Institute for Regional Development and Research, University of Joensuu, pp. 55–72.

GCRR (Grand Canyon Railway and Resort) (2003) *The Grand Canyon Starts Here: the Grand Canyon Railway*. Williams AZ: Grand Canyon Railway and Resort <http://www.thetrain.com>.

Gilmore, J.H. and Pine, B.J. (1999), *The Experience Economy*. Boston: Harvard Business School Press.

Gwili Steam Railway (2003) *Gwili Steam Railway*. Carmarthen: Gwili Steam Railway <http://www.gwili-railway.co.uk/>.

Hall, D. (1999) Conceptualising tourism transport: inequality and externality issues. *Journal of Transport Geography*, 7(4), 181–188.

Halsall, D.A. (2001) Railway heritage and the tourist gaze: Stoomtram Hoorn-Medemblik. *Journal of Transport Geography*, 9(2), 151–160.

IGE (Interessengemeinschaft Eisenbahn) (2003) *Eisenbahn-Souvenirartikel*. Hersbruck: IGE Bahntouristik <http://www.bahntouristik.de/cms/?cms_p=20|&cms_c=81&cms_a=81>.

Indian Steam Railway Society (2003) *Indian Steam Railway Society*. New Delhi: Indian Steam Railway Society <http://www.indiansteamrailwaysociety.org>.

Jokioinen Museum Railway (2003) *Jokioinen Museum Railway*. Jokioinen: Jokioinen Museum Railway <http://www.jokioistenmuseorautatie.fi/>.

Keighley and Worth Valley Railway (2003) *Santa Steam Specials*. Keighley: Keighley and Worth Valley Railway <http://www.kwvr.co.uk/events/santa.htm>.

Kotler, P., Haider, D.H. and Rein, I. (1993), *Marketing Places: Attracting Industry, Investment and Tourism to Cities, States and Nations*. Glencoe: The Free Press.

LCGB (Locomotive Club of Great Britain) (2003) *Overseas Tours 2004*. Norwood Green: LCGB <http://www.lcgb.net/html/overseas_.html>.

MacCannell, D. (1974) Staged authenticity: arrangements of social space in tourist settings. *American Journal of Sociology*, 79(3), 589–603.

MÁV Nostalgia (nd) *Trip to the Gypsy Village of Solt*. Budapest: MÁV Nostalgia Tourist, Trading and Services Ltd.

MÁV Nostalgia (2000) *MÁV Nostalgia Tourist, Trading and Services Ltd*. Budapest: MÁV Nostalgia Tourist, Trading and Services Ltd <http://www.miwo.hu/partner/old_trains/eindex.htm>.

Mid-Hants Railway (2003) *The Watercress Line Official Website*. Arlesford: Mid-Hants Railway <http://www.watercressline.co.uk>.

Orient Express (2003) *Orient Express*. London: Orient Express <http://www.orient-express.com>.

Ostróda-Elblag Navigation (2003) *Ostróda-Elblag Navigation 1860–2003*. Ostróda: Ostróda-Elblag Navigation <http://www.zegluga.com.pl/ang/index_ag.htm>.

Page, M. (1975) *The Lost Pleasures of the Great Trains*. London: Weidenfeld and Nicolson.

Pine, B.J. and Gilmore, J.H. (1998) Welcome to the experience economy. *Harvard Business Review*, July-August, 97–105.

Pirin Tourism Forum (2000) *Welcome to the Pirin Tourism Forum*. Sandanski: Pirin Tourism Forum <http://www.travel-bulgaria.com/ptf/>.

Roberts, L. and Hall, D. (2001) *Rural Tourism and Recreation: Principles to Practice*. Wallingford: CAB International.

Ronedo (1998) *Adventures with Steam in Romania*. Piatra Neam: Ronedo.

Rosiak, A. and Szarski, T. (1995) *Wenecja: Narrow Gauge Railway Museum*. Wroclaw: ZET.

SteamRanger (2003) *SteamRanger*. Mount Barker, South Australia: SteamRanger <http://www.steamranger.org.au/>.

Tenterden Railway Company (2003) *Kent & East Sussex Railway*. Tenterden: Tenterden Railway Company <http://www.kesr.org.uk/>.

Urry, J. (1995) *Consuming Places*. London and New York: Routledge.

Wilson, G. (2003) Terrorism fear derails train-spotters. BBC News Online, 28 May <http://news.bbc.co.uk/1/hi/uk/2943304.stm>.

Questions

1 Briefly examine the major roles of transport as tourist attractions.
2 Explain some of the ways in which transport tourism as a niche interest has broadened its markets.

Further recommended reading

Lumsdon, L.M. and Page, S.J. (2004) *Tourism and Transport*. Oxford: Pergamon.

Websites

www.automotive-links.com/ent/bus/fan.htm: list of and web links to more than 200 bus enthusiasts' sites

www.planespotting.com: forum for plane spotters: directory of some 140 from 12 countries, airport index; various links including those to military and government aviation sources

www.staff.ncl.ac.uk/m.h.ellison/bls/raillink.html: list of and links to around 470 rail website addresses

Glossary

BAAT   Bulgarian Association for Alternative Tourism
DGEG   Deutsche Gesellschaft für Eisenbahngeschichte (German Association for Railway History)
GCRR   Grand Canyon Railway and Resort
IGE   Interessengemeinschaft Eisenbahn (German Railway Enthusiasts' Society)
LCGB   Locomotive Club of Great Britain
LRT   Light Rail Transit
MÁV   Hungarian State Railways

Part II
Tradition and culture-based tourism

Recent tourism trends have been characterised by an increasing interest in natural and cultural heritage. As a consequence to this, a set of opportunities have appeared on the market involving also what the European Commission defines as 'non-traditional destinations' (European Commission (2002) *Using Natural and Cultural Heritage to Develop Sustainable Tourism in Non-traditional Destinations*, Brussels: Enterprise Directorat-General). *Tradition and culture-based tourism* engages those tourists who have the desire to learn, to experience, to discover and to be part of the host environment. This form of tourism stimulates a range of mechanisms certainly beneficial for the local economy of destination; however, due to the close contact between the visiting and the host community, this may often produce loss of authenticity and commodification of resources. These elements will be highlighted in the chapters presented in this part of the book, where a variety of theoretical issues, locations and examples are discussed. 'Tribal', 'cultural heritage', 'peripheral regions', and 'research' tourism will be the key themes of this section, presenting an extremely diverse international perspective and a valuable contribution for further consideration.

8

Tribal tourism 'Cannibal Tours'
Tribal tourism in hidden places

Peter M. Burns and Yana Figurova

There is nothing so strange in a strange land, as the stranger who comes to visit it (O'Rourke, 1987).

Introduction

This chapter reflects on what MacCannell (1992), in ironic mood, called 'ex-primitives' and tourism drawing on a case study, Dennis O'Rourke's documentary film, *Cannibal Tours*. At a surface level, the film documents the interactions between a group of tourists and tribal people as they try to understand each other within the context of being 'hosts' and 'guests'. This chapter attempts to delve beneath the surface looking for motives, meanings and implications of tribal tours to hidden places. But, just like the case study, there are no objective truths or scientifically based (normative) conclusions that can be drawn. Rather, the chapter will try to make some sort of meaning about the consumption of tourism within the context of a particular market niche. *Cannibal Tours* is a film portraying not only the two different worlds of the Western tourists and the Iatmul people who live along the Sepik River, Papua

New Guinea, in Melanesian South Pacific, but also the world of the filmmaker (O'Rourke) who is at one time situated as mediator between 'hosts' and 'guests' and then in another world of the potential TV audience as he sits in the cutting room constructing the film from the film stock. The film supposedly explores the desires of the tourists to see the 'primitives', the exotic, the 'other' as Said (1978) might have called it, but of course the filmmaker constructs what we see just as a tour guide constructs our view during a trip. While the film was shot in Papua New Guinea, the multiple meanings and connotations (as well as the multiple voices), could have come from tribal peoples anywhere: Africa, Asia, South America, or as far north as the Sami peoples of Finland. The chapter concludes with some thoughts about race, social identities, stereotyping and role-play in the other worlds of hidden places.

Theoretical position

'Tribal tourism' is a loaded phrase and fraught with difficulties, not least of which revolve around definitional and social problems with the use of the word tribal. Moreover, there are paradoxes about assigning motivations to the 'tribal' peoples, tourists and businesses alike. The easy option is to presume that tribal tourism to hidden places is a manifestation of the claims that some tourists are motivated by a search for authenticity to be found in the early works of MacCannell (1976) and Urry (1990) which linked the postmodern condition, described by Selwyn (1996: 29) as where tourists 'are driven by instincts of undiluted consumerism and the pursuit of commodities... [and is] the post-modern tourist just another consumer junkie, infantilised, schizoid and rendered cognitively and intellectually unable to distinguish between different types of knowledge'. This notion of fragmentation is a position also taken by MacCannell (1976) in the context of postindustrialising societies. However, both views focus on the *tourist* and do not do justice to the complexities of *tourism* with its power to construct and reduce social identities, place and space, and systematically arrange poorer parts of the world (through the agency of travel firms and governments) for the benefit of richer (restless, bored?) populations (in current discourse termed the 'North-South' debate) in a symbiotic relationship described by Jafari (1987: 158) as an 'interdependence of the [tourism] systems'.

As visual evidence, the ethnographic film can be described as a tool that can be used to learn more about various cultures. In the case of *Cannibal Tours*, we are presented with multi-layered data in the tradition of Geertz's (1973) 'thick description': what we see on the surface (just like in a tour) is not an accurate reflection of what is going on underneath. Even in thinking about the location of the film, in the Sepik region, it cannot be a coincidence that the renowned American anthropologist Margaret Mead (along with Gregory Bateson) had made an extensive study of the Iatmul people in 1938 (Kline Silverman, n.d.). Silverman (2001: 4) described the work of Meads and Bateman as having a 'keen awareness of the emotional nuances of gesture, posture, and glance' – qualities easily ascribed to O'Rourke's sensitive work. Moreover, Silverman (2001: 4) goes on to say, 'Indeed, Mead was at her best in perceiving the significant meanings that people silently convey through fleeting bodily expressions. For her, the truly distinctive humanism of a community was particularly evident in how it performs the everyday things that unite us all into a common humanity. Such commentary about Mead's approach and intuitiveness is very 'filmic' and could almost be a description of O'Rourke's work. Just as we have to question why particular locations are chosen for tours, we should also question the filmmaker's motivation in choosing locations. In this sense, part of the theoretical position for the present chapter owes allegiance to Geertz's (1973) idea of 'thick description'. Taking this theme a little further, and since ethnography can be defined as 'the systematic observation of social groups' (Clark *et al.*, 1998: 139), the ethnographic film is a 'text' or visual representation based on observation of a particular culture or cultures. *Cannibal Tours* can be looked at as an ethnographic film, even though many anthropologists and ethnographers would argue otherwise, as indeed Dennis O'Rourke does himself as will be shown later in the chapter. Ota (1994: 887) in particular, reiterates O'Rourke's own plea for the film to be seen as text, which, incidentally, is the position of the present author.

Case study: *Cannibal Tours*

The case study is divided into two distinct parts. First, a general discussion on the film, the type of tribal tourism it represents and the ways in which it has engaged a number of researchers. Second, a short series of vignettes (playfully described here as 'Brief Encounters') describing a series of host-guest encounters.

Cannibal Tours centres around the journey of a group of seemingly rich Western tourists travelling on a luxury cruise ship along the Sepik River in Papua New Guinea, a trip being promoted in 2003 at $1,750 for 5 nights, not including flight fares to Papua New Guinea (MTS Papua New Guinea, 2004). The tourists visit a number of villages along the way and a number of host-guest encounters occur when cultural and economic exchanges take place which may act as a sort of metaphor for local-global encounters — but not in the way that might at first be thought. The title of the film derives from the tourists' fascination with cannibalism that used to be a tradition amongst the Iatmul people. The tourists want to see and feel and touch the places where cannibalism was once practised; however, they would prefer to do it from a safe point of view, from a point of luxury tourism (Bruner, 1989).

Literature on *Cannibal Tours* is filled with such contention. Ball (1998: 5) considers the film to 'explore the notion of the "Other" ... [that] raise[s] fascinating questions concerning authority within accounts of encounters between cultures'. O'Rourke himself however, in an interview, described the film as a 'meditation on tourism', thus emphasising a 'more directly self-reflexive' (Lutkehaus, 1989: 423) style of filmmaking than previous works, and evident from the increased presence of himself in his own films, not so much as neutral ethnographer, but culture-broker and teasing intermediary. The promotional text for *Cannibal Tours* (video cover notes) states, 'This gently ironic film neither condones nor condemns the tourists or the Papua New Guinea' (Bruner, 1989: 443), Bruner however disagrees, drawing attention to 'O'Rourke's view ... that tourism is neo-colonialism and that the New Guineans are exploited' (1989: 443–444). As we will see, this dichotomy is not the only competing narrative in this particular niche tourism outing.

Brief Encounters 1: The Arrival

The opening scene of the film (or the arrival of the tourists) is a very slow panning shot showing thickly wooded hills on the horizon across an expanse of the calm Sepik River. The film dissolves into a face shot of a young local boy looking into the camera. The background track moves very cleverly from a Mozart strings piece to (as the boy appears) the haunting sound of an Iatmul nose-flute; all interwoven with the sound of a short-wave radio being tuned in across (pre-Perestroika) Radio Moscow, Radio Australia and the BBC World Service. The scene shifts to include black and white photographs of German colonialists of the region. So, this encounter, or pre-encounter — for the tourists have not yet reached their destination but are in sight of it — has been framed by history, ideology, globalisation, and contrast between 'us' and 'them'. The filmmaker — or perhaps 'culture-broker' — remains as yet unseen.

Brief Encounters 2: Searching for Cannibals

The second major scene in the film is the introduction of one of the main characters, a German tourist. He is walking across a village space heavily laden with all the trappings of a well seasoned tourist: camera, bags, tropical hat, sensible shoes, etc. He is talking to a local villager who is guiding him. He is anxious to take some very specific photographs. But first he shows the local some old photographs of German colonial occupation — one wonders where he got them from, were they from Dennis O'Rourke with a view to setting up a scene? In talking about the photos, the German says 'They were good, the Germans, Yes? . . . They were very popular'. The local nods in embarrassed agreement. Here the tourist is affirming his own roots and in a sense reminding the local of former power relations (modalities) and that under such conditions things were pretty good. Now the German is pointing to and stroking a large phallic-looking stone and asking questions about cannibalism, 'Where did they kill the people, here?' True to role, the local responds, 'At those stones we would dance and cut off heads.' The tourist looks happy, the local looks smug. Both sides consider the conversation a victory. Later on in the film, at the same location, the German tourist lists the countries he has visited just to show his credentials as a 'traveller' rather than 'tourist'. 'Lebanon, Iran, India, Thailand, Burma, China, Japan, the Philippines, Indonesia, the Pacific Islands, Australia — two times, once to New Zealand, South Africa and Rhodesia, all of South America. Next year I'll go to Central America and Panama'. He turns to camera and gives a big smile.

Brief Encounters 3: The Conversation

Back on the boat, three Italians are leaning on the gunwale with the sound of the engine and views of the river in the background. Their group comprises one older man on the left, a younger man on the right and a young female as centre shot. They are discussing the local Iatmul people and their lives (the conversation is in Italian with English sub-titles). The older man says, 'What do you think of these primitive people whose lives are so different from ours?' Before the younger man has a chance to respond, the young female, who is smoking, says, 'Look at the camera when you speak'. This is her entire contribution to the scene. After the interjection, the younger man responds, 'Truly living with nature, in a way they don't really live . . . I wonder though if their way of life is really better than ours, yes, really living with nature, well not really living, more like vegetating . . .' The older man says, 'Looking at them, they don't seem sad . . .' 'No, no' the younger one says 'The experts assure us they are satisfied . . . more than satisfied, they are delighted. What can we say, happy and well fed'. To which the older man adds, 'And they don't have to worry about thinking of tomorrow'.

Brief Encounters 4: Talking Head

From a face seemingly battered by poverty and teeth blackened by betel nut juice an old man speaks about the past, cannibalism and the coming of the white man: 'We were not born, it was our parents who saw the first Europeans; they were Germans and they came in a big ship up this river. Everyone was afraid, they said "Our dead ancestors have returned." They didn't know about you European people. They cried out "The spirits of our dead have come back!" Some ran away, others went out to see the ship saying "What is it that has brought them, that moves on the water? — It's Sanguambi!" They gave it [the ship] the name of our crocodile spirit [Sanguambi], they did. And some were crying, saying our dead have come back! That was our parents who were there at the time. So now, when we see tourists we say about them, "The dead have returned!" That's what we say, they are our dead ancestors, they went and got a new face and skin, and now they come and see us. We don't seriously believe they are our dead ancestors, but we do say it!' The man's commentary is interesting because it gives valuable insights into how the local/global clash of cultures gets taken into contemporary localised myths and legends. The expression on the man's face throughout the talking head shot — especially at the end — is one of knowing, and gentle irony.

Brief Encounters 5: Consuming Culture

The next encounter is between a large group of the tourists in the middle of the village and a variety of locals. They watch a group of dancers perform a once-sacred crocodile dance in a hesitant, almost reluctant style. As the tourists then pick their way through the spirit house, they attempt to categorise and show tacit knowledge about buildings and carving, 'They use a lot of curves here . . . in the Sepik they use a lot of curves.' Outside, a group of women tourists look hot and bothered by mosquitoes as they attempt to purchase souvenirs, 'What was the first price?' 'Fifteen Kina.' 'The son said twenty-five Kina!' They are discussing an exquisite, Modigliani-esque mask about a metre high with intricate markings. An off-camera remark, 'I've seen like this stuff in Africa'. As the deal is done, the tour guide places an orange sticker on the mask to indicate the mask has been sold, in some ways like a formal art gallery the tourists would find in their own home towns . . . except of course they would be unlikely to attempt bargaining the price down.

Brief Encounters 6: What do they want?

An old villager and his friend are musing as to the motivation of the tourists. The bearded one says, 'What do they come for?' The other replies, 'To see if we are civilized or not'. 'And what do they find?' 'Do they read about us in books?' 'Behind me is the spirit house of our ancestors which we still use, is this what they want? I'm confused'. This sense of confusion is clearly felt on both sides as they struggle to understand each other.

Brief Encounters 7: Be Polite!

If the German tourist in Brief Encounter 2 ('Searching for Cannibals') is a major character on screen, then the 'angry woman' is another. The scene pans onto the face of an old woman furiously chewing a lime stick and betel nut and pulls back to reveal she is sitting in front of some shell necklaces and other hand-made ephemera laid out on a woven mat. Her misshapen, broken fingers indicate that she is possibly a widow. Off camera (and in Pijin) a voice is heard to warn her, 'Think carefully before you speak!' She responds disdainfully in her own language, 'I'm telling him [O'Rourke] that the tourists never buy our things'. The off-camera voice insists, 'Speak slowly or they won't understand, and be polite'! The 'angry woman' continues her story, 'I'm explaining that they don't buy our handicrafts...we hurry down here with things for the tourists ['tell him straight' says a mocking, laughing voice off camera] but the tourists only look, they don't buy ['don't be too angry' say her companions]... I'm talking in my dialect [the woman has turned from angry to ferocious by this stage, her tone and voice rising] and he [O'Rourke] doesn't seem to hear... these tourists come but they don't really help us, I'm sorry to say. We have nothing [she switches from her dialect to Pijin and looks directly at the camera] we have nothing, "*white fella 'e got moni*" [only you white people have money]'. Her friends are laughing (she must be known as a character) and they encourage her, 'Tell them!' She slips back into her dialect language, 'I'm trying to do that! I keep saying we have no money, we need it! You white people, you have all the money, we village people have no money. You people [pointing at O'Rourke] have money, not us, that's why I complain. [The camera pans away from the close up of her and her anger to show the shell necklaces again] I'm talking about these things here. The tourists ignore them. They don't buy from us and that's a problem'. At this stage the camera pans upwards to what are presumably her children and she goes on to talk about needing money for the children's education and school books.

Brief Encounters 8: Final Contact

The final scene of the film is quite extraordinary. The soundtrack resumes its W.A. Mozart string quartet theme while the moving images are slowed and blurred to reveal the tourists' white faces being painted with delicate brush strokes the muddy, ochre colours of the Sepik by black hands. Slowly the faces of the tourists are hidden behind the swirls and intricate patterns characteristic of the area. The scene continues in slow motion as the tourists dance. It seems that as their faces are masked, their Western inhibitions are stripped away and for a moment they 'become' the 'other' they are searching for; movements of sexuality, aggression and freedom are all apparent as they dance clumsily around the upper deck of the ship. Photos are taken, the anchor is weighed and the tourists slip back into their normal lives.

Implications for management

The implications for the management of 'tribal tourism to hidden places' can be seen from two distinct perspectives; both framed by expectations. On the one hand, it is quite clear from the 'brief encounters' reported above – and there are of course many more in this hour-long film – that the local villagers, the Iatmal people, had high economic expectations from tourism. The question to ask is 'where did these expectations come from?' The answer must be 'from the tour operating company'. Organising visits to tribal lands in Papua New Guinea is complex and assumptions can be made on the fact that protracted negotiations took place during the time when promises were made on both sides. It can be seen – or rather assumed – that the promises on the part of the villagers were likely to have been: access to hidden (i.e. sacred or formerly sacred places), dance performance, the wearing of traditional dress so as to provide photo opportunities, the provision of handicrafts for sale. The promises to the villagers on the part of the tour operator would be likely to include some form of payment – but to whom and how this was shared is not known, showing up with the tourists at the agreed date and time, indications that the tourists would buy goods, in the form of souvenirs and maybe soft drinks and services, in the form of payment for photographs.

On the other hand, promises were made to the tourists and their expectations of seeing 'primitive peoples in hidden places' were high. These tourists would draw on their own cultural mythologies about *'primitive other'* helped along by the advertising promotion which promotes other worldliness by using such words as 'paradise', 'unspoilt' and 'unique'.

The implications for management are quite clear and can be summarised in a single phrase that would suit any business in its relations between suppliers and customers: *'Honest and clear communication'*. In the particular case of arranging tours to places where local culture has limited exposure to dealing with the outside world there are ethical and moral dimensions that cannot be ignored – especially with tourism given its invasive nature. An approach could be to set up a joint NGO to act as the interface between business dealings and the local population, to ensure fair play and managed expectations on both sides. Another approach would be for the villagers themselves to have far more detailed discussions among themselves to try and identify what they want from tourism and what they are willing to give up in order to achieve this. This has been attempted in the US and Canada where the Alliance of Tribal Tourism Advocates have come up with a mission and set of goals:

Mission: The Alliance of Tribal Tourism Advocates is an association of Tribes, Indian and non-Indian individuals, agencies and organizations that are concerned about responsible tourism development on the reservations and in off-reservation Indian communities. Organized in 1993 by tribal governments in the South Dakota region, the consortium works to enhance and promote tourism as a means of economic development and growth, while maintaining respect for tribal traditions and lands (ATTA, 2003).

The mission statement is supported by a set of goals and organisational beliefs.

Our overriding goal is to enhance tourism development prospects for tribes, thereby providing employment and economic benefits for Indian people on the reservations and in off-reservation Indian communities...

- Support cultural integrity and traditional values in the development of tribal tourism
- Acknowledge the sovereignty of tribes
- Preserve the sanctity of sites, artefacts, rituals, and ceremonies considered sacred by tribes
- Protect the natural environment of tribal homelands
- Assist in tourism code and policy development
- Publish and distribute intertribal tourism materials
- Host tribal tourism workshops and training
- Provide technical assistance to members in developing publicity materials and tour packages
- Sponsor national and international marketing efforts and trade missions
- Develop inter-tribal tour packages (ATTA, 2003).

While the example from North America is not an exact fit, it does demonstrate the need for the modalities, or power relations to change from a balance which clearly benefits the tour operating company to one that gives much greater benefit to the host communities. At the same time, tour companies and tour guides must take far greater responsibility in managing the expectations of their customers (the tourists) and getting the balance right between useful levels of economic exchange and limited social intrusion.

Final considerations

The face-painting scene (Brief Encounter 8, above) serves as an allegory for niche tourism that points up the central paradox for 'tribal tourism to hidden places'. At the surface level, niche tourism, just like the face-painting scene, is about cultural interaction and mutual benefit. However, what lies beneath is a complex set of power relationships driven by commerce. The paradox, thus far unresolved, is that this type of 'tribal' niche tourism demands new experiences that are not framed by mainstream tourism; it is off the beaten track, yet as we know from colleagues who deal with the natural environment, that beaten track soon becomes a paved road over a short period of time. So genuine cultural encounters full of mutual and genuine quest for knowledge about 'Other' on both sides soon become, without thoughtful management and access control, a human zoo. The niche 'travellers' (as they might term themselves) soon become (in a metaphoric sense rather than literal) just another bunch of whining tourists demanding their rights and are seen by locals as just another set of faceless rubberneckers who deserve only to be ripped off. This process is not inevitable; the management strategies outlined above could contribute to ameliorating such problems, but evidence suggest that there is a thin line to be drawn between 'characteristic' and 'inevitable' processes.

References

ATTA (2003) *Mission, Goals, and Beliefs* http://attatribal.com/attatribal/the-experience_page3.htm [accessed 29/09/03].

Ball, M., Critical Design (1997) *Understanding What We See: Subject, Author and Audience in Visual Anthropology* http://www.criticaldesign.com/anthropo/visual/visanth.htm [accessed 8 February 2002].

Bruner, E.M. (1989) Of cannibals, tourists and ethnographers. *Cultural Anthropology*, 4(4), 438–445.

Clark, M., Riley, M., Wilkie, E. and Wood, R. (1998) *Researching and Writing Dissertations in Hospitality and Tourism*. London: International Thompson Business Press.

Geertz, C. (1973) *The Interpretation of Cultures*. New York: Basic Books.

Jafari, J. (1987) Tourism models: the sociocultural aspects. *Tourism Management*, 8(2), 151–159.

Klinc Silverman, E. (n.d.) In the field: The Iatmul Tourism and Totemism in Tambunum, Sepik River http://www.interculturalstudies.org/IIS/iatmul.html (accessed 14 January 2004).

Lutkehaus, N. C. (1989) 'Excuse me, Everything is not all right': On ethnography, film, and representation. *Cultural Anthropology*, 4(4), 422–437.

MacCannell, D. (1992) *Empty Meeting Grounds: The Tourist Papers*, London: Routledge.

MacCannell, D. (1976) *The Tourist*. New York: Shoken.

Mead, M. (1988 [1928]) *Coming of Age in Samoa: A Psychological Study of Primitive Youth for Western Civilization*. New York: Quill.

MTS Papua New Guinea (2004) www.mtspng.com (accessed 3 March 2004).

O'Rourke, D. (1987) (Produced, directed and photographed) *Cannibal Tours*, 70 minutes. 35 mm and 16 mm. Color. Film editor: Tim Lichtenfeld. Distributed by Direct Cinema, P.O. Box 69799, Los Angeles, CA 90069.

Ota, Y. (1994) Cannibal Tours [review essay] *Annals of Tourism Research*, 21(4), 886–891.

Said, E. (1978) *Orientalism: Western Concepts of the Orient*. London: Routledge and Kegan Paul.

Said, E. (2001) *Power, Politics, and Culture: Interviews with Edward Said* (edited by Gauri Viswanathan). New York: Pantheon.

Selwyn, T. (ed.) (1996) *The Tourist Image: Myths and Myth Making in Tourism*. London: Wiley.

Silverman, D. (2000) *Doing Qualitative Research: A Practical Handbook*. London: Sage.

Silverman, E.K. (2001) 'In the Field: The Iatmul' *Continuing Work in Mead's Research Sites* http://www.mead2001.org/iatmul.html.

Urry, J. (1990) *The Tourist Gaze*, London: Sage.

Questions

1   Given the problems described above, would it be best to stop these tribal tours?
2   To what extent can we use films, including documentary films such as *Cannibal Tours* as evidence in researching tourism?

Further recommended reading

Burns, P.M. (1999) *An Introduction to Tourism and Anthropology*. London: Routledge.
Butler, R. and Hinch, T. (1996) *Tourism and Indigenous Peoples*. London: International Thomson Business Press.
Gosden, C. and Knowles, C. (2001) *Collecting Colonialism: Material Culture and Colonial Change*. Oxford: Berg.
Pink, S. (2001) *Visual Ethnography: Images, Media and Representation in Research*. London: Sage Publications.

Websites

Australian Film, Television and Radio School (2001). *Dennis O'Rourke: Professional Associate*. North Ryde. Available at: http://www.aftrs.edu.au/departments/documentary/doco_orourke.htm
Bacigalupo, A.M., University at Buffalo (1999). *Introduction to Cultural Anthropology*. Buffalo. Available at: http://icarus.ubetc.buffalo.edu/users/apy106/film/cannibaltours.htm
Ball, M., Critical Design (1998). *Subject, Author and Audience Revisited: Ethnographic Film Study*. Available at: http://www.criticaldesign.com/anthropo/ethno/ethno.htm

9

Cultural heritage tourism
Being, not looking: beyond the tourism
brochure of Greece

Eugenia Wickens

Introduction

The Chalkidiki region in Northern Greece is promoted primarily for its sun, sea and sand, rather than
as a cultural destination. Travel brochures and other
advertising material convey information about
beaches, the number of hours of sunshine, location
and facilities of the accommodation and details of
the nightlife. Less emphasis is given to 'tradition
and culture based' tours to nearby cities such as
Thessaloniki and to ancient sites and museums,
which might inform the foreign visitors to Greece
with special interests in the culture and heritage of
this destination. Both policy-makers and the tourist
industry view culture as one part of the total tourism
product, rather than as a distinct market segment to
be developed (Kalogeropoulou, 1996).

Visiting other villages and historical monuments,
taking walks amongst the hills in the hinterland and/
or doing a lot of 'foot-slogging' in the evenings
around the back streets of Kalimeria to see the 'true
way of Greek life' are some of the main holiday
activities undertaken by special interest tourists,
who want to experience something new, whether
it is the cultural traditions or ethno-history (way of
life) of Chalkidiki. Fieldwork clearly indicates that
'Cultural Heritage' tourists are active participants,

learning and experiencing the 'other' they visit. This indicates that cultural tourism in Chalkidiki may be regarded as a form of special interest tourism. It is an experiential type of tourism in the sense of seeking an encounter with the authentic 'other'.

Tourism in Greece

Greece has a long tradition of tourism, attracting travellers fascinated by the art, philosophy and literature of ancient Greece. In terms of historic sites, Greece is undoubtedly one of the richest in the world with a plethora of ancient and Byzantine monuments and artistic treasures.

> Perfect travel... demands two qualities in a country – that it shall be full of beauty; and that it shall be full of ghosts. Lands with too little past may thrill the eye, but not the memory... Since the Romantic Age, and before, Greece has constituted a spiritual landscape, the embodiment both of wild beauty and of antique wisdom (Eisner, 1993: 13).

According to Eisner (1993) the majority of early foreign visitors to Greece were scholars, including classicists and archaeologists, visiting places such as Athens, Marathon, Sparta and Delphi. Drawn by Greece's classical heritage and cultural attractions, these early travellers were however, few in numbers (Lytra, 1987). Influenced by the classical Greek texts, these early travellers were willing to brave the dangers and discomforts of travel in order to see the tangible remains of Greece's past in the form of archaeological sites and monuments (Lytra, 1987; Yale, 1991; Eisner, 1993; Pettifer, 1993). According to Lytra (1987) cultural motivations for travel have been a significant factor since the early sixteenth century and he documents how Greece was featured as a destination in the 'Grand Tour' undertaken by many of the European elite. The history of foreign travel to Greece clearly shows that the culture and heritage attractions have long played a role in the development of tourism in Greece. Recent evidence from Chalkidiki suggests that culture as displayed in buildings, architecture, music and dance, festivals, cuisine and language is still a major draw for a particular type of tourist.

In addition to its cultural attractions, Greece has many picturesque islands, dramatic mountainous landscapes and a wide variety of sports activities. It represents: 'something infinitely desirable to most visitors, a combination of unsurpassed natural beauty and antiquity and perhaps most of all, warmth and security – Byron's sweet south' (Pettifer, 1993: 70).

With around 9,000 miles of coastline, some 2,000 islands, and its mild climate, Greece is very attractive to foreign visitors with an interest in the archaeology, art, the natural beauties and the cultural traditions which combine to make up the cultural heritage of this destination. More than half of all arrivals to Greece occur in the summer months of June, July and August. Approximately 90% of foreign visitors to Greece originate from Northern Europe, with the UK, Germany, Austria, France, and Italy being the major tourist-generating countries (Pettifer, 1993).

The literature: some generalisations

Several analysts argue that Greece's natural beauties, particularly its sunny beaches, are preferred to its culture and historic monuments (Leontidou, 1991; Komilis, 1994; Coccossis and Parpairis, 1996). For instance, Leontidou (1991: 84) writes:

> If Greece is one of the cradles of Western civilisation . . . this is hardly evident in the nature, destination and seasonality of tourist flows. Instead, the country's mild climate . . . its natural beauty and especially the clear sea are preferred to its culture, heritage, myths and historic monuments.

Likewise, Komilis (1994) argues that 'sun-lust' tourism is the predominant form of tourism in Greece. 'Sun-lust' tourists on a 2-week sun, sea and sand holiday do not come into contact with local people. It is further argued that lack of knowledge, understanding and sensitivity on the part of tourists to the local culture of the host community characterises the sun-lust tourist. Such research assumes that culture is not a primary motivation for visiting Greece. The beautiful landscapes and the climate are said to be the main attractions. For many analysts, it is obvious that people go to Greece to have fun in the sun.

This perspective is commonplace amongst those thinkers who bemoan the growth of tourism and who prefer to use secondary sources, such as travel brochures and books, as their main source of information on this phenomenon. A key characteristic of research to date is that many scholars, in recognising the key role that travel brochures and advertising material play in informing as well as influencing tourists' wants, appear to be content to use such secondary sources as evidence in support of their arguments on why people visit destinations such as Greece. For instance, in their analysis of travel from the aristocratic Grand Tour through to the age of mass tourism, Turner and Ash (1975: 11) assert that modern tourists, as opposed to travellers of the past, are only interested in pleasure, escape, and sunshine. For them, holiday places such as Greece: 'roll across the page evoking images of sun, pleasure and escape . . . we are offered these destinations as retreats to a childlike world in which the sun always shines, and we gratify all our desires' (Turner and Ash, 1975: 11).

While an analysis of travel brochures may be necessary in order to gain an insight into contemporary tourism in Greece, on its own it is insufficient for a full understanding of this complex cultural phenomenon. A major failing of many existing studies arises because they are grounded within traditional methodological 'single paradigm' frameworks, rather than the more appropriate multi-paradigm approach adopted by the Chalkidiki study (Wickens, 2002). Evidence from such multi-paradigm grounded research suggests that the tourist is a polymorphous consumer and different tourist types experience the same host community in different ways. One of the key findings of the Chalkidiki study is that cultural attractions and the traditional aspects of Greek authentic life, religion and history are still a continuous source of fascination to some foreign visitors. The 'Cultural Heritage' tourists are attracted to Chalkidiki for its historical and cultural characteristics as well as its sunny weather.

The research setting

Chalkidiki is a well-established destination for foreign visitors. The coast of this thickly wooded area comprises three peninsulas: Kassandra, Sithonia, and Mount Athos (the 'Holy Mountain'), which is a monastic republic. Kassandra is surrounded by the Aegean Sea and edged by curving beaches that give the visitor a feel of being on an island. Chalkidiki has a number of thriving beach resorts with extensive modern tourist accommodation, including several small family-run hotels and lots of self-catering apartments/studios (Wickens, 1999).

Chalkidiki is full of contrasts. Travelling around this area, one can see that much of the inland region of Chalkidiki is still wild and unspoilt. The whole region has a plethora of cultural attractions. For instance, the ancient site of Stagira, the birth place of Aristotle; traditional villages such as Arnea, found on the slopes of Mount Holomon and Afitos built on the slopes of an ancient citadel; archaeological sites and museums found in the Thessaloniki region; the Petralona caves with their paleontological interest. Other attractions include sandy beaches and clear, pollution-free seawater. However, Chalkidiki, like the rest of Greece, is marketed primarily as an area of long, golden beaches, which can guarantee the sun. It is not surprising therefore, that the whole region of Chalkidiki, including Kalimeria, a coastal village towards the foot of Kassandra, becomes congested during the summer months with both foreign and domestic visitors.

Kalimeria is approximately an hour's drive (c.105 km) from Thessaloniki airport, a main arrival point for tourists. According to the President of the village, the total resident population of Kalimeria is 1,150 inhabitants. In addition, during the summer period, second home owners mainly from Thessaloniki and migrant workers from other parts of Greece temporarily take up residency in the village. Kalimeria is reasonably representative of the village resorts found in Chalkidiki. Because of its size and the level of tourist development, it provided an ideal location for the study of tourists' motives and experiences of the visited host community.

Today in Kalimeria, there are some 250 tourist enterprises, including tavernas, restaurants, bars, supermarkets, souvenir and jewellery shops, hotels and self-catering apartments. In addition, there are a number (unrecorded) of rooms available for rent in private houses. Due to the existence of this undeclared accommodation, overnight stays are usually underestimated by at least a quarter. This 'black economy' in tourism renders it difficult to estimate exactly the number of foreign visitors to Kalimeria. It is important to note here that estimates vary wildly – from a few thousand visitors to more than 30,000.

Study methods

The locus of fieldwork was Kalimeria, in Kassandra, Chalkidiki. Kalimeria attracts package holidaymakers of various nationalities, primarily British, Austrian and Germans. This meant that semi-structured interviews could be conducted with the English-speaking respondents at various sites, including tavernas, cafes and bars. The majority of interviews were taped with the consent of the participant, and subsequently transcribed. Where a participant was unwilling to be recorded, the researcher kept field notes of conversations. A snowball sample was used.

This is common in studies of mobile populations such as tourists (see Bernard, 1988; Lazaridis and Wickens, 1999). In addition, other sources of information were utilised, including the Chalkidiki Tourist Authorities, E.O.T. publications, travel brochures, newspaper articles, and travel guides. The information so collected was subsequently analysed in an attempt to explore the way Chalkidiki was advertised to foreign visitors.

In research of this kind the co-operation of tourists is crucial. In total, 86 British tourists participated. The profile of participants indicates that the majority were in professional managerial occupations. The vast majority of the respondents had come on holiday with other people. Just over half of the respondents stayed in self-catering accommodation. All the participants stayed in the resort for a fortnight. Fieldwork also revealed that a significant proportion reported that they visited Greece on a regular basis. An overwhelming majority reported that they were on a package holiday. Further, the travel brochure was the major source of information for these visitors to Chalkidiki.

The technique of clustering data was used for placing 18 participants (couples with young children) into the category of 'Cultural Heritage' tourist. This process involved a constant examination of differences and similarities in participants' accounts. Clustering helped to identify a number of tourist types – the Cultural Heritage, the Lord Byron, the Raver, the Heliolatrous, and the Shirley Valentine – presented in the 'The sacred and the profane: a tourist typology' (Wickens, 2002). Each of these clusters is characterised by the dominant themes identified by participants for their choice of holiday, the types of holiday activities they indulged in, and the views they expressed about the host community. For the purpose of this chapter only one of these tourist types – the 'Cultural Heritage', will be considered.

The case of the 'Cultural Heritage' tourist

Within this category all participants placed a strong emphasis on the cultural aspects of the host country. Although this was their first visit to Kalimeria, all of these participants had some previous holiday experience of Greece and knowledge of Greek culture and ancient history. In comparing Kalimeria with other Greek communities which they had previously visited, participants told me that 'this place is less touristy than Corfu'; 'I like the casualness of the place, the general atmosphere of the whole place'; 'the place is not swamped by big hotels and so you can see the Greek people, the true way of life and not an artificial way of life'; 'the old village is real Greek, it still has several old buildings'; 'it preserves features, for instance old buildings, churches, tavernas of an authentic Greek village'. The theme of an 'authentic Greek village' was common in conversations with Cultural Heritage tourists.

Participants identified the culture and history of Greece as well as its natural beauties as the primary reasons for their visits. As one female participant put it:

> 'The classical sites, the Greek way of life, the food, the language, the music . . . the plant life, the animal life . . . a lot of wild birds, some of them en route, on migration . . . the beautiful sunsets, Greece has so many things to offer . . . Because of these special sites, . . . the classical archaeology is a particular draw for people who are specifically interested in that type of holiday – an interest holiday. And so Greece can provide a

number of things . . . the interest holiday side of things – sailing and water sports, cultural attractions, traditional hospitality, as well as the conventional, sunbathing type – it has a lot to offer to people'.

Their interest in 'Greekness', such as the Greek way of life, is reflected in many of their holiday activities. For example, with Kalimeria as their base, and using public transport, they visited other villages located away from the coast. One such village, Aghia Paraskevi, was described as a 'typical Greek village', as a 'lovely and peaceful place' and as a place 'not geared towards tourism'. This is how one participant described Aghia Paraskevi:

'Yes, we did travel around the peninsula and although some parts are touris-ty . . . Kalithea is very commercialised – you can go 2 or 3 miles away from the main coastal road – and find places which I can describe as the true Greek way of life . . . Aghia Paraskevi was very casual, friendly and very quiet – no bars or discos'.

Another participant said:

'We enjoy travelling around on our own . . . it is very special for us. . . . Like an adventure, because we don't know exactly where we are going to go next . . . we have a rough idea and we like to visit other villages and ancient sights . . . and we don't know the time of the buses or how we are going to get there, or how we are going to get back to Kalimeria, we just have to work it out on our own and off we go . . . and I like it – my wife likes it – it's like an adventure'.

Organised excursions to the historical monuments of Thessaloniki, to Stagira, and to the Petralona caves were also undertaken by Cultural Heritage tourists. As one female participant who was travelling with her husband expressed it:

'You can always escape . . . we try to get about on the local bus and that's quite a good experience . . . it's also nice listening to the Greek people, yapping to each other, especially the old women in their black clothes . . . yesterday, we were in Thessaloniki . . . oh yeah, we spend most of our time sightseeing and visiting other villages'.

Similarly this participant said:

'We had a car for 10 days and toured around the peninsula . . . we've visited Mount Athos, and a small village on top of a mountain – I can't remember the name . . . and Paliouri. Paliouri is a nice place with lots of old buildings that have a lot of character. We also went on an organised trip to Thessaloniki but that was a bit of a let down . . . didn't have enough time to visit Aghia Sophia . . . Yes, we also spent some days by the sea relaxing'.

In actively seeking to sample the village life in Kalimeria, these special interest tourists also come into contact with locals and Greek holidaymakers. Interactions with their hosts occur in tavernas, cafes, shops, but also on the beach. The 'unexpected friendliness' and hospitality of their hosts was a common theme to arise in our conversations. This is illustrated in the following extract from a conversation with a female participant who was holidaying with her husband and two children.

'Last night we just happened to be getting off the boat and walking up along the beach and these people. . . just dragged us . . . into their party. There were lots of Greek people dancing on the beach and they were cooking the little fish – and they shared the fish with us and it was a wonderful experience, it was just wonderful. So you still get the spontaneity here and I like that ... Oh, it was a lovely experience ... That wouldn't happen in England'.

This is how another participant described her encounter with Greek hospitality:

'I was admiring somebody's flowers ... in a little garden and saying to her how beautiful they were, and we were invited in and given a drink and the lady picked some of these flowers – you know – and handed them to us – it was a very special experience of Greek hospitality ... this wouldn't happen in England'.

Fieldwork suggests that Cultural Heritage tourists are motivated by the desire to experience the 'Greek way of life'. Furthermore, their narratives show that they are not isolated from the host environment, as has been suggested in previous studies (Komilis, 1994). The absence of big hotel complexes, which tend to isolate tourists from the local culture, seems to increase the opportunities for social interaction between tourists and their hosts in Kalimeria. When asked if they would return to Kalimeria, a common response from participants was that they would like to 'visit other parts of Greece'. For example: 'Oh I'd come again, perhaps, in a few years time ... but I'd like to see other places in Greece as well'.

Similarly:

'We will come to Greece. We'd like to see other parts of Greece, maybe some of the islands. We'd very much love to visit Crete next year. One of our friends who's been to Crete, said it was a lovely island, not very touristy with lots of historical monuments to see ...'

The 'very special sites of Greece', the 'classics', 'archaeology' and 'Greek folklore', were identified by Cultural Heritage tourists as significant 'pull factors' for visiting Kalimeria. However, being in a Greek village and sampling its culture (i.e. food, drink, music, and language) was also a strong motivational factor and this was reflected in their narratives. It is also clear that in pursuing 'Greekness', they also come into contact with their hosts. Other factors identified by them were interpersonal, such as the desire to meet Greek people and make new friends, or simply to pursue one's interests.

The case of the Cultural Heritage type provides evidence that tourists can achieve a meaningful cultural experience through their interactions with their Greek hosts. Indeed these foreign visitors are travelling to Greece for the express purpose of understanding and experiencing a culture that is somehow different from their own. Their narratives reveal that they are interested in the 'other', that is, in the history and culture of the whole region of Chalkidiki, including local food, Greek folk music, handcrafts, architecture and the Greek language. As a consequence, they come into close contact with local people. These findings contrast with the prevailing view that package holidaymakers to Greece are only interested in the sun and having fun.

Final considerations

There are several studies, which show that 'cultural authenticity' is not perceived by the travel industry to be a prime motive of tourists visiting Greece. Instead the theme of escape to the 'sandy beaches' of Greece is frequently found in travel brochures and other advertising material (E.O.T., 1997). It is not surprising therefore, that previous studies on the motives and profiles of foreign visitors to Greece assume that all tourists seek sun and fun.

However, the Chalkidiki study shows that although many foreign visitors are concerned with the 'authentic' sunny weather, there is also evidence that a significant number – the Cultural Heritage type – are interested in the culture and history of this area. Their narratives show that they combine sightseeing with a holiday on the beach. They do not view their travel as simply a holiday in the sun where the principal goal is rest and relaxation, but they want to do something unique on their holiday, such as visiting other villages and historical monuments, taking walks in the hills in the hinterland, and/or doing a lot of foot-slogging in the evenings around the back streets to see the 'true way of Greek life'. Data on the holiday activities undertaken by them is useful for shedding light on tourists' wants and involvement with the host community. The analysis clearly shows that it would be wrong to assume that the themes found in travel brochures reflect also people's holiday activities.

The interest in the 'other' is a strong motivational factor for many visitors to Chalkidiki, which suggests that it should be used as a marketing tool promoting the local culture, traditional hospitality and warm welcome of Greeks. Travel brochures are missing opportunities by focusing only on the sun, sea and sand appeal of Chalkidiki. Emphasis should also be given to details of 'traditions and culture-based' tours to nearby cities such as Thessaloniki, and to ancient sites and museums.

Since travel brochures are one of the key elements in communicating the tourist product for a destination such as Chalkidiki, tour operators need to rethink marketing strategies by conveying the culture and heritage of this destination in their promotional information. Heritage sites in Chalkidiki are uniquely placed to respond to the growing interest of tourists expecting authentic travel experiences.

Furthermore, in an increasingly competitive tourism market, it is vital for the tourist industry to know and understand not only who travels, but also how tourist locations such as Chalkidiki are experienced by individual visitors. Detailed knowledge of tourists' motivation can be used to promote and market Chalkidiki appropriately, recognising and giving visibility to key 'niches', which would offer unique experiences especially to foreign visitors.

References

Bernard, H. (1988) *Research Methods in Cultural Anthropology: Qualitative and Quantitative Approaches*. London: Sage.

Boniface, P. (1995) *Managing Quality Cultural Tourism*. London: Routledge.

Briassoulis, H. (1993) Tourism in Greece. In W. Pompl and P. Lavery (eds) *Tourism in Europe: Structures and Developments*. Wallingford: CAB International, pp. 285–302.

Bryman, A. (1992) *Quantity and Quality in Social Research*. London: Routledge.

Buckley, P. and Papadopoulos, S. (1986) Marketing Greek tourism: the planning process. *Tourism Management*, 7, 86–100.

Cassons, L. (1974) *Travels in the Ancient World*. London: Allen & Unwin.

Coccossis, H. and Parpairis, A. (1996) Tourism and carrying capacity in coastal areas: Mykonos, Greece. In G. Priestley *et al.* (eds) *Sustainable Tourism? European Experiences*. Wallingford: CAB International.

Eisner, R. (1993) *Travellers to an Antique Land, The History and Literature of Travel to Greece*. USA: The University of Michigan Press.

E.O.T. (1997) Tourist advertisement in the *Telegraph Magazine*, 19 April, p. 31.

Kalogeropoulou, H. (1996) Cultural tourism in Greece. In G. Richards (1996) *Cultural Tourism in Europe*. Wallingford: CAB International, pp. 183–197.

Komilis, P. (1994) Tourism and sustainable regional development. In A. Seaton *et al.* (eds) *Tourism the State of the Art*. Chichester: Wiley.

Lazaridis, G. and Wickens, E. (1999) Us and the others: the experiences of different ethnic minorities in the Greek cities of Athens and Thessaloniki. *Annals of Tourism Research*, 26, 632–655.

Leontidou, L. (1991) Greece: Prospects and contradictions of tourism. In the 1980s, In A. Williams and G. Shaw (eds) *Tourism and Economic Development, Western European Experiences*. London: Belhaven Press.

Lytra, P. (1987) *The Sociology of Tourism*. Athens: Interbooks. (In Greek.)

Pettifer, J. (1993) *The Greeks: The Land and People Since the War*. Harmondsworth: Penguin.

Richards, G. (1996) *Cultural Tourism in Europe*. Wallingford: CAB International.

Robinson, H. (1976) *A Geography of Tourism*. Plymouth: Macdonald and Evans.

Turner, L. and Ash, J. (1975) *The Golden Hordes: International Tourism and the Pleasure Periphery*. London: Costable.

Wickens, E. (1999) Tourists' voices: A sociological analysis of tourists' experiences in Chalkidiki, Northern Greece. Unpublished PhD dissertation, Oxford Brookes University.

Wickens, E. (2002) The sacred and the profane: a tourist typology. *Annals of Tourism Research*, 29(3), 834–851.

Yale, P. (1991) *From Tourist Attractions to Heritage Tourism*. Huntington: ELM Publications.

Further recommended reading

European Commission (2002) *Using Natural and Cultural Heritage to Develop Sustainable Tourism in Non-traditional Destinations*. Brussels: Enterprise Directorat-General.

Questions

1 Bearing in mind the tourist typologies and market characteristics highlighted in this Greek case study, identify similar European cases, focusing on tourism implementation strategies and general management issues.

2 In the research for this chapter, clustering helped to identify a number of tourist types – the Cultural Heritage, the Lord Byron, the Raver, the Heliolatrous, and the Shirley Valentine – presented in the paper 'The sacred and the profane: a tourist typology' (Wickens, 2002). By way of examples critically analyse the above tourist types, using other European contexts.

10

Tourism in peripheral regions
Discovering the hidden histories of Italy

Rosalina Grumo and Antonietta Ivona

Introduction

In Italy, the past 20 years of tourism development has been characterised by strong plans followed by investments in areas already well established from a tourism market perspective. These areas have been able to generate a high demand for tourism, due to the presence of relevant resources, either in the form of their cultural features – especially cities of interest to art lovers with buildings of historical significance – or natural characteristics – such as the climate, the sea and the mountains. In the course of time, certain destinations have consolidated their role as Italian leaders in tourism. However, a selection of smaller inland destinations have recently started becoming the centre of development initiatives, which have given them visibility in the market. A more diversified tourism portfolio, both in terms of activities and of locations, has become the focus of their tourism strategies.

These initiatives are aimed at enhancing the visibility of those 'non-traditional destinations' (see European Commission, 2002) rich in tourism potential. In this way, they are given the opportunity to become part of special itineraries based on identified common themes and be included in the wider tourist circuit. This type of tourism is considered as a valuable form of 'niche' tourism, aiming at the

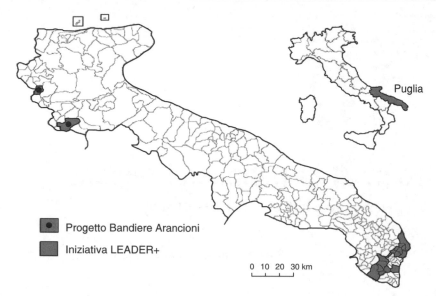

Figure 10.1 Areas included in the 'Orange Flags Project' and the 'LEADER + Initiative' in Apulia.

enhancement and promotion of territorial and cultural values of certain less known regions and municipalities lagging behind others in terms of resources, organisation, market visibility and economic development.

The need for implementing forms of tourism that involve not only the well-established coastal areas is strongly felt in the southern Italian region of Apulia. If on the one hand, this region is fairly well known for its seaside resorts, on the other hand there are numerous inland villages that could be enhanced through the use of their heritage. In relation to this, appropriate policies in line with sustainable tourism development and with the preservation of local resources should be identified. Apulia has notable historical and architectural resources which could be viewed as elements around which to organise and better exploit forms of tourism involving towns of artistic interest, smaller centres and rural villages.

The two cases examined in this chapter, namely the *EU LEADER Initiative* and the *Orange Flags Project*, reflect a search for alternative and innovative forms of tourism based on interesting historical and cultural traditions (Figure 10.1).

The LEADER Initiative in the southern part of Apulia

The European Community LEADER Initiative (Liaisons Entre Actions de Développement de l'Economie Rural) has undergone three phases: LEADER I (1991–1994), LEADER II (1994–1999) and the ongoing LEADER + (2000–2006), the aim of which is to further develop the method adopted in the previous programmes through pilot strategies and catalysing themes (GU, 1991, 1994, 2000). The *territorial innovation* elements identified are different in the experience of areas involved. Starting from the way the LEADER Initiative has been set out, its basis is the creation of a Local Action Group (LAG), an organisation of *local components*, whose task is to define and put into action a Local Action Plan (LAP). This involves selected actions by both private and public bodies. The Initiative itself could include *multi-sectorial actions* consisting of attempts to achieve the integration of production and service activities, *the decentralisation of financing* from the European Commission, to the Member States and the Regions, the realisation of a *connected network* of the areas involved, and the introduction of forms of exchange between the rural and urban environment.

The elements of integration and transfer, launched at the Cork Conference in 1996, have been implemented through this Initiative, which emphasises that policies for rural development should focus on an integrated approach involving the development of agriculture, economic diversification, management of natural resources, promotion of culture, tourism and recreational activities (AEIDL, 1997). The *LEADER I* was carried out in 217 territorial areas of the European Union defined as in Objective I (less-favoured) and Objective 5b (rural) regions (AEIDL, 1997–1998). The *LEADER II* covered a greater area and involved 1,000 localities. It provided stronger support for aspects concerning trans-national cooperation, networking and innovation (INEA, 1994; AEIDL, 1999). Moreover the various elements of an area, whether material or immaterial, are at the heart of the LEADER + approach (2000–2006).

The attempt to promote and develop the marginal areas follows a general outward-looking trend and starts from a consideration of local interests, whereby consent among the local population is created so that they have a stake in becoming directly involved (LEADER European Observatory, 2001). In Apulia, the LEADER + concerns 14 Local Action Groups (LAG), throughout the region (Ministry for Agriculture and Forests, 2000).[1]

Part of this chapter analyses the Local Action Group of Capo Santa Maria di Leuca, which started in 1991 in the province of Lecce and involves the southern area of Apulia, called Salento (Figure 10.1). It is a representative example of good practice which has produced significant signs of development.

The area itself lies between two seas, the Ionian and the Adriatic. Santa Maria di Leuca, *'finitibus terrae'*, marks the point where the two seas meet and is where different cultures mingle. Its geographical position can be seen as the synergetic result of all the historical, cultural, gastronomic and natural variables of this area. The Salento has always been a frontier region where peoples from different ethnic backgrounds merge, at a point where the Mediterranean Sea acts as a crossroads for its commerce and the future of its inhabitants. The land of Leuca is one of the most ancient areas of Apulia (Novembre, 1973).

Nineteen centres were involved in the LAG of Capo Santa Maria di Leuca in the early part of the programme (1991–1994).[2] The most significant measures of the LEADER I project were applied in the sector of farm accommodation, in an area where this type of activity was not yet known, and also in the hotel accommodation sector with the launching of an innovative project within a local, and sustainable approach. This is the so called 'extended hotel' development carried out in the town of Specchia, where the local dwellings have been updated and turned into hotel accommodation. The village of Cardigliano is another example of 'niche' accommodation, where signs of human presence go back to the Messapian period and continue till 1920, when it became a village inhabited by families who were employed on an agricultural scheme for the manufacture of tobacco. Up until 1970, the village was gradually abandoned because of the decline in agriculture. The LEADER Initiative has facilitated the transformation from its original purpose to tourist accommodation structure. In fact, the former tobacco storehouses and the homes of the agricultural workers have been transformed into accommodation for tourists. A further innovative element in this area is the pilot project developed by the Ministry of the Environment, whereby the village is supplied with electricity from wind, photovoltaic and solar energy sources.

Special attention has been paid to the preservation and protection of the *Mediterranean maquis* areas. The latter project was carried out in an area where a type of essence still exists and is found nowhere else in Europe (Trono, 1995; GAL Capo Santa Maria di Leuca, 1999).

The LEADER II Initiative (1994–1999) at the LAG of Capo di Leuca involved 15 towns.[3] This programme includes features aimed at improving the knowledge of the area. The ultimate purpose is in developing a sense of identity in the local population and promoting a series of measures involving and integrating both the inland and coastal areas, in order to spread the benefits to a wider area. This would also help to create off-peak tourism in the Salento area and promote the cultural, historical, architectural and environmental attractions of Capo di Leuca. A number of initiatives have taken place, such as the development of 'Small country hotels', and of 'Farmhouse accommodation', the creation of facilities for 'Stopover in the historical centres' and the realisation of 'The sea at Capo di Leuca' boosting knowledge of the sea, recreational fishing as well as trips along the Adriatic and Ionian coasts. Among the Measure C projects entitled 'Projects for International Cooperation' is the 'Vacation in our European Village', which is the result of a partnership with Austria, Greece, Great Britain and Cyprus.[4] The same Measure proposes the 'Promotion of the Regions of the 40th Parallel', developed in partnership with two LAG from Sardinia, 17 from Spain and five from Portugal (GAL Capo Santa Maria di Leuca, 2001).

The LEADER + (2000–2006) involves 16 towns, part of the LAG of Capo di Leuca.[5] These include a number of inland towns and others on the Adriatic Sea and Ionian Sea. In this area the main activity is agriculture, but tourism also plays an important role. Also included are the coastal towns of Otranto, Santa Cesarea Terme, and Ugento, and other villages offering an alternative to the excessively exploited beaches and providing better services and greater tranquillity. They have recently been included in itineraries of historical interest, highlighting the local traditions, culture and architectural heritage and also sustaining the natural beauty.[6]

Provisional hypotheses for development

In this area the tourism organisation will significantly take root if it succeeds in boosting 'niche tourism'. This should start from consideration given to the local identity and its distinctive features as something that is unique to that area and goes beyond an interest that is merely local in scale. However, certain aspects that could hold back initiatives from development need to be removed. In those places where their geographical position has given origin to the nickname of 'land between two seas', the essential development of the marina in Gallipoli e Santa Maria di Leuca is still lagging behind plans and construction work is still not completed. While connections with the inland areas are still poorly integrated and the railway connection is not so efficient, Brindisi airport is about 25 kilometres from Lecce, with daily flights from Rome and Milan, and a number of seasonal charter flights. As part of an overall improvement project a number of initiatives are planned for Santa Maria di Leuca. General efforts are being made to stimulate off-season tourism through the development of alternative tourism attractions outside the seasonal seaside resorts. Equally important is the need to create a more efficient promotional campaign in line with local resources. These include farm holidays, culture, nature, sports, food and wine based tourism activities. In this context, strengths of the area are to be found in the high quality of products and in their variety, extending to the less known smaller towns (Grumo and Novelli, 2001).

The LEADER Initiative aims mainly at taking full advantage of the heritage, bearing in mind the local features and grafting on its unique elements as innovative method and measures to adopt. This would contribute to increasing development and new job opportunities. This is extremely important for the young generation of this area, which has problems of high unemployment. To this end, favourable conditions for creating enterprises are offered. Other objectives involve the development of an integrated information system and of research into new opportunities for development; they also include greater participation of the local inhabitants in the growth process, a stronger sense of identity and better image of the area in terms of its environment, culture and lifestyle. All this creates a visible and easily identifiable quality tourism product based on local traditions, heritage and culture.

Orange Flags Project for Apulia

In June 2001 the Apulian towns of Alberona and Sant'Agata di Puglia, in the administrative area of Foggia (Figure 10.1), were awarded the Italian Touring Club's (TCI) recognition named 'Orange Flag'. This initiative was introduced in 1999 and certifies the quality of tourism and the environment of small inland towns. The award is set for towns with no more than 20,000 inhabitants, and is similar to the 'Blue Flag'[7] awarded to coastal towns.

The World Tourism Organization has selected the Orange Flags Project as the only successful Italian experience in the field of sustainable tourism (WTO, 2001).

The award is presented to centres that conform to set standards of tourism and environmental aspects. This project is not only part of an overall strategy for the development of tourism, based on the quality of local products and enterprises, but it also aims at a wider sustainable development policy focused on the benefits to be gained by the local community. At the heart of the policy there is the conservation and enhancement of the existing resources, whether these are related to the landscape, the local history or local customs and traditions.

The local landscape, the environment and environmentally friendly actions play a key part in the strategy, which is fully supported by local administrations and communities. This is known to be extremely effective, especially in Northern Europe, often being the source for tourists' choices. The areas chosen are strategic to the development of quality tourism and compatible with the characteristics of the inland areas involved. Cultural heritage, environmental protection, hospitality, local food production, data collection, and availability of information are key parts of the initiative.

Overall the project sets out to confirm a line of development oriented towards integrating coastal tourism with inland areas. By being introduced to inland small towns, tourists have an additional option, which can respond to their niche tourism interests with hitherto unknown places.

The procedure by which the TCI implements the award (Figure 10.2) consists of an analysis of the following parameters: tourist reception (tourist information and suggestions, accessibility and transport); lodging and accommodation and complementary services (hotels and other alternatives, complementary services such as tours, guided visits and excursions); tourist attractions (scenery, historical, cultural and social resources, organisation of events); sustainability and quality of the environment (green areas, water, air, energy, noise, refuse); qualitative evaluation (town amenities, hospitality, traditions, food and wine) and additional comments of the assessors. Those towns reflecting the list of mentioned requisites can obtain the Orange Flag. The award is temporary and subject to maintaining the 'qualities' that were ascertained when the original assessment was made. Those towns that do not obtain a sufficient 'score' at their first assessment have the chance to try to comply with the standards recommended by the assessors in order to receive the quality award at a future attempt. Local administrators and assessors can in fact agree on a brief 'improvement plan' (TCI, 2003), where critical parameters on tourist reception, tourist accommodation and complementary services, tourist attractions, environmental quality and overall qualitative assessment are pointed out. A plan is devised showing the targets still to achieve, together with a series of the short, medium and long-term measures needed to attain them.

In September 2001, the Province of Foggia approved the realisation of an 'Orange Flags Project' in the inland areas under its administration after the Italian Touring Club had presented the proposal to the Local Tourism Board and the Ministry of Environment. The first stage of the project involved the preliminary identification of places that had the minimum standards required for their candidature. Forty-three small centres with fewer than 20,000 inhabitants in the

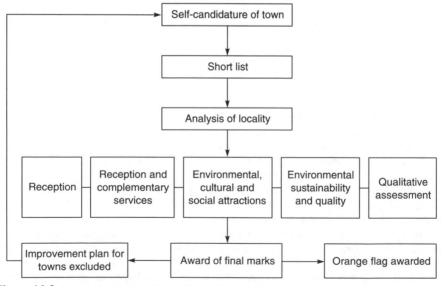

Figure 10.2 Scheme for award of 'Orange Flags'. (*Source*: TCI, 2003: 7.)

inland Daunian area were selected. At a later phase 26 of these entered as potential final candidates.

The data presented in the application forms were then processed and closely examined in order to assess their overall value as areas of historical, cultural, scenic interest and tourist appeal. The forms were also analysed for their completeness, the number of inhabitants, and the availability of tourists' accommodation. Following this second assessment, a short list of six towns was drawn up. These towns underwent further investigation during an on-the-spot visit.

During the first part of the visit, inspectors from the TCI simulated a tourist excursion to test its feasibility; this started with the information provided by the local tourist information centre and then proceeded to the use of the services offered by the municipalities; in the second part a meeting was held with the local stakeholders to gain further information. The final assessment was then reached whereby the Orange Flag was awarded to the towns of Alberona and Sant'Agata di Puglia, while an improvement plan was recommended for the others. A series of measures were suggested in order to reach the standards required for gaining the recognition. One of the main aims of the programme is to make the local administrations aware of the requirements for sustainable tourism development and management.

The recognition given to the towns of Alberona and Sant'Agata di Puglia may well be a unique opportunity to increase the flow of tourists and enhance their economic and social development. Following the recognition, these two centres have been using the 'Orange Flags' logo, which can be displayed for 2 years from the award date, for non-profit and promotional activities.

The purpose of the Orange Flags Project is precisely to give visibility to smaller centres where tourism is as yet undeveloped and to promote them as alternative and additional attractive areas to the established tourist destination, usually located by the sea. Redistribution of tourist flows, better use of local resources, reinforcement of local identity and identification of authentic experiences for the visitors are the ultimate objectives of the initiative.

What lies ahead?

Local development has a greater strategic importance in the context of globalisation. It emphasised the importance of the local dimension by highlighting the need to link any outside interventions to a selected area with those from within the area itself. It is important to include single factors (i.e. natural and human resources) in the system, assess their potential and monitor their results in the light of a deeper understanding of the area involved.

The towns of Alberona and Sant'Agata di Puglia in particular will be enabled to develop a niche type of tourism also aimed at encouraging visitors to stay for longer periods rather than just for a day excursion. Furthermore, due to their limited infrastructures, they will be promoted in conjunction with other neighbouring towns, sharing with them the benefits of the award. The 'Orange Flag' could be stimulus for the implementation of a local system of opportunities for the communities of those towns that have been given the quality award as well as their surrounding ones. Nationally, the recognised 52 Orange Flag towns are grouping themselves into a cooperative company which, among other things, would enable them to have access to financial resources made available by the European Union.

In relation to this, smaller centres are increasingly seen as having a balancing function, which is often facilitated if they have the advantage of being situated not far from a centre with strong appeal for the tourist, as in the case of Alberona and Sant'Agata di Puglia.[8]

Thus increasing what the smaller tourist centres can offer also means:

- reducing pressure on the coastal centres and therefore lessening congestion and degradation
- enhancing the architectural and historical rural heritage generally
- safeguarding the historical values of the landscape by preserving the 'natural-ness' of many places, for which there is increasing demand
- creating cultural and tourist itineraries to better use the rural amenities of the area
- exploiting the material culture of the municipalities and their products (Manzi, 2000).

It also means promoting the spread of tourism over the whole area by shifting its focus towards resources other than those connected to the sea and coast.

The development of tourism cannot follow standardised models, especially in the case of less economically developed peripheries. Moreover, as McCannel (1976: 122) states, 'Tourism cannot be reduced to a mere aggregate of commercial activities, it is also an ideological interconnection of history, nature and tradition which has the power to grant new forms to the need for culture and nature'. Planners' focus should be towards a form of tourism that is not oriented only at economic profit, but strongly involves ecological and social aspects, in respect of the hosting communities. Hence the development of tourism can be seen as something that is no longer ephemeral and of short duration but rather a serious opportunity for diversifying the economy of weaker areas.

Final considerations

The reflections to be drawn from the case studies examined regard two hypotheses for development in areas up until now considered peripheral from a national tourism perspective. There is no doubt that some coastal and inland towns included in the LEADER initiatives in the Province of Lecce may have had only spontaneous development. This is the case of Otranto, Santa Cesarea Terme and Tricase, which are all coastal resorts that have a reasonably strong flow of tourism connected to the sea. There is also no doubt that development in this area has become more integrated only by means of an innovative and wide-ranging overall plan, as well as geographical and marketing considerations (relations between coast and interior and the creation of itineraries). This has contributed to creating off-season tourism, not only in general terms, but strongly related to the local area, where nature, history, traditions and local products are the key attractive factors. At the same time, the local identity has been strengthened, the resources of the area been efficiently used and wider European networks encouraged. The province of Lecce, therefore, despite a few weak points, which still need to be eliminated, has made use of the LEADER initiatives as a 'practice run' for planning, experimenting and employing innovative tourism strategies.

In Apulia, local private and public operators seem to be working together to develop a niche tourism portfolio, which aims to maintain quality and ecological balance and at the same time provide diversified tourism products (Novelli, 2003). This appears to be present particularly in the Orange Flags Project in the towns of Alberona and Sant'Agata di Puglia. This is seen as an opportunity to increase the flows of tourists towards those areas regarded as of little interest to mass tourists.

It is felt that further projects are needed to enhance the urban centres and bring out their 'uniqueness', connecting them to themed itineraries without attempting to enter into competition with other more important tourist centres. Besides, all forms of tourism that establish significant connections between places, the history of towns and activities for the well-being of tourists during their stay, require the presence of skilled and conscientious managers. In the light of the two case studies analysed, it is hoped that more will be planned and implemented through public/private collaboration for the long-term benefit of similar peripheral areas.

Notes

1 The GAL projects in Apulia are: Nord Salento Valle della Cupa, Piana del Tavoliere, L'Uomo di Altamura, Polis rurale, Nord Ovest Salento, Terra dei Messapi, Monti Dauni, Murgia degli Svevi, Comprensorio Rurale Jonico, Consorzio di Sviluppo dell'Arco Jonico Tarantino, Murgia Tarantina, Meridaunia, Alto Salento.
2 The towns that are part of LEADER I are: Alessano, Andrano, Castrignano, Castro, Corsano, Diso, Gagliano del Capo, Montesano, Morciano, Ortelle, Patù, Poggiardo, Ruffano, Salve, Santa Cesarea Terme, Specchia, Spongano, Tiggiano, Tricase.
3 The towns participating in LEADER II are the same as in LEADER I, except for Castrignano, Montesano, Morciano, Patù, Santa Cesarea Terme and Spongano and with the additions of Acquarica del Capo and Presicce.
4 These are in Austria the GAL 'Kleinregion Feldbach', in Greece the GAL 'Anaptixiaki Eteria Parnona A.E.', in Great Britain the GAL 'North Pennines' and in Cyprus the tourist operator 'Cyprus Village'.
5 The towns adhering to LEADER+ are: Acquarica del Capo, Giuggianello, Giurdignano, Minervino di Lecce, Otranto, Poggiardo, Ruffano, Salve, Sanarica, San Cassiano, Santa Cesarea Terme, Specchia, Supersano, Tricase, Ugento e Uggiano La Chiesa.
6 Five itineraries of this type have been developed: 'Le Serre, rural landscapes, churches and small towns of artistic interest'; 'Environment and health, treasures of nature in the inland areas'; 'The Adriatic coast, grottoes and other rock formation'; 'The Ionian coast, stretches of sand'; 'The origins of the Leuca area from the Messapians to the civilization of the middle ages'.
7 The award is given by the FEEE, Foundation for Environmental Education in Europe; it is given for sea water quality, quality of the coast, services and safety measures and environmental education.
8 Alberona and Sant'Agata di Puglia: distances of some important tourist resorts in the Provinces of Bari and Foggia:

Towns	Distance from Alberona (km)	Distance from Sant'Agata di Puglia (km)
San Giovanni Rotondo	8	95
Vieste	129	143
Peschici	130	169
Rodi Garganico	116	155
Lucera	25	75
Margherita di Savoia	114	81
Andria (Castel del Monte)	122	88

References

AEIDL (1997) *Leader Magazine, Speciale Conferenza di Cork: un mondo rurale che vive*, n. 13, European Commission, Bruxelles.

AEIDL, LEADER Magazine (1997–1998) *Speciale Convegno LEADER, Per una nuova iniziativa comunitaria per lo sviluppo rurale: 800 leader a confronto*, n. 16, European Commission, Bruxelles.

AEIDL LEADER Magazine (1999) *La cooperazione trasnazionale tra territori rurali*, n. 21, European Commission, Bruxelles.

European Commission (2002) *Using Natural and Cultural Heritage to Develop Sustainable Tourism in Non-traditional Destinations*. Brussels: Enterprise Directorat-General.

GAL Capo S. Maria di Leuca (1999) *Leader I e II. Interventi in materia ambientale nel Capo di Leuca*.

GAL Capo S. Maria di Leuca (2001) *Terra di Leuca 'Conoscere, Crescere, Innovar'*, Periodico di informazione del GAL, anno I, da n. 5 a n. 10.

GU Delle Comunita' Europee (1991) *Comunicazione agli Stati membri recante orientamenti per la concessione di sovvenzioni globali integrate sulla base di proposte che gli Stati membri sono invitati a presentare nel quadro di un'iniziativa comunitaria in materia di sviluppo rurale*. Bruxelles.

GU Delle Comunita' Europee (1994) *Comunicazione degli Stati membri recante gli orientamenti per la concessione di sovvenzioni globali o per programmi operativi integrati sulla base di richieste di contributo che gli Stati membri sono invitati a presentare nell'ambito di un'iniziativa comunitaria in materia di sviluppo rurale-LEADER II*. Bruxelles.

GU Delle Comunita' Europee (2000) *Comunicazione della Commissione agli Stati membri del 14 aprile del 2000 recante gli orientamenti per l'iniziativa comunitaria in materia di sviluppo rurale LEADER +*. Bruxelles.

Grumo, R. and Novelli, M. (2001) *Progetto RINTUR, Ricerca-Innovazione per lo sviluppo competitivo del turismo*. Lecce.

INEA (1994) *Leader II, Dossier informativo*, Roma.

Manzi, E. (2000) Centri minori tra geografia, urbanistica, beni culturali e ambiente. Spunti per una ricerca e un dibattito. *Rivista Geografica Italiana*, fasc. 2, 255–272.

McCannel, D. (1976) *The Tourist. A New Theory Of The Leisure Class*. New York: Schocken Books.

Ministero per le Politiche Agricole e Forestali (2000) *Linee guida per l'applicazione del Leader + in Italia*, Roma.

Novelli, M. (2003) Niche Tourism: a sustainable option for tourism development in peripheral Southern Italy?. *International Conference Taking Tourism to the Limits*, Waikato, New Zealand, December 2003.

Novembre, D. (1973), *Geografia urbana della Puglia. Ricerche sul popolamento antico del Salento con particolare riguardo a quello messapico*. Bari, Adriatica.

Osservatorio Europeo LEADER (2001) *Leader da un'iniziativa ad un metodo, Guida didattica all'impostazione LEADER*, European Commission, Bruxelles.

TCI (2001) *Progetto Bandiere Arancioni: Provincia di Foggia – Report delle attività svolte*. Milano.

TCI (2003) *Bandiere Arancioni*. Milano.

Trono, A. (1995) Risorse locali e programma L.E.A.D.E.R I per lo sviluppo delle aree rurali con particolare riferimento all'esperienza pugliese. In Viterbo, D., *Turismo e territorio*. Lecce, Argo, pp. 265–299.

Viterbo, D. (1995) *Turismo e territorio*. Lecce, Argo.

WTO (2001) *Sustainable Development of Tourism. A Compilation of Good Practices*, Madrid.

Acknowledgements

The introduction and the Final Considerations of this chapter were co-authored. While the sections 'The LEADER Initiative in the southern part of Apulia' and 'Provisional hypotheses for development' were written by Grumo, the 'Orange Flags Project for Apulia' and 'What lies ahead?' were by Ivona.

Questions

1 What is the function of the European Union Initiatives in relation to local development and promotion of peripheral areas?
2 How can the small centres help the diffusion of the sustainable tourism'?

Further reading

Girolami, M. (2002) Bandiere Arancioni. Un marchio di qualità turistico ambientale dell'entroterra. In *Atti della Conferenza Internazionale di Rimini sul Turismo Sostenibile,* Rimini.
Gubert, R. and Pollini, G. (2002). *Turismo, fluidità relazionale e appartenenza territoriale.* Milano: Franco Angeli.
Todisco, E., Pezzulli, S., Carlin, P. and Melchiorri, C. (2000) L'importanza dei siti turistici: un tentativo per stabilirne il valore. *Bollettino della Società Geografica,* Serie XII, V, Roma.

Websites

www.europa.eu.int
www.galcapodileuca.it
www.touringclub.it

11

Research tourism
Professional travel for useful discoveries

Angela Benson

This chapter attempts to examine the concept of 'research tourism' and provides a framework showing why this should be considered as an emerging niche market. Research tourism will be contextualised within the 'alternative tourism paradigm', but more specifically, the educational, scientific and volunteer sectors will be examined and within this research tourism will be characterised. In order to establish research tourism in context, a case study will be used to illustrate an example of this type of tourism. The case study which describes the organisation, the participating scientists and the volunteer tourists, will be examined by drawing upon qualitative evidence that was undertaken during fieldwork in Indonesia in 2002.

Alternative tourism paradigm

After three decades of popular tourism (Cohen, 1972; Turner and Ash, 1975; Poon, 1993) it is considered to be socially, culturally and environmentally destructive, although the economic benefits are acknowledged. In the latter part of the twentieth century, academics, governments and members of the public became increasingly concerned, at both global and local level, at the changes and degradation (Russo, 1999) of the environment. As a result of this, popular or 'mass' tourism was no longer considered best practice and the move towards more alternative approaches has emerged (Burns and Holden, 1995). Alternative tourism is the vogue and although still debated, the literature characterises it as being a significant area within the tourism sector (Holden, 1984; Cohen, 1987; Weiler and Hall, 1992; Douglas *et al.*, 2001; Wearing, 2001). The characteristics of alternative tourism can be seen in Table 11.1, which contrasts with popular or 'mass' tourism that is typified as a standardised, rigid package with no flexibility, mass marketing to an undifferentiated clientele, consumed *en masse* and with little regard for the effects upon the destination (Poon, 1993) or for the host community (Urry, 1990).

The alternative tourism paradigm is seen as an overarching umbrella term, under which the diversity of other forms of tourism or niche markets lay; this is demonstrated in Figure 11.1. The next section concentrates on three of these subsets: educational, volunteer and scientific.

Table 11.1 Characteristics of alternative tourism

- Small scale of development with high rates of local ownership
- Minimised negative environmental and social impacts
- Maximised linkages to other sectors of the local economy, such as agriculture, reducing a reliance upon imports
- Retention of the majority of the economic expenditure from tourism by local people
- Localised power sharing and involvement of people in the decision-making process
- Pace of development directed and controlled by local people rather than external influences

Source: Holden (2000: 192).

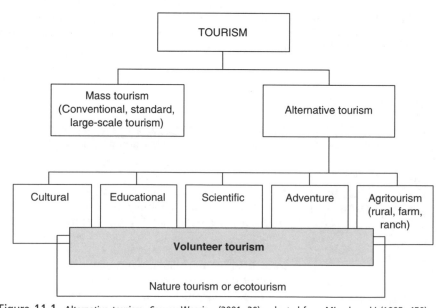

Figure 11.1 Alternative tourism. *Source:* Wearing (2001: 30), adapted from Mieczkowski (1995: 459).

Educational, volunteer and scientific tourism

This section begins by reviewing growing but fragmented literature that is uneven in quality. However, such an assessment is necessary, even if preliminary and partial in order to establish the framework in which research tourism will be contextualised. The educational, volunteer and scientific tourism examined here generally acknowledges that these niches fall both inside and outside the wider ecotourism construct (Boo, 1990; Cater and Lowman, 1994; Lindberg and McKercher, 1997; Epler Wood, 1998; Fennell, 1999; Weaver, 2001; Page and Dowling, 2002) and is demonstrated in Figure 11.1.

Educational tourism

The Grand Tour is recognised as the beginning of educational tourism (French *et al.*, 2000; CTC, 2001) where scholars and aristocracy undertook world tours as part of their education. Modern educational tourism evolved with colleges and universities offering opportunities to travel and study overseas and has continued to diversify into other interested groups. In order to examine the niche of educational tourism and distinguish it from other forms of tourism, it is necessary to define education and therefore, establish travel that has an educational purpose. Smith (1982: 47) defined education as 'the organised, systematic effort to foster learning, to establish the conditions, and to provide the activities through which learning can occur'. Kulich (1987) concurs with this but also notes that learning is a natural process, which occurs throughout one's life and is quite often incidental, whereas education is a more conscious, planned and systematic process dependent upon learning objectives and learning strategies. Educational tourism includes: school trips and language schools (Carr and Cooper, 2003); university and college students in terms of study abroad, fieldtrips and exchanges (Carr, 2003), and the adult and seniors' market, including cookery, art and gardening courses in exotic locations, and specialist organisers like Elderhostel in the USA. There has also been a growth in nature-based and cultural educational tourism programmes, as tourists have become more sophisticated; whale watching tours and other wildlife programmes with educational aspects are well known and documented (Ritchie, 2003).

Volunteer tourism

Whilst the concept of volunteering has a long and established history, the niche of volunteer tourism is relatively new. The generic term 'volunteer tourism' applies to those tourists who, for various reasons, volunteer in an organised way to undertake holidays that might involve aiding or alleviating the material poverty of some groups in society, the restoration of certain environments or research into aspects of society or environment (Wearing, 2001: 1). Examples of volunteer tourist operations, as defined by themselves as offering volunteer opportunities, are: Earthwatch, Coral Cay Conservation, Operation Wallacea (see case study below), British Trust for Conservation Volunteers (BTCV), and Operation Raleigh. These organisations display the characteristics of ecotourism and many have won industry awards to demonstrate this. Volunteer tourism often takes place in developing countries with many of the above companies offering the opportunity to travel to areas of high biodiversity. Volunteering opportunities are often linked to charitable organisations; however, within the tourism sector, whilst some are charitable others are profit-making companies, although they often display strong leaning towards social responsibility. Also, unlike volunteering in other sectors, the opportunities available for volunteer tourists usually involve payment, with a few being in line with the price of an elite and exotic holiday. Payment often excludes flights, insurance and other incidentals. Volunteer opportunities may be for the period of 1 or 2 weeks (as in Earthwatch) but are often for longer periods and may even be for up to a year (Coral Cay Conservation, Operation Wallacea, Operation Raleigh). These organisations may place restrictions upon the participants in that the volunteers cannot participate over a certain age (Operation Raleigh) or they may target a particular segment in order to recruit sufficient volunteers; for example, Operation Wallacea targets university students.

Scientific tourism

Although scientific tourism often receives a notional mention in environmental literature related to tourism, the area lacks depth or breadth. Whilst scientific tourism is a recent phenomenon, Morse (1997) believes that its origins lay in the late nineteenth century when the different science disciplines that depended on field expeditions started to explore the world in a search for knowledge. The expeditions were funded largely by wealthy individuals, or sometimes by the scientists themselves. As a result of this, major scientific institutions emerged and researchers found employment in scientific pursuits. Funding was initially from government money and private donations. This enabled research and study centres to be built in various locations worldwide, which facilitated research to be conducted in remote locations. Although it was not anticipated, the research publications created an interest and image of the country which has since appealed to ecotourists (Rovinsky, 1993). In order to survive, in the face of diminishing scientific funding, scientific research aligned itself with education and learning and the modern study tour emerged (Morse, 1997). This is validated by Mieczkowski (1995: 465) who views 'scientific tourism as a form of ecotourism that helps to preserve the environment relatively undisturbed ... interest of individuals or groups visiting various ecosystems under the leadership of highly qualified scientists has been increasing ...'. Scientists may work for a government, an organisation or be university-based, they may also be travelling on research visas, or often in the case of university-based scientists, travel on tourist passports/visas. Scientists are often a feature of the organisations outlined above in the volunteer section; they are sometimes employed directly by the organisation, or are university-based scientists conducting their own research, which may or may not need volunteers in the collection of that data; they often 'work' without payment, although expenses may be paid. In the case of university-based scientists, it can be clearly seen that they do not travel with tourists as outlined in the definition by Mieczkowski (1995) and Morse (1997) above; furthermore they also do not fall into the definition outlined by Hall (1992: 2): 'all existing human activities other than those directly involved in scientific research and the normal operation of government bases', or in the definition of polar tourism: 'all travel for pleasure or adventure within polar regions, exclusive of travel for primarily governmental commercial, subsistence, military or scientific purposes' (Hall and Johnson, 1995). It would appear that university-based scientists seem to fall between the two distinct sets of definitions; nevertheless they need to be included and considered as part of this subset.

Research tourism

The specialist organisations as outlined in the volunteer section above have steadily grown in number over the past decade. With this growth has come innovation and a range of programmes that is often complex and diverse, with each company seeking a uniqueness, whether this is through targeting certain participants, the location of the programme, or the range of activities offered. However, regardless of these differences, the organisations display a range of characteristics that are featured from educational, volunteer and scientific tourism; this means that the organisations are, at present, situated in niche markets that overlap. It is argued here that when an organisation displays the characteristics outlined in Table 11.2 and demonstrates that educational, volunteer and scientific subsets overlap (Figure 11.2), the consequence of this overlap is an emerging niche – research tourism.

Table 11.2 Characteristics of research tourism

- Characteristics of alternative tourism are present
- Scientific teams or individual scientists are engaged in research pursuits
- The fostering and active promotion of learning and education in relation to participants is evident
- The facilities (e.g. research centre) support and enhance the opportunities for learning and education (e.g. labs, library, lecture theatre, computer equipment, etc.)
- Participants volunteer to participate, although this may or may not involve payment
- The opportunity for participants to conduct their own research is available, with support from the scientific team or individual scientist

Source: The Author, based on fieldwork.

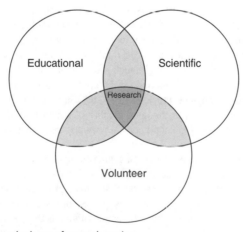

Figure 11.2 A conceptual schema of research tourism.

Figure 11.2 offers a conceptual schema of research tourism: the shaded area represents ecotourism, demonstrating that educational, volunteer and scientific tourism fall outside the ecotourism concept but that research tourism falls within it.

Case study: Operation Wallacea, South East Sulawesi

The following case study on Operation Wallacea outlines the organisation, the participating scientists and the volunteer tourists. It also highlights the problem of definition faced by participants when trying to describe the type of tourism they are involved with. It is argued then, that the following case study has been chosen to illustrate the characteristics shown in Table 11.2 and therefore, clearly demonstrates what may be described as 'research tourism'.

Operation Wallacea is a UK organisation that runs a series of biological and social science expeditions that are used to underpin conservation aims. Operation Wallacea has been operating in South East Sulawesi since 1995. The key objective of the organisation is for paying volunteers, primarily from universities, to provide the financial support for a team of worldwide university scientists to gather data, which will help in the identification of priority areas for conservation and in their subsequent management (Coles, 2003). Operation Wallacea is a profit-making company, although it has now set up the Operation Wallacea Trust (charity number 1078362) which was launched in April 2000 at the British House of Commons. The Trust was established in order to support activities that could directly contribute towards the conservation of biodiversity in the Wallacea region of Eastern Indonesia. The idea behind the charity was to attract additional funding from the private sector and funding agencies, for the community development projects currently being run under the Operation Wallacea Project banner. The organisation was instrumental in collecting the baseline data in order to set up the Wakotobi Marine National Park (1996). Operation Wallacea has won two industry awards: Best Conservation Project 1998 in the SE Asian region from ASEANTA, and the British Airways Tomorrow Award for the best World Ecotourism Project in a National Park.

The organisation has a system of utilising scientists from a range of UK, USA, Australian and Indonesian institutions. Whilst the research is used to achieve conservation aims, the scientists also see this as an opportunity to publish papers in academic journals, and due to the biodiversity of the area, scientists have found new species or sub species endemic to the area. The university-based scientists travel during their summer vacation, which may be taken as leave or research study time, although if the latter is the case, publications are a necessity rather than a luxury. It is normal for the university-based scientists to have their airfare paid, board and lodgings provided free, and after several years a small loyalty remuneration may be paid. Due to the large number of scientists working together, there are often spin-offs in terms of collaboration on projects, research grant applications and joint papers.

Participants join as general volunteers. This enables them to work alongside and assist an expert research team, which allows the individual volunteer to gain invaluable field experience. In the 2004 season, there were 40 main projects available that general volunteers can join with a team of 75 scientists, guides, divers and support staff to enable this to happen. A further addition to the programme offered is the opportunity to complete

---

an independent piece of research for students who would like to undertake a dissertation for undergraduate or masters level courses. The company are keen to boast that 'over 60% of students completing their Honours or Masters level dissertations with Operation Wallacea have gained Firsts or Distinctions ...' (Operation Wallacea, 2004: 1). Training projects are also available to support field projects, for example; an Indonesian language and culture course; forest acclimatisation; PADI open water dive training and/or a reef ecology course. Operational Wallacea operates from May to October, although they are trying to extend the season. As the project has developed, the visitor numbers, although small, have steadily grown from under 100 in 1995, to 320 booked in the 2004 season. The volunteers can stay on the programme for between 2 and 8 weeks, the cost being £900 and £2,700 respectively, excluding flights and insurance. Most participants stay at least four weeks, which is due, in part, to the remote location of the Research Centres but also the length of the particular project the volunteer will be involved with.

Operation Wallacea have two main research stations in Indonesia, one marine and one forest. The location chosen for the Forest Research Centre is Buton Island. This island also acts as a stepping-stone in the travel itinerary to the Marine Research Centre on Hoga Island. The Forest Research Centre is based at Labundo Bundo and is well placed for the Lambusanga and Kakenauwe Forest Reserves. The Forest Research Centre includes a computer room with networked laptops, scanning and printing facilities. There is also a 'wet lab' and an 'ecology lab', each equipped with microscopes and other equipment for processing animal and plant samples. Three, 1-kilometre square, study plots have been established in the reserves. Volunteers stay in local village houses in Labundo Bundo and walk into the forest, although for work on two of the grids volunteers camp out for several nights. Evening meals are taken together, either in the local village hall near the Research Centre, or in a communal tent in the forest. There are lectures available most evenings given either by academics or volunteers talking about their project.

The Marine Research Centre is based on Hoga Island and offers volunteers the opportunity of staying and diving in the Tukang Besi Archipelago, a remote island group off Southeast Sulawesi, which contains all of the major reef formations—atolls, barrier, fringing and patch reefs. There is a fully equipped dive centre, networked computers, wet lab, library, lecture theatre, eating area and bar. Volunteers stay in locally owned bungalows, which have been built to accommodate the growth of volunteers on the island. There are lectures taking place on most evenings about the different research projects. Whilst the hub of activity is based around the Marine Research Centre, two smaller satellite sites have been set up, one in the small township of Ambeua on Kaledupa which concentrates on social science projects, and the other in the village of Sampela, which focuses on Bajau cultural and fisheries projects. Sampela is a separate village built on stilts over the reef flats between Hoga and Kaledupa and is inhabited by the Bajau, sometimes referred to as sea gypsies.

Participants acknowledged that they were paying volunteers but also used the terms 'ecotourist' and 'researcher' when talking about themselves. However, when discussing the organisation there was little consensus over terminology, the following terms were used, often interchangeably: 'culturally sensitive and caring type of organisation'; 'ecotourism minded rather than being a commercial diver resort'; 'expeditions'; 'wilderness feel controlled tourism'; 'conservation and science'; 'tour operator'; 'offering volunteer opportunities'; 'research tourism'; 'research facilities'; 'business with a moral conscience' and 'science-based'. It can be seen quite clearly, that the actual type of tourism the organisation is involved in is not clear-cut; it is also interesting that education and learning were not terms that were used, although this clearly took place on a daily basis.

Final considerations

The alternative tourism paradigm is an important and significant area within the tourism sector, and it is characterised by a series of niche markets. This chapter argues that the present niche markets, namely, educational, volunteer and scientific, are unable to account for the diverse nature and the complexity of the programmes currently offered by specialist organisations. This situation is not aided by the fact that the literature is already scant in this area and the specialist organisations have evolved, leaving the literature even further behind. The chapter goes some way to addressing this, attempts to close the void in the literature, and suggests that 'research tourism', although an emerging niche, is already established, as demonstrated in the case study.

References

Boo, E. (ed.) (1990). *Ecotourism: The Potential and Pitfalls*. Washington, DC: World Wildlife Foundation.

Burns, P.M. and Holden, A. (1995) *Tourism: A New Perspective*. Hitchin: Prentice-Hall.

Canadian Tourism Commission (CTC) (2001) *Learning Travel: 'Canadian Ed-Ventures' Learning Vacations in Canada: An Overview*. Ontario: Canadian Tourism Commission.

Carr, N. (2003) University and college students' tourism. In B.W. Ritchie Clevedon (ed.) *Managing Educational Tourism*. UK: Channel View Publications.

Carr, N. and Cooper, C. (2003) Schools' educational tourism. *Managing Educational Tourism*. In B.W. Ritchie Clevedon (ed.) UK: Channel View Publications.

Cater, E. and Lowman, G. (eds) (1994) *Ecotourism: A Sustainable Option?* Chichester: John Wiley & Sons.

Cohen, E. (1972) Towards a sociology of international tourism. *Social Research*, 39(1), 164–182.

Cohen, E. (1987) Alternative Tourism – a critique. *Tourism Recreation Research* 12, 13–18.

Coles, T. (2003) *Proposed Management of Wakatobi and the Proposed Kakenauwe/Lambusango National Park against Biological and Social Objectives*. Operation Wallacea.

Douglas, N. and Cerrett R. (eds) (2001) *Special Interest Tourism*. Singapore: John Wiley & Sons.

Epler Wood, M. (1998) New directions in the ecotourism industry. In K. Lindberg, M. Epler Wood and D. Engeldrum (eds) *Ecotourism: A Guide for Planners and Managers*. North Bennington, Vermont: The Ecotourism Society, 2, pp. 45–61.

Fennell, D.A. (1999). *Ecotourism: An Introduction*. London: Routledge.

French, C., Craig-Smith, S. and Collier, A. (2000) *Principles of Tourism*. French's Forest, Australia: Pearson Education.

Hall, C.M. (1992) Tourism in Antarctica: activities impacts and management. *Journal of Travel Research*, 30(4), 2–9.

Hall, C.M. and Johnson, P. (1995) Introduction: pole to pole: tourism impacts and the search for a management regime in polar regions. In *Polar Tourism: Tourism in the Arctic and Antarctic Regions*. Chichester: John Wiley & Sons, pp. 1–26.

Holden, A. (2000) *Environment and Tourism*. London: Routledge.

Holden, P. (ed.) (1984) *Alternative Tourism: Report on the Workshop on Alternative Tourism with a Focus on Asia*. Bangkok: Ecumenical Coalition on Third World Tourism.

Kulich, J. (1987) The university and adult education: The newest role and responsibility of the university. In W. Leirman and J. Kulich. (eds) *Adult Education and the Challenges of the 1990s*. New York: Croom Helm, pp. 170–190.

Lindberg, K. and McKercher, B. (1997) Ecotourism: a critical overview. *Pacific Tourism Review*, 1(1), 65–79.

Mieczkowski, Z. (1995) *Environmental Issues of Tourism and Recreation*. New York: University Press of America.

Morse, M.A. (1997) All the world's a field: a history of the scientific study tour. *Progress in Tourism and Hospitality Research*, 3, 257–269.

Operation Wallacea (2001) What is Operation Wallacea? *Operation Wallacea 2001 Programme*.

Page, S.J. and Dowling, R.K. (2002) *Ecotourism*. Harlow: Pearson Education Ltd: Prentice-Hall.

Poon, A. (1993) *Tourism, Technology and Competitive Strategies*. Wallingford: CAB International.

Ritchie, B.W. (2003) *Managing Educational Tourism*. Clevedon, UK: Channel View Publications.

Rovinsky, Y. (1993) Private reserves, parks and ecotourism in Costa Rica. In *Nature Tourism: Managing the Environment*. Washington, USA.

Russo, M.V. (ed.) (1999) *Environmental Management: Readings and Cases*. New York: Houghton Mifflin.

Smith, R. (1982) *Learning How to Learn*. Chicago: Follett.

Turner, L. and Ash, J. (1975). *The Golden Hordes: International Tourism and the Pleasure Periphery*. London: Constable.

Urry, J. (1990) *The Tourist Gaze: Leisure and Travel in Contemporary Societies*. London: Sage.

Wearing, S. (2001) *Volunteer Tourism: Experiences that make a Difference*. Wallingford: CAB International.

Weaver, D.B. (ed.) (2001) *The Encyclopedia of Ecotourism*. Wallingford: CAB International.

Weiler, B. and Hall, C.M. (eds) (1992) *Special Interest Tourism*. London: Belhaven Press.

Questions

1 Examine the extent to which the case study – Operation Wallacea – fulfils the characteristics of research tourism as outlined in Table 11.2.

2 Assess the applicability of the conceptual schema of research tourism (Figure 11.2) on one of the other organisations discussed in the chapter.

Further reading

Christ, C. (1998) Taking ecotourism to the next level: taking a look at private sector involvement with local communities. *Ecotourism: A Guide for Planners and Managers*. K. Lindberg, M. Epler Wood and D. Engeldrum. Vermont: The Ecotourism Society. 2, pp. 183–195.

Wearing, S. and Neil, J. (2000) Refiguring self and identity through volunteer tourism. *Loisir et Societe/Society and Leisure*, 23(2), 389–419.

Weiler, B. and Richins, H. (1995) Extreme, extravagant and elite: a profile of ecotourists on earthwatch expeditions. *Tourism Recreation Research*, 20(1), 29–36.

Websites

Operation Wallacea www.opwall.com
Coral Cay Conservation www.coralcay.org
Earthwatch www.uk.earthwatch.org

Part III
Activity-based tourism

Tourists in search of new experiences seem to look for a wide range of diverse activities which motivate them to visit certain destinations. Sailing, sightseeing, hunting, fishing, attending sport events, participating in nature conservation and in adventure recreation are only some examples. Some of them may be highly seasonal, others can be done all year around; some may require particular skills and permits, in others the visitor is only a spectator, some may require a short period of time, others could involve weeks of activities. '*Activity-based tourism*' may be defined as a form of tourism, which involves consumers whose holiday choice is inspired by the desire to pursue an activity. The visitor may be involved at different levels (i.e., adventure: very high; sport event attendance: very low). These elements will be presented in the chapters offered in this part of the book, where some key activity-based tourism will be discussed in relation to a set of management issues and sector implications. 'Small ship cruising', 'sport', 'wildlife', 'volunteer' and 'adventure' will be the key themes of this section, offering an original international perspective of cases and an interesting set of issues often ignored.

12

Small ship cruising
From muddy rivers to blue lagoons

Ngaire Douglas and Norman Douglas

Introduction

In the world of cruise ships, big is often better. Twenty-first century ships can accommodate more than 3,000 passengers and keep them entertained with a combination of attractions that borrow freely from theme parks, Las Vegas and Broadway. The ship has become the destination. In 2002 *The World of Residensea* launched the first apartments-at-sea concept. A combination of fully equipped two and three bedroom apartments and traditional staterooms, *The World* is a floating community appealing to the rich and famous. The next development is said to be *Freedom Ship*, a floating city of 17,000 resident families, up to 20,000 daily visitors and 3,000 commercial enterprises. With apartments, hospital, landing strip for aircraft, bicycle paths, yacht marina for private boats and education facilities (Park, 2002), *Freedom Ship* is definitely one of the latest inventions. Even if downsized because of financial and other possible constraints, it heralds yet another dimension in the expanding world of cruise ships.

However, not all cruise companies compete in the race to be biggest, best and busiest. Fortunately for niche product developers, there are many people who seek a cruise experience to satisfy quite a different range of travel and relaxation needs. They want to avoid the huge, overpopulated floating resorts, and seek a more intimate, challenging – even educational – experience. Some want to be seen as 'daring to be different' with their holiday choices. Others are nervous of deep water and of being out of sight of land, and so look for cruises in sheltered waters. They want a rewarding, enriching, adventurous and learning – REAL tourism (Read, 1980) – cruise experience. These are the target markets for niche cruise companies.

This chapter examines three niche cruise companies in the South Pacific. Captain Cook Cruises (CCC), Blue Lagoon Cruises (BLC), and Melanesian Tourist Services (MTS) operate respectively in Australia and Fiji, Fiji, and Papua New Guinea (PNG). The geographical and cultural contexts of each company are outlined along with their historical growth and market segments. Management implications and similarities are discussed. For this study the focus for CCC is on its operation in Northern Queensland, Australia. Its Fiji cruise business is similar to that of BLC.

Geographical and cultural contexts

The three countries form a triangle in the south-west Pacific Ocean. Australia is a vast island continent with a population of nearly 20 million. It is industrially well developed, while politically and culturally it is arguably ambivalent. Its historical association is proudly British; its geographical location is distinctly Asia Pacific and its cultural proclivity is decidedly American. Its main industries are mineral extraction, agriculture – including wool, wheat, dairy and meat production – and tourism.

Fiji, a British colony until 1970 and an independent member of the Common-wealth until 1987, is now a republic following the military coups of that year. It consists of three main islands – Viti Levu, seat of the capital, Suva, Vanua Levu and Taveuni – along with some 320 other islands. The population of 857,000 is multi-cultural, with Fijians comprising the largest ethnic group (50%). Its economy is based on sugar, fishing, gold mining, manufacturing (particularly garments) and tourism.

PNG was under Australian administration until 1975 when it became an independent state and member of the Commonwealth. It consists of the eastern half of the large island of New Guinea and numerous offshore islands. The majority of the population of 5.2 million is Melanesian. Its economy is dominated by mineral extraction and agriculture, although its fortunes fluctuate because of ongoing political instability. Tourism remains underdeveloped. All three countries have tropical weather (a large part of Australia lies within the tropics) with hot, wet summers and marginally milder, drier 'winters'. Many Northern Europeans would find the two seasons barely distinguishable. CCC cruises the World Heritage listed Great Barrier Reef which lies along the coast of Queensland. It is a mixture of low coral islands, high islands and vast coral reefs below the water's surface. BLC charts its course through similar islands and many small coral reefs in Fiji's Yasawa group, while MTS offers both island-focused cruises and its special cruise up the mighty, muddy Sepik River.

The three tourism sectors have marked differences. Australia has a highly developed, very diverse tourism industry. Its main markets are Asia-based with Japan at the forefront. The United Kingdom, United States and New Zealand are also strong generating regions. Australia is well serviced by the world's major airlines either directly or through partnerships and code sharing. The various catastrophes of these early years of the twenty-first century have affected the tourism industry's previously optimistic forecasts, but given that about 75% of Australia's tourism is domestically generated, the effects have been cushioned to some degree. CCC's product has a strong market base in the domestic sector as well as a sound international base.

Fiji's tourism industry, on the other hand, is entirely inbound and therefore more susceptible to the vagaries of international airlines and personal travel decisions in times of crises and uncertainties. Australia, New Zealand and USA are the main tourist markets. For Fiji, factors affecting its tourism sector are both international and domestic; seasonal cyclones as well as political coups and unrest keep potential visitors away. It can, however, claim a very strong approach to crisis recovery and control, evidenced by its ability to recoup its visitor losses quite quickly (King and Berno, 2001). Fiji's tourism product is based near, on and under water, with island and coastal resorts, water sports of all kinds and small ship cruising in protected chains of islands such as the Yasawas and the Mamanucas. Thus, BLC is a significant part of the tourism sector.

In PNG, MTS is a major player in a struggling tourism sector. While it has the potential to be one of the greatest cultural and adventure tourism destinations in the region, PNG's widely publicised troubled social and political environments and poor infrastructure are the sector's biggest handicaps (Douglas, 1998). Tourist numbers are very low: those who choose to visit are young Australians, Europeans or Americans seeking the renowned scuba diving locations, or decreasing numbers of Germans and Japanese, respectively making pilgrimages to a former colony, or searching for relics and bones from the Pacific War. Small numbers of Americans and Europeans find their way on board *Melanesian Discoverer* for the great Sepik adventure.

Entrepreneurs and their visions

Entrepreneurs are people who are influenced by market forces and who, in turn, influence society by creating new ventures (Holt, 1992). 'The essence of entrepreneurship,' said Schumpeter in 1928 (cited in Filion, 1998: 3) 'lies in the perception and exploitation of new opportunities in the realm of business.' Filion himself (1998: 4) describes entrepreneurs as detectors of opportunities, creators of enterprises, risk-takers and coordinators of resources. Not only do they satisfy market demand for new products and services, but they also create demand where none exists (Hing, 2001: 58). The psychology of entrepreneurs, however, has only been the object of empirical research for the past 50 years and there is no agreement yet on a distinctive set of entrepreneurial traits. Hing (2001: 60) summarises the literature and concludes that entrepreneurs can generally be characterised by:

- a high need for achievement, particularly for personal accomplishment; they enjoy solving problems and achieving targets and goals
- an internal locus of control; they strongly believe that success is attributed to personal effort and skill. Luck has nothing to do with it
- a propensity to take calculated risks; they confront immediate risk where they have some control over the outcome
- a high tolerance of ambiguity; they can thrive in conditions of uncertainty.

Captain Trevor Haworth, Captain Trevor Withers and Sir Peter Barter were such men. These entrepreneurs and risk-takers saw the potential opportunities that fledgling tourism industries of the 1960s promised. Their names remain indelibly associated with the companies they founded. The public stories of all three emphasise initiative and perseverance.

Captain Cook Cruises

Trevor Haworth began his sea career with the British Merchant Service. He left it in 1961 and settled in Sydney, subsequently buying a boatshed with slipways and becoming partner in a ship delivery business. In 1969 a cruise on New York's waterways spurred on his interest in a tourism idea he had been thinking about, and in 1970 Haworth chartered a World War II motor gunboat that had been converted for day cruising on Australia's Great Barrier Reef. He renamed it *Captain Cook*, registered a company in that name, and took advantage of a few already scheduled charter cruises on Sydney Harbour. Vigorous promotion and canny public relations made a success of the coffee and lunch cruises and by late 1981 CCC had expanded its Sydney Harbour fleet to four.

In 1988, the year of Australia's bicentenary celebrations, CCC made a significant move with the acquisition of three vessels with accommodation. This decision had two major consequences: it expanded the operations of CCC geographically and set it on a more ambitious path towards small ship cruising. That direction received additional impetus in 1989, when, to capitalise on a rapid growth of interest in the Northern Queensland city of Cairns, the Australian flag carrier, Qantas, proposed a joint venture to discuss 'the advantages to be gained by placing a small liner in Cairns to explore the Great Barrier Reef' (Goldsack, 1995: 91). The advantages seemed obvious, but serious obstacles, legal and technical, delayed progress on the construction of the vessel. Work on the 'small liner' at the Fiji Government shipyards in Suva began in 1989 but was not completed until 1995. Marketing of the Barrier Reef cruiser, which had begun in early 1990, resulted in bookings for the schedule of cruises for 1992 having to be met by the remodelling of an existing Captain Cook vessel. It was eventually replaced in late 1995 by the Fiji-built *Reef Endeavour*.

The immediate success of the enterprise suggests that the market was certainly ready for it. *Reef Endeavour* was the first vessel purpose built for the company that fully met the now accepted concept of small ship cruising. Its appearance is, without modification, that of a modern liner, necessarily scaled down; it has permanent ocean going capability; it has sleeping accommodation of various configurations for 168 passengers; it carries on and off board recreational facilities and engages the appropriate specialists to enhance passenger experience, including a marine biologist and a diving instructor. In 1995 CCC ventured into small ship cruising in Fijian waters in direct competition with BLC – a story that need not be dealt with here.

Blue Lagoon Cruises

Trevor Withers and an adventurous, entrepreneurial friend, aviator Harold Gatty, arrived in Fiji just after World War II, planning to establish a tuna fishing business. Fiji, then a British

Crown Colony, had little tourism infrastructure although it had a long history of hosting visitors in transit on their way to somewhere else, initially by sea and then in the post-war airline development era, by air. While assessing the potential for tuna fishing, Fijian protocol and tradition demanded that the two men make a special visit to the islands to pay their respects to the local chiefs before proceeding. Difficulties in communication were overcome with help from an interpreter. Withers managed to obtain full support from the Yasawa people for his fishing venture and established firm friendships with the chiefs. Later this association became crucial to BLC.

Fiji, however, was not yet ready for a tuna fishing industry. But with entrepreneurship undaunted, Gatty went on to establish Fiji Airways, the forerunner to Fiji's national airline, Air Pacific. Withers turned his attention to the possibility of taking visitors on cruises through the Yasawas, a chain of beautiful islands in western Fiji. With the enthusiastic support of the chief who had supported his fishing scheme, Withers purchased his first boat from the New Zealand Civil Aviation Authorities in Fiji and named his new enterprise after a 1948 film, *Blue Lagoon*, made partly in the Yasawas.

The first cruise date was scheduled and advertised – and brought a complete lack of response. Withers, though tempted to cancel, was reluctant to disappoint the islanders awaiting the ship's arrival. He invited six Fijian men on the wharf who had previously assisted him to become his first cruise passengers. For the first month, Withers sailed every Monday, often carrying Fijians to their Yasawa villages but lacking any paying customers. Ten days into his second month of operation he secured his first charter.

During the following 3 months, however, only 27 passengers were carried on the cruise. Facing bankruptcy, Withers made a final gamble. After obtaining an agreement with airlines flying the Pacific to undertake a joint promotion in North America, he sold his possessions to finance a whirlwind promotional visit to travel agents in the USA and Canada. The gamble succeeded and by 1966 BLC had established an international reputation. Withers, suffering poor health, retired after selling the business. He died in 1981. By then the company had changed hands twice, and its vessels were being purpose built.

Melanesian Tourist Services

Peter Barter's involvement with tourism dates back to 1967 when he set up Talco Tours, then owned by Territory Airlines and based in Goroka, PNG. By 1975 Talco had become the largest inbound tourist operator in PNG and pioneered tourism to many regions in the country. It also operated a number of tourist hotels and lodges. In 1975 the Barters moved their operation to Madang and shortly afterwards acquired the Hotel Madang (now the Madang Resort) and the ownership or management of other lodges and visitor services. Maintaining something of the adventure mythology of small ship operations, the Sepik River cruises are said to have started in 1972 with two dugout canoes tied together and covered with canvas and mosquito netting to form a 'houseboat'. In 1976 the company, now known as Melanesian Tourist Services, purchased the first of four vessels to operate expeditionary cruises, naming it *Sepik Explorer*. Each vessel became more sophisticated and comfortable until in 1988 the twin-hulled *Melanesian (MTS) Discoverer* was constructed in Perth, Western Australia, especially to meet the needs of river and open water cruising in PNG. On-board facilities include auxiliary craft such as inflatables, a speedboat, and at times a small helicopter. It can make its own drinking water – from either the sea or the Sepik – a valuable resource if the copious supply of liquor on board ever runs out. Earlier successes inspired the appearance in 1989 of a smaller competitor, the 18-passenger *Sepik Spirit*, which offers a slightly different itinerary.

MTS has assisted many locally owned tourist enterprises and has received a number of awards for cultural preservation and sustainable tourism through the work of the Melanesian Foundation, an organisation which directly and indirectly provides assistance to people living in remote rural areas of PNG. The directors of the company are mainly Barter family members, although a number of managerial positions are held by indigenous Papua New Guineans. Peter Barter, who has held ministerial posts in the national government of PNG at various times, was most recently minister for inter-governmental relations. He received a knighthood some years ago.

The nature of tourism enterprises in the Pacific Islands and the generally successful record of the company mean that the Barters are not without their public critics. In 1987 Australian film-maker Dennis O'Rourke produced *Cannibal Tours* (see Chapter 8 of this book), having taken several trips on *Melanesian Discoverer* to secure the footage he required, according to Lady Janet Barter, cruise director and qualified anthropologist (personal communication). The resulting 77-minute film presents a fairly cynical view of the vessel's 'typical' passengers and the brief relationship between them and the villagers on the itinerary, implying strongly that the visitors are guilty of both cultural ignorance and exploitation, implications that reflect on the management of the enterprise.

Markets

Small ship cruising, like every other tourism sector, is market driven and these niche product operators must work hard to ensure that their advertising reaches the best possible passenger generating segments. Pizam and Mansfield (1999) suggest that the majority of studies on why people become tourists generally agree that motivation determines not only *if* consumers will engage in a tourism activity, but also when, where and what type of tourism experience they will seek. Hudson (1999) concludes that consumer behaviour research in tourism has focused on motivations, typologies, destination choice and the decision process itself. Dickman (1997) cites a study by Roy Morgan and Ogilvy and Mather that proposes ten value segments relating to potential consumers (Table 12.1). The accompanying insights into the psychographic elements of social class, personal values, stages in the life-cycle and consumer attitudes are valuable tools for niche product companies trying to both expand their market base and to understand the needs of their various markets. Of the ten segments, Dickman indicates that five of these would be important target areas for such companies.

Cartwright and Baird (1999: 103) developed three broad categories to describe people who choose to cruise. Their *niche cruises*: *explorers/seeker* market segment should ideally describe the clientele of these three small ship operations. These people, according to Cartwright and Baird, are seeking experiences very different from the traditional cruise holiday. The experience is more important than comfort

Table 12.1 Value segments of interest to niche product developers

Value segment	Features	CCC	MTS	BLC
		Dickman's niche consumers		
1. Basic needs (4% of population)	Hold traditional views of life, enjoy passive activities; fairly satisfied with life; generally retired, pensioners, widowers, people on low incomes.			
2. Fairer deal (5%)	Relatively dissatisfied with life; includes highest level of unskilled workers; pessimistic, cynical, insecure; think everyone else has all the fun and they miss out; feel anger and disillusionment; often hostile to authority.			
3. Conventional family life (12%)	Life home focused; goal to provide children with life opportunities they deserve; place high value on time with family and friends; strive for financial security; making money will secure lifestyle.			X
4. Traditional family life (19%)	Over-50 'empty-nesters'; strong commitment to family roles and values and extended family; life centres on home, garden and traditional activities; cautious about new things and ideas.	X	X	X
5. Look at me (13%)	Young, active, unsophisticated, self-centred, peer-driven; seek fun and freedom and prosperous life; generally unmarried with no children; fashion and trend conscious; socially active; take leisure and sport seriously; not interested in causes.			X
6. Something better (8%)	Probably well-educated; have responsible jobs; confident, ambitious, progressive; want good things of life; prepared to over-extend financially to have things now.	X		X
7. Real conservatives (7%)	Conservatives in most things, asset rich, income poor; interested in security, tradition, stability; hold conservative social, religious, moral and ethical views.	X	X	X
8. Young optimists (8%)	Generally optimistic about future; view themselves as middle to upper class; primarily students, computer technologists and professionals; career building and travel.	X	X	X
9. Visible achievers (16%)	Generally over 30 with above average incomes; want personal recognition of success; collect visible signs of achievement; in control of lives; interested in public affairs and politics; self-focused.	X	X	X
10. Socially aware (10%)	Socially responsible, community minded; involved in environmental groups; seen as progressive and open-minded; enjoy new products and ideas; take global view of world and political issues.	X	X	

Source: Dickman (1997) plus original research.

151

and merit. They will stray from the 'comfort bubble' of a traditional ship but still require a base from which to have new experiences. Each company in this study was asked to indicate where their markets might align with Table 12.1 value segments. In terms of Dickman's five likely market segments, traditional family life emerged as the strongest category. Categories 8, 9, and 10 were strongly aligned across the three companies. Overall, however, it would appear that the small ship cruising experience in the South Pacific appeals to older, general conservative people (categories 4 and 7).

The marketing literature of all three companies emphasises the quality of the facilities on their ships. Good food, en suite facilities in spacious cabins, well appointed lounges, bars, etc. are highlighted. After a day of sea and sand activities or visiting villages in tropical heat, all three ships present a cool, clean and comfortable retreat. Cruising tradition is maintained with the captain's farewell dinner. CCC and BLC focus on water in their promotion, including activities above and below the surface. Descriptions of coral cays, white sandy beaches, sea life, tropical vegetation and birds abound. Both refer to major eighteenth century-historical figures that sailed through their respective areas – CCC to Captain James Cook and BLC to Captain William Bligh. Opportunities for romance and 'sybaritic pleasures' are indicated. In short, the ship is part of the destination with most activities happening in, on and under the water while at anchor, interspersed with forays ashore for some beach-based activity or short, educational experiences with tropical island flora and fauna. CCC provides a marine biologist or similar expert on board to enhance the Barrier Reef experience. BLC includes cultural highlights of the tourist kind, namely the opportunity to buy locally produced souvenirs, play volley-ball with the locals or go to church. MTS, on the other hand, is very focused on the culture contact component of its Sepik trip. Words like 'jungle' (as opposed to the more gentle-sounding 'rainforest' of the other two), 'cultural canvas', 'anthropological', 'adventure' and 'last frontier' pepper its advertising. Unlike the other two case studies, *Melanesian Discoverer* does not promise an idyllic experience, but rather is 'penetrating deep into the essential PNG'. Nightly lectures review the day's encounters and prepare the passengers for the next day's sometimes confronting cultural exposure. 'Expect the unexpected' is a favourite line. The product has particular appeal for high level educational tourism experiences such as organised groups from the Smithsonian Institute in Washington. The authors of this chapter, who have wide experience of both cruise and cultural tourism products, suggest that this small ship experience is one of the very best of the specialist kind.

Management issues

CCC and MTS continue to be family operated companies with various sons, daughters and in-laws of the founders holding a range of management positions. Outside expertise is employed where and when required. Staff training and skills transfer are actively pursued by both companies. BLC has had the majority of its shares (54%) held by Fiji Holdings Limited (FHL) since 2001. FHL itself was established in 1984 by the Fijian chiefs and on behalf of their people as an avenue for indigenous Fijians to become stakeholders in the mainstream economy of the country. The majority of Blue Lagoon's staff is Fijian. In-house training is regular and food and beverage training is continuous. Other training courses include upgrades in engineering, international safety management practices, first aid, fire-fighting and cooking. Employees also participate in courses conducted by the Fiji National Training Council, which range from those concerning seamanship to aspects of hotel and catering.

The three companies in this study share, either across all three or in pairs, a number of characteristics. There are always resident experts on board CCC and MTS; romance and coral cays are promised by CCC and BLC; all three provide very comfortable facilities. They sail within sheltered waters; they were founded by strong personalities whose philosophies pervade the companies' promotional materials decades later; they give employment opportunities to indigenous crews and in administration; they provide opportunities to people in remote locations who would otherwise have few cash-earning options; they use small, specifically designed vessels of similar high standards in quality and facilities. Each company assists in dispersing the benefits – and occasionally the costs – of tourism development to a wider range of communities within the country. They also provide emergency transport for supplies and people in the case of cyclones, volcanic eruptions and other disasters. For BLC and MTS the markets are strictly inbound apart from occasional expatriate residents in Fiji and PNG who seek a brief respite from the urban environments where they mostly work. CCC, on the other hand, has a strong position in the domestic market and this may well strengthen even further as Australians choose to holiday at home as an outcome of the uncertainties of these early years of the twenty-first century. Over 75% of Australia's tourism business is domestically generated.

The focus for each company is the destination rather than the vessel. However, the three waterways and their scattered islands, reefs, lagoons and villages each represent a continuous destination – the vessel is in/at the destination the whole duration of the cruise. The experiences include both environmental and cultural contacts which need to be managed for sustainability. Both Sepik River settlements and Fijian villages on far-flung islands are potentially at risk of over-exposure to tourists who are so extremely different in every respect to the villagers. But as both Douglas (1996) and film-maker Dennis O'Rourke (1988) indicate, these so-called 'primitive' people that tourists come to gaze at show remarkable insights into western behaviour. On a CCC cruise, a visit to Cooktown in far North Queensland could be an equally fascinating 'meet the locals' experience for an American or European or Sydney-based Australian.

Final considerations

Small cruise vessels have great potential to disburse some of the benefits of tourism out to remote and isolated communities. They have minimal expensive and scarce resource-diverting infrastructure requirements and their environmental and social impacts are controllable by responsible management practices. This type of tourism can provide opportunities for many communities located on or near navigable waterways as long as the vessel has reasonable access to one appropriately developed port suitable for providoring, maintenance, bunkering and embarkation and disembarkation of passengers. This last requirement usually means the port has to be easily accessible from an international airport, or, at the very least, a sizeable domestic one. As a niche market product, small ship cruising can satisfy the tourist seeking soft adventure, comfort, cruising, education and culture (Douglas and Douglas, 2003).

References

Cartwright, R. and Baird, C. (1999) *The Development and Growth of the Cruise Industry*. Oxford: Butterworth-Heinemann.

Dickman, S. (1997) *Arts Marketing: The Pocket Guide*. Sydney: Centre for Professional Development and Australia Council.

Douglas, N. (1996) *They Came for Savages: 100 Years of Tourism in Melanesia*. Lismore: Southern Cross University Press.

Douglas, N. (1998) Tourism in PNG: past, present and future. *Pacific Tourism Review*, 2(1), 97–104.

Douglas, N. and Douglas, N. (2001) The short, unhappy life of an Australia-based cruise line. *Pacific Tourism Review*, 5(3), 131–142.

Douglas, N. and Douglas, N. (2003) *The Cruise Experience: Regional and Global Issues in Cruise Tourism*. Sydney: Pearson Education Press.

Filion, J. (1998) From entrepreneurship to entreprenology: the emergence of a new discipline. *Journal of Enterprising Culture,* 6(1), 1–23.

Goldsack, R. (1995) *A Silver Jubilee: Captain Cook Cruises*. Sydney: Fendwave, 17–18.

Hing, N. (2001). Entrepreneurship and small business. In N. Douglas., N. Douglas and R. Derrett (eds) *Special Interest Tourism: Context and Cases*. Brisbane: John Wiley, pp. 57–85.

Holt, D.H. (1992) *Entrepreneurship: New Venture Creation*. New Jersey: Prentice-Hall.

Hudson, S. (1999) Consumer behaviour related to tourism. In A. Pizam and Y. Mansfield (eds) *Consumer Behaviour in Travel and Tourism*. New York: Haworth Hospitality Press.

King, B. and Berno, T. (2001) Transforming negative publicity into positive communication. Tourism recovery in Fiji. Paper presented at World Tourism Organisation Tourism and Economics Conference, Cheju Island, Republic of Korea. June, 2001.

O'Rourke, D. (1987) *Cannibal Tours*, Film Australia.

Park, M.Y. (2002) Setting sail on a giant, floating city. *Fox News Channel*, www.foxnews, accessed on 13 March 2004.

Pizam, A. and Mansfield, Y. (1999) *Consumer Behaviour in Travel and Tourism*. New York: Haworth Hospitality Press.

Read, S.E. (1980) A prime force in the expansion of tourism in the next decade: special interest travel. In D.E. Hawkins, E.L. Schafer and J.M. Rovestad (eds) *Tourism, Marketing and Management Issues*, Washington, DC: George Washington University, pp. 193–202.

Questions

1 Dwyer and Forsyth (1998) identify two main categories of expenditure when a cruise ship visits a port. Within these two categories, there are a number of specific areas where economic input might happen, depending on the nature of the port. Your first task is to locate these categories and their sub-sectors. Your second task is to get a brochure outlining an itinerary of a typical small ship cruise of the type discussed in this chapter. A travel agent or a quick search on the web will turn up such an example for you. Your next task is to determine what areas the economic input might come from for each of the ports on the itinerary.

2 Why should local, regional or national government interested in developing their tourism product diversity look at small ship cruising as a viable option?

Further recommended reading

Forsyth, P. and Dwyer, L. (1998) Economic significance of cruise tourism. *Annals of Tourism Research*, 25(2), 393–415.

Websites

www.bluelagoon.com
www.captaincook.com
www.melanesiantouristservices.com

13

Sport tourism

Small-scale sport event tourism: the changing dynamics of the New Zealand Masters Games

Brent Ritchie

Introduction

This chapter introduces readers to the niche market of sport tourism and outlines the growing interest in sport tourism by government, industry and academics. The chapter considers specialist niche markets under the broad umbrella of sport tourism and notes that literature and research has concentrated largely on large-scale sporting events. However, it argues that small-scale sporting events can be a useful tool to help towns and cities attract visitors and create economic development in times of urban restructuring. The second part of the chapter examines the role and dynamics of a small-scale sporting event (the New Zealand Masters Games) in what could be termed a peripheral city (Dunedin). It discusses results from several years of event evaluation and research and considers the strategic development and changing direction of the event, which may be of use to other destinations using small-scale sporting events as development and marketing tools.

Growth of sport tourism as a niche market

Researchers have recognised that people have been travelling to participate in or watch sport for centuries (see Delpy, 1998; Gibson, 1998). Today sport and tourism are among the 'developed' world's most sought-after leisure experiences and are becoming very important economic activities. Research has indicated that the contribution sport makes to the gross domestic product (GDP) of industrialised nations is between 1 and 2%, while the contribution of tourism is between 4 and 6% (WTO, 2001). Research conducted on sport tourism has been undertaken at international and national levels by researchers, government and non-governmental organisations, thus illustrating the growing importance and recognition of sport tourism as a tourism market.

At the international level the World Tourism Organization (WTO, 2001) concluded that German tourists accounted for 32 million sport-orientated trips a year, or 55% of all outbound travel, while 52% (7 million) of all trips made by Dutch tourists included a sport component. French tourists were less motivated by sport holidays, although 23% or 3.5 million trips still included a sport component. Across the English Channel, the British Tourist Authority and the English Tourism Council (now VisitBritain) claim that as many as 20% of tourist trips are directly related to sports participation, while 50% of holidays contain some form of incidental sports participation (DISR, 2000). However, this development is not simply a European trend. In the United States, event sport tourism generates an estimated US $27 billion a year (Travel Industry Association of America, 2001) and two-fifths of the population (75 million) reported attending a sports event as either a participant or spectator while travelling in the past 5 years (TIA, 1999).

Research conducted in Canada during 1998 demonstrated that 37.3% of the 73.7 million domestic recreational journeys were undertaken for attendance at a sports event. In 1996, a Canadian Sports Tourism Initiative programme was developed to increase the tourism potential of sports events in Canada (Canada Tourism, 2000). Similarly, in South Africa, 4% of the domestic tourism market comprises sport tourism, and the potential to develop the international sport tourism market can be best seen by the recent inauguration of South Africa Sports Tourism (SAST), a joint initiative by the Ministry of Environmental Affairs and Tourism and the Ministry of Sport and Recreation in South Africa. In Australia, the Bureau of Tourism Research (2000) has shown that a total of 12.9 million domestic trips were undertaken to participate in, watch, or organise a sporting event in Australia during 1999. It is evident from the above discussion that government and researchers have tended to focus on sporting events at the expense of other sub-segments of sport tourism, which will be discussed in the next section.

Sport tourism definitions and segments

Sport tourism includes travel to participate in a *passive* sport holiday (e.g. sports events and sports museums) or an *active* sport holiday (e.g. scuba diving, cycling, golf), and it may involve instances where *either* sport or tourism are the dominant activity or reason for travel. Standevan and De Knop (1999: 12) therefore define sport tourism as 'all forms of active and passive involvement in sporting activity, participated in casually or in an organized way for non-commercial or business/commercial reasons that necessitate travel away from home and work locality'. Pitts (1999: 31) believes that from a sport marketing and management perspective, sport tourism consists of two broad product categories:

- *sports participation travel* (travel for the purpose of *participating* in a sports, recreation, leisure or fitness activity)
- *sports spectatorial travel* (travel for the purpose of *watching* sports, recreation, leisure or fitness activities and events).

However, Gibson (2002) suggests three possibly overlapping categories of sport tourism including active sport tourism, event sport tourism, and nostalgia sport tourism. Active sport tourism consists of several activities including skiing (see Hudson, 2000 and Gilbert and Hudson, 2000), bicycle touring (Ritchie, 1998a; Ritchie and Hall, 1999), adventure tourism (Fluker and Turner, 2000) and active participation events such as Masters Games and other sporting tournaments (Green and Chalip, 1998). According to Standeven and De Knop (1999) this segment of the travelling population comprises approximately 10–30% of the total market. The WTO (2001) noted that favourite physical activities on active holidays ranged from skiing and snowboarding in winter, to hiking, mountaineering, climbing, water sports (scuba diving, snorkelling, swimming) and cycling in summer. Active sport tourism overlaps with Pitt's (1999) concept of sports participation travel. Furthermore, the settings in which active sport tourism can take place include attractions (such as indoor summer ski arenas), resorts (for skiing, golf and fitness activities), cruises (for snorkelling and sports facilities) and adventure tourism (such as hiking and snowboarding) as noted by Kurtzman (2000).

Event sport tourism has provided the vast majority of research and scholarship in the field of sport tourism. Higham and Hinch (2002) note that the majority of research conducted in the field of sport tourism examines sport events tourism (or event sport tourism) and within this category mainly large-scale 'mega' or 'hallmark' events such as the Olympic Games and other major sporting tournaments.

With respect to nostalgia sport tourism, both Gibson (2002) and Gammon (2002) consider nostalgia sport tourism as a separate category, yet it has received less scholarly attention than other categories of sport tourism. Examples of nostalgia sport tourism cut across the various sport tourism categories noted by Kurtzman (2000) to include sport halls of fame and museums, sport tourism tours to famous sporting stadium or facilities (such as Twickenham for Rugby Union and Lords for cricket), and sport theme vacations on cruise ships or at resorts with sporting professionals (sometimes referred to as fantasy camps).

These three categories of sport tourism noted by Gibson (2002) can overlap (Figure 13.1), and it is possible to have an active sporting event that involves participants rather than spectators, as well as a theme vacation or fantasy camp between both active and nostalgia sport tourism categories. However, the remainder of this chapter considers small-scale active sport event tourism which fits between Gibson's (2002) event and active sport tourism categories, and is an area which has received little attention to date.

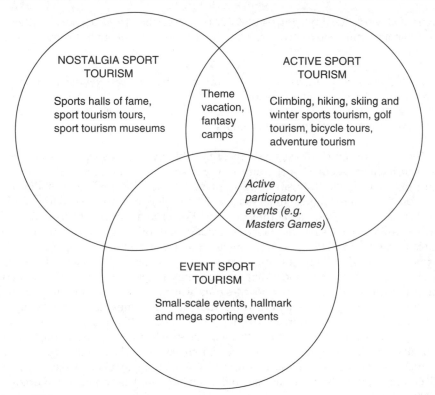

Figure 13.1 Sport tourism segments and categories.

Small-scale sport event tourism

Higham (1999) suggests that small-scale sport events can produce positive impacts for host communities without a number of negative impacts often associated with large-scale 'hallmark' or 'mega' events such as the Olympic Games. Larger events may have downsides or long-term negative consequences such as displacement of residents; large opportunity cost can often be politically driven and may impact negatively upon host community quality of life (see for instance Hall, 1992; Hiller, 1998; Olds, 1998). As Essex and Chalkley (1988: 19) suggest, large-scale events may become 'a self-serving commercial circus of property developers, construction companies, equipment suppliers and commercial sponsors who do not have the local community's best interests high on their agendas'.

According to Higham (1999: 87) small-scale sport events include 'regular season sporting competitions (ice hockey, basketball, soccer, rugby leagues), international sporting fixtures, domestic competitions, Masters or disabled sports, and the like'. However, as Gibson *et al.* (2003: 182) rightly note:

> The distinction between small-scale and hallmark events is not simply related to the size of the event, but is also related to the fact that regular season games do not tax the resources of the host city in the same manner as hosting a mega event.

Higham (1999) suggests that these smaller events may use existing infra-structure, require reduced investment of funds, can minimise tourism seasonality, and are more manageable than larger 'hallmark events'. They can also be just as important for developing the national or regional sport tourism industry and can provide marketing and economic development for small destination regions. Small-scale sporting events should complement existing infrastructure and resources of the local destination, and, in doing so can minimise displacement of visitors, locals and the large costs often associated with hosting larger-scale sporting events. However, to date little research has been conducted into small-scale event sport tourism and its implications for destinations, despite the potential for marketing and attracting economic development in an era where cities are competing against each other to attract investment and tourism (Kotler et al., 1993).

Furthermore, research undertaken on small-scale sport event tourism has tended to focus on spectators rather than participants or active sporting events. Irwin and Sadler (1998) noted the tourism potential of fans travelling to view university sport events in the United States with emphasis on fans' travel planning and expenditure patterns. Walo et al. (1996) examined the National University Games in Australia in 1995 and noted that the event acted as an attraction for the local region. However, Garnham (1996) suggested that although the Ranfurly Shield Rugby Union match in New Zealand produced high levels of spending by visitors there were winners and losers, with the retail sector missing out as visitors were 'partying rather than shopping'. Gibson et al. (2003) also discovered the potential use of small-scale sport events by examining fans attending the University of Florida football matches.

Concerning active small-scale sport event tourism, Higham and Ritchie (2001) noted a growth of small-scale rural sporting events in Southern New Zealand, which mirror the growth in sport event tourism in New Zealand and other countries such as Australia. Sport event organisers used the landscape and physical resources of the region to host active sporting events such as marathons and endurance races at little or no cost and were able to showcase the local destination and attract tourists. Other research, such as that undertaken by Green and Chalip (1998), examined participants in a flag football tournament in the United States and in particular the motivation and desire of participants, while Pitts (1999) examined gay and lesbian sport tourists at the Gay Games. However, despite this research, the detailed examination of active small-scale sport event tourism is rare. Nevertheless, the potential marketing and economic development benefits for destinations are similar, but smaller in size and scope than 'hallmark' or 'mega' sporting events which tend to generate the most interest from researchers, policy makers and planners alike. Furthermore, because of the size and scale of such events little ongoing research and evaluation is undertaken and many event organisers may not use the event strategically with respect to their local resources available. As Higham and Ritchie (2001) noted in their research, only 25% of event organisers undertook research related to their events and only 10% had a strategic plan related to the event.

More recently research has been undertaken on the Super 12 Rugby Union competition in New Zealand (Higham and Hinch, 2002) and in Australia (Ritchie et al., 2002) suggesting the potential of this competition to attract domestic and international visitors, their resulting expenditure as well as their ability to contribute towards destination image and branding. Furthermore, as Gibson *et al.* (2003: 188) note from their study on college sports events, they can attract a significant proportion of fans from outside of the local community and their findings support the growing attention within the tourism literature concerning the benefits of small-scale sporting events for the tourism industry. This assumption is also examined in the remainder of this chapter through the examination of the development and economic impact associated with the New Zealand Masters Games (an active sport tourism event) held every alternate year in Dunedin, New Zealand.

The New Zealand Masters Games: setting the context

The New Zealand Masters Games (NZMG) have been in existence since 1989 where participant numbers started at 1,650 and rose to over 8,000 participants in 2002 (Table 13.1) making it the largest multi-sport event in New Zealand for people over 30 years of age. However, Dunedin has only been involved in hosting the games in alternate years since 1992 and the event is held every other year in Wanganui in the North Island of New Zealand. During this period numbers have grown in Dunedin from 3,600 in 1992 to 8,120 participants in 2002 and now over 70 sports are represented at the Masters Games. The event has been scheduled for 8 days in February (summer) of each year and includes social activities and entertainment for participants.

The NZMG have undergone major changes in their organisation and management over the past decade, particularly with respect to becoming more formalised and professional. The NZMG in Dunedin have progressed to a formal organisational structure with the appointment of a full-time manager occurring in 1997 prior to the 1998 event. The manager is assisted by financial resources from the local Dunedin City Council Economic Development Unit and by human resources from the City Council who provide office support. The Dunedin Masters Games Organising Committee consists of the Games manager, local business people, city councillors and academics from the local University of Otago. The Dunedin organisers have realised the tourism and publicity potential of the Games and have attempted to increase the number of non-local visitors to the event, and in particular visitors from the North Island of New Zealand and overseas. They have done this through increasing their marketing and promotional efforts to these source markets despite competition increasing from both within and outside of New Zealand in the past decade.

Dunedin is a peripheral city located near the bottom of the South Island of New Zealand and has been through a number of economic and social changes in

Table 13.1 Number and ratio of local and non-local participants

Origin	Games participants 1994	Games participants 1996	Games participants 1998	Games participants 2000	Games participants 2002
Dunedin	2848 (64%)	2932 (56%)	3450 (55%)	3817 (50%)	4295 (53%)
Non-local	1602 (36%)	2323 (44%)	2803 (45%)	3798 (50%)	3825 (47%)
Total	4450 (100%)	5255 (100%)	6253 (100%)	7615 (100%)	8120 (100%)

the past two decades. Dunedin has struggled to keep a number of its industries and as a result of international pressures and restructuring it has lost a number of businesses to the North Island core centres of Auckland and Wellington. However, Dunedin has a unique natural and cultural heritage and a large student population base that comprises approximately 10% from its 120,000 population. In the last 15 or so years, Dunedin has actively sought to attract new economic activities and investment, with tourism being a key driver in this strategy. Within the development of tourism, the use of events and in particular sporting events such as Rugby Union competitions and the multi-sport NZMG have played an important role not only in attracting visitors, but also branding the city and attracting inward investment.

The strong economic imperative for Dunedin illustrates the particular significance of its sporting events. However, with limited resources and access to markets, Dunedin has had to use its existing natural, cultural and sporting resources to the best of its ability. However, increasing competition from within New Zealand and overseas illustrates that the Masters Games organisers need to develop the event strategically and make decisions based on relevant data, suggesting the need for constant event evaluation and feedback, and this is what the organisers have done. A number of strategic developments linked to research and evaluation have helped make changes to improve the experience for participants and to leverage the opportunities from the small-scale event using local resources and infrastructure. However, changing dynamics also pose new challenges, which arise from an analysis of data related to the event collected from 1994 to 2002 (from Moore, 1995; Ritchie, 1996, 1998b; Langley, 2000; Low, 2002). Although the data collection method has had some changes over the years, some comparisons can be made and the implications of these findings are considered in the following sections.

Changing markets and potential displacement

Because of Dunedin's geographical location and limited access to markets in a geographical sense, the organisers had in the past relied on visitors from the surrounding area and provinces. However, a number of developments have enabled the event organisers to broaden out their access, and target participants from further away such as the North Island of New Zealand and from Australia. For instance, Project Gateway was established to provide Dunedin as a gateway for Australian business and facilitated the introduction of low cost flights, and at the time of writing six direct flights occur to and from Australia. Table 13.1 illustrates the changing demographics of participants in the Dunedin event and demonstrates an increase in non-local participants from 36% of participants in 1994 to 47% in 2002. Furthermore, participant numbers as a whole have nearly doubled from 1994 to 2002.

Table 13.2 shows the origins of participants from 1994 until 2002 and demonstrates that although the organisers have sought to target participants from overseas, in percentage terms there has been little increase over the years, although both Australian and North Island competitors increased substantially in 2000 when the event was branded the Millennium Games to take advantage of the year 2000. However, the actual numbers of participants from Australia, other

Table 13.2 Origins of non-local Masters games participants

Origin	Games participants 1994	Games participants 1996	Games participants 1998	Games participants 2000	Games participants 2002
Otago	320 (20%)	611 (26%)	704 (25%)	223 (6%)	616 (16%)
Southland	530 (33%)	665 (29%)	761 (27%)	936 (24%)	960 (25%)
Canterbury	497 (31%)	591 (25%)	632 (23%)	1078 (28%)	1436 (38%)
Other South Island	17 (1%)	55 (2%)	73 (3%)	634 (17%)	117 (3%)
North Island	224 (14%)	295 (13%)	550 (20%)	583 (16%)	542 (14%)
Australia	5 (<1%)	89 (4%)	66 (2%)	290 (8%)	110 (3%)
Other International	9 (<1%)	17 (<1%)	17 (<1%)	54 (1%)	44 (1%)
Total	1602 (100%)	2323 (100%)	2803 (100%)	3798 (100%)	3825 (100%)

international and North Island of New Zealand have all increased in real (numeric terms) although not proportionally compared to the total numbers.

Research suggests that those from further away tend to have a larger number of accompanying persons (those that do not compete) than those closer to Dunedin with accompanying people calculated at 2,174 (from 3,825 actual participants) in 2002 (Low, 2002). Another assumption is that visitors from further away may stay longer in Dunedin and provide a larger economic impact. An examination of the length of stay suggests that the average length of stay in days has gone down from 5.1 in 1994 to 4.4 in 2002 with a brief increase to 5.7 in 1996 although the event is held over 8 days in total. In line with this the average length of stay in nights has gone from 4.6 in 1994 to 3.8 in 2002 with an increase of 5.1 in 1996. However, those from markets further away appear to stay longer on average compared to those who live geographically closer. For instance, Australians' average length of stay in nights was 8.4 in 1996, 6.9 in 1998, 6.8 in 2000 and 7.0 in 2002.

As discussed earlier, the event occurs in the peak tourist season and therefore has the capacity to displace traditional summer visitors at accommodation and attractions. However, Ritchie (1996) stated that the event complemented the current tourist product despite the fact that it was held in the peak summer season because it replaced a drop in local spending as a result of the student summer vacation. Furthermore, because the majority of participants were from surrounding areas and provinces they had less interest in the key attractions and a significant proportion stayed with friends and relatives. Therefore, the market was complementing rather than competing and displacing other summer visitors (unlike many 'hallmark' events). However, Ritchie (1998) warned that an increase in numbers from further away (as a result of increased marketing initiatives) could result in pressure on commercial accommodation and key visitor attractions, especially the natural heritage (such as penguins, seals and albatross) located on the Otago Peninsula. Table 13.3 illustrates the tourist attraction and activity behaviour and illustrates the level of potential displacement from event visitors.

Table 13.3 also highlights that Masters Games visitors are less likely to visit wildlife and the Otago Peninsula area, which are popular for traditional visitors and are the key icon attractions of Dunedin. Traditional attractions such as Larnach Castle, the Taieri Gorge Train journey and the historic buildings of Dunedin are also less frequently visited by event visitors. However, an increased number of participants had undertaken shopping, visited the University of Otago,

Table 13.3 Comparison of attraction and activity behaviour of non-local Masters Games participants 1996, 1998, 2000, 2002 (%)

	1995 Summer visitor	1996 Masters Games visitor	1998 Masters Games visitor	2000 Masters Games visitor	2002 Masters Games visitor
Wildlife	74	30	21	23	17
Peninsula	49	7	9	10	9
Shopping	39	47	38	48	69
City Centre Walk	33	18	18	27	16
Larnach Castle	29	13	10	12	–
Taieri Gorge Train	26	5	5	8	5
Historic Buildings	22	9	9	13	2
Olveston	20	10	5	4	4
Botanic Gardens	15	17	9	12	8
University	13	13	19	29	50
Beach	13	18	22	21	19
Wilsons Distillery	8	1	2	2	–
Early Settlers Museum	5	6	3	3	3
Railway Station	3	12	10	19	11
Baldwin Street	2	7	5	9	3
Otago Museum	–	–	8	10	7
Dunedin Casino	–	–	–	11	14
Speights Brewery	–	–	3	9	9

Note: Summer Visitor Survey 1995 was conducted on a sample of summer visitors and is used as a benchmark to compare Masters Games visitors against.

the railway station and the beach. An analysis of attraction and activity participation by visitors indicates little change over time in their travel behaviour apart from a reduction in visiting wildlife (which is a core attraction for summer visitors) and an increase in shopping and visiting the University of Otago. Based on these results, it appears that despite an increase in real numbers of visitors from overseas and the North Island of New Zealand, the small increase has made little difference to visitor travel behaviour.

Displacement is unlikely to occur with respect to visitor attractions and sites, especially as the results show a decline in viewing wildlife in a key number of sites along or close to the Otago Peninsula. Furthermore, displacement or congestion at commercial accommodation (as a result of increased visitors) has also been limited through the organisers' use of empty student halls of residence/accommodation over the student vacation period. Initiated in 2002 for the first time to limit congestion in commercial accommodation and provide closer access to the Games village, 19% of Games visitors used university accommodation in 2002 compared with 21% who used friends and family and 44% who used a motel or hotel, again limiting the potential displacement of other summer visitors.

Economic development issues

The limited investment by the local council appears to have paid off, with the economic impact of the event growing. However, in 2002 the direct economic impact reduced, and this could be partly because of an exclusion of the Souvenirs and Merchandise sector in the survey, and a drop in the average length of stay overall. But what is more likely to be the cause is due to a change in methodology which asked for total expenditure of participants (as opposed to daily spending in previous surveys) resulting in a possible under-estimation of expenditure patterns.

Although a significant proportion of visitors stayed in university accommodation, Table 13.4 shows that there is still a large amount of spending on accommodation. Shopping spend in 2002 has reduced substantially from previous years, despite 69% stating shopping as an activity in Table 13.3, but could be due to methodological differences. An employment multiplier shows how many full-time equivalent job opportunities are supported in the community as a result of the visitor expenditure. With respect to employment, for every NZ$1 million of direct spending, or part thereof, employment figures for the year can be calculated using employment multiplier tables from the Dunedin City Council. A drop in direct economic impact by event visitors reduces the amount of people employed in various economic sectors in 2002. However, it should be noted that this figure might be misleading, as local businesses are likely to respond to additional demand by using their existing staff in a greater capacity. It is unlikely that businesses would hire additional staff because the extra business demand only lasts for the duration of the event. Hence, the extra employment was probably either casual workers or current labour that worked longer hours during the event.

There are also two other important points in relation to the economic impact. As stated earlier, students have left Dunedin for their summer vacation resulting in a decline of spending on the retail and food and beverage sector, especially in North Dunedin where the university and Games village is located. Therefore, for these two economic sectors although the event occurs in peak summer season it helps to boost revenue during a low period. Furthermore, since the production of local souvenirs and merchandise for participants, this sector has grown rapidly (although no data were collected in 2002), helping to support a number of local jobs (see Table 13.5).

Table 13.4 Total estimated direct spending by participants 1994, 1996, 1998, 2000, 2002 (NZ$)

Economic sector	1994 Games	1996 Games	1998 Games	2000 Games	2002 Games
Shopping	$219,895	$523,329	$1,371,597	$1,032,111	$527,793
Souvenirs and merchandise	–	$263,311	$662,232	$510,924	–
Accommodation	$138,094	$399,586	$492,779	$813,387	$836,271
Miscellaneous	$370,359	$186,231	$487,905	$774,007	$670,479[1]
Food and beverage (outside accommodation and Games village)	$176,998	$473,101	$439,387	$463,513	$492,579
Entertainment	$45,435	$143,234	$374,904	$472,860	$156,110
Food and beverage (inside accommodation and Games village)	$64,850	$107,340	$333,684	$408,883	$369,187
Transport	$90,149	$237,971	$329,746	$419,330	$79,617
Total	$1,105,631	$2,334,103	$4,492,234	$4,865,015	$3,132,036
Per capita spend	$690.16	$998.76	$1602.66	$1248.67	$564.77

[1]A registration and sports fee of $242,419 was added to this total in 2002.

Table 13.5 Employment generated by the Games based on direct economic impact (full time equivalents)

Economic sector	1998	2000	2002
Shopping	31 jobs	24 jobs	12 jobs
Souvenirs and merchandise	14 jobs	12 jobs	0 jobs
Miscellaneous	11 jobs	18 jobs	24 jobs
Entertainment	10 jobs	12 jobs	4 jobs
Food and beverage (inside accommodation and Games village)	8 jobs	10 jobs	9 jobs
Accommodation	6 jobs	10 jobs	10 jobs
Transport	6 jobs	7 jobs	1 job
Food and beverage (outside accommodation and Games village)	5 jobs	6 jobs	6 jobs
Total	91 jobs	99 jobs	66 jobs

Capacity and organisational challenges

One of the major characteristics of small-scale sporting events is that they often use existing infrastructure, and in this case local sporting facilities and infrastructure. However, as the numbers of participants increase and the number of sports involved in the event also increases, this puts increasing pressure on existing infrastructure. In Ritchie's 1998b study, the largest group of concerns that emerged from visitors were related to logistical factors such as the timing and scheduling of events (19% of those that answered), and sports venues themselves (10%). In 1998 10% of respondents mentioned the poor organisation of sports and named golf and soccer especially. Further evidence of logistical problems relating to the growth of the event was evident in that 90% in 1998 and 91% in 2000, but only 77% in 2002, stated that they would return to the next Dunedin event. In 1998 reasons for this were related to poor organisation of the event, poor venues and volunteer staff that were needed to organise and referee many of the sports. In fact visitors from the North Island and overseas were statistically more likely to be critical of sport organisers and general staff as many other factors in a satisfaction question (Ritchie, 1998b). Following these results the event organisers have introduced a volunteer management and induction scheme to ensure that volunteers are well trained and better able to deal with visitors (further evidence of professionalism and more formal organisation).

Despite some concerns by participants over scheduling and the venues, there is a view by the event organisers that they can comfortably host up to 9,000 participants in future events. However, without the infrastructure it may be better to concentrate on increasing the length of stay of visitors rather than increasing the number of participants, which could put pressure on venues. Another strategy may be to host a number of sporting events throughout the year to use existing resources more effectively. On the basis of the successful summer Masters Games in Dunedin the council are planning to attract visitors during other times of the year where there may be more capacity to attract sports visitors without displacing summer visitors. They are hoping to host a World Winter Masters Games in August 2005 and the council believe that they could host 12 major events each year.

Final considerations

This chapter has outlined the growth of sport tourism as a niche market. However, it has noted that within the broad umbrella of sport tourism many sub-segments or niche markets exist, including event sport tourism, active sport tourism, and nostalgia sport tourism consisting of both active and passive involvement. The majority of interest and research has been associated with event sport tourism, and large-scale sporting events especially. Questions concerning the costs of staging these events and who actually benefits have seen the discussion of small-scale sporting events as alternatives which use local facilities and infrastructure and do not tax local resources or displace local residents or visitors.

This chapter discussed the development and changing dynamics of the NZMG held in Dunedin, New Zealand, and found that it provides an economic boost for the local economy through using local infrastructure and providing increased revenues for the food/beverage and retail sector which is depressed due to a loss of student spending. However, although strategies have been undertaken to expand the participation of the event to overseas participants, and although real numbers have grown, the percentage of those from further away is still low. This should perhaps be viewed positively as visitors from further away tend to be more critical and at this point in time do not appear to displace traditional summer visitors. However, although the event has become more professionalised and better managed, there are still questions over whether the city can host more participants as some venues are at capacity and participant loyalty appears to be declining. Nevertheless, continued consistent event evaluation linked to strategy development has been implemented in the past, and may be useful in the future to help reduce these potential problems as a result of the changing dynamics of the small-scale event.

References

Bureau of Tourism Research (BTR) (2000) *Sports Tourism: An Australian Perspective.* Tourism Research Report (3rd edn). Canberra: BTR.

Canada Tourism (2000) *The Canadian Sports Tourism Initiative.* http://www.canadatourism. com/en/ctc/partner_centre/partnering/sports_initiative.htm (online accessed 23/11/00).

Delpy, L. (1998) An overview of sport tourism: building towards a dimensional framework. *Journal of Vacation Marketing*, 4, 23–38.

Department of Industry, Science and Resources (DISR) (2000) *Towards a National Sports Tourism Strategy* (Draft). Canberra: Commonwealth of Australia.

Essex, S. and Chalkley, B. (1998) Olympic Games: catalyst of urban change. *Leisure Studies*, 17(3), 187–206.

Fluker, M. and Turner, L. (2000) Needs, motivation, and expectations of a commercial whitewater rafting experience. *Journal of Travel Research*, 38(4), 380–389.

Gammon, S. (2002) Fantasy, nostalgia and the pursuit of what never was. In S. Gammon and J. Kurtzman (eds) *Sport Tourism: Principles and Practice.* Eastbourne: Leisure Studies Association, pp. 61–71.

Garnham, B. (1996) Ranfurly shield rugby: an investigation into the impacts of a sporting event on a provincial city, the case of New Plymouth. *Festival Management and Event Tourism*, 4, 145–149.

Gibson, H. (1998) Sport tourism: a critical analysis of research. *Sport Management Review*, 1(1), 45–76.

Gibson, H. (2002) Sport tourism at a crossroad? Considerations for the future. In S. Gammon and J. Kurtzman (eds) *Sport Tourism: Principles and Practice*. Eastbourne: Leisure Studies Association, pp. 111–128.

Gibson, H., Willming, C. and Holdnak, A. (2003), Small-scale event sport tourism: fans as tourists. *Tourism Management*, 24, 181–190.

Gilbert, D. and Hudson, S. (2000) Tourism demand constraints: a skiing participation. *Annals of Tourism Research*, 27(4), 906–925.

Green, B.C. and Chalip, L. (1998) Sport tourism as a celebration of subculture. *Annals of Tourism Research*, 25(2), 275–291.

Hall, C.M. (1992) *Hallmark Tourist Events: Impacts, Management and Planning*. London: Belhaven.

Higham, J.E.S. (1999) Sport as an avenue of tourism development: an analysis of the positive and negative impacts of sport tourism. *Current Issues in Tourism*, 2(1), 82–90.

Higham, J. and Hinch, T. (2002) Tourism, sport and the seasons: the challenges and potential of overcoming seasonality in the sport and tourism sectors. *Tourism Management*, 23, 175–185.

Higham, J. and Ritchie, B. (2001) The evolution of festivals and other events in rural southern New Zealand. *Journal of Event Management*, 7(1), 51–65.

Hiller, H. (1998) Assessing the impacts of mega-events: a linkage model. *Current Issues in Tourism*, 1(1), 47–57.

Hudson, S. (2000) The segmentation of potential tourists: constraint differences between men and women. *Journal of Travel Research*, 38(4), 363–368.

Irwin, R. and Sadler, M. (1998) An analysis of travel behaviour and event-induced expenditure amongst American collegiate championship patron groups. *Journal of Vacation Marketing*, 4, 78–90.

Kotler, P., Haider, D.H. and Rein, I. (1993) *Marketing Places: Attracting Investment, Industry, and Tourism to Cities, States, and Nations*. New York: The Free Press.

Kurtzman, J. (2000) Sport and tourism relationship: a unique reality In B. Ritchie and D. Adair (eds) *Sports Generated Tourism: Exploring the Nexus*. Proceedings of the First Australian Sports Tourism Symposium. Canberra: Tourism Program, University of Canberra, pp. 5–22.

Langley, M. (2000) New Zealand Masters Games economic impact study. Unpublished Report: Centre for Tourism, University of Otago.

Low, W. (2002) New Zealand Masters Games economic impact study. Unpublished Report: Department of Tourism, University of Otago.

Moore, N. (1995) 1994 National Mutual Masters Games, economic impact assessment, Dunedin, 13–15 February. Unpublished Dissertation: Centre for Tourism, University of Otago.

Olds, K. (1998) Urban mega-events, evictions and housing rights: the Canadian case. *Current Issues in Tourism*, 1(1), 2–46.

Pitts, B. (1999) Sports tourism and niche markets: identification and analysis of the growing lesbian and gay sports tourism industry. *Journal of Vacation Marketing*, 5(1), 31–50.

Ritchie, B.W. (1996) How special are special events? The economic development and strategic value of the New Zealand Masters Games. *Journal of Festival Management and Event Tourism*, 4(3/4), 117–126.

Ritchie, B.W. (1998a) Bicycle tourism in the south island of New Zealand: planning and management issues. *Tourism Management*, 19(6), 567–582.

Ritchie, B.W. (1998b) The development of the New Zealand Masters Games: the economic impact and satisfaction of event participants, In J. Kandampully (ed) *Proceedings of New Zealand Tourism and Hospitality Research Conference*. Akaroa, New Zealand.

Ritchie, B.W. and Hall, C.M. (1999) Cycle tourism and regional development: a New Zealand case study. *Anatolia: An International Journal of Tourism and Hospitality Research*, 10(2) 89–112.

Ritchie, B.W., Mosedale, L. and King, J. (2002) Profiling sport tourists: the case of Super 12 rugby union in the Australian Capital Territory (ACT), Australia. *Current Issues in Tourism*, 5(1), 33–44.

Standeven, J. and De Knop, P. (1999) *Sport Tourism*. Champaign, IL: Human Kinetics.

Travel Industry Association of America. (1999) Profile of travelers who attend sports events. http://www.tia.org.com (online accessed 22/9/03).

Travel Industry Association of America. (2001) Travel statistics and trends. http://www. tia.org.com (online accessed 22/9/03).

Walo, M., Bull, A. and Breen, H. (1996) Achieving economic benefits at local events: a case study of a local sports event. *Festival Management and Event Tourism*, 4, 95–106.

World Tourism Organization (WTO). (2001) *Sport and tourism shaping global culture*. http://www.world-tourism.org/newsroom/Releases/more_releases/R0102901.html (online accessed 3/4/01).

Questions

1 The chapter discussed how event organisers wish to increase the number of participants but may face organisational challenges with respect to facilities and venues. Balancing increased participants with using local resources can be problematic for small-scale sport event organisers. What other alternatives exist for the organisers to increase the number of participants? What suggestions would you provide to them to help them increase participant numbers through using existing local resources?

2 The case study also illustrated how the length of stay of non-local participants and per capita spend has declined over time, yet the local economy needs this expenditure as students leave for their summer vacation. What suggestions could you provide to event organisers to increase the length of stay of non-local participants and their expenditure?

Further recommended reading

Gibson, H., Willming, C. and Holdnak, A. (2003) Small-scale event sport tourism: fans as tourists. *Tourism Management*, 24, 181–190.

Higham, J.E.S. (1999) Sport as an avenue of tourism development: an analysis of the positive and negative impacts of sport tourism. *Current Issues in Tourism*, 2(1), 82–90.

Ritchie, B.W., Mosedale, L. and King, J. (2002) Profiling sport tourists: the case of Super 12 rugby union in the Australian Capital Territory (ACT), Australia. *Current Issues in Tourism*, 5(1), 33–44.

14

Wildlife tourism
Wildlife use vs local gain: trophy hunting in Namibia

Marina Novelli and Michael N. Humavindu

This chapter outlines the growth and development of certain tourism activities as part of a broader nature-related macro-niche: the wildlife tourism segment. Namibia will provide the case study, within the frame of consumptive and non-consumptive forms of recreation and tourism. Trophy hunting will be considered in the context of nature conservation. Background information will be given in order to provide readers with a context for wildlife and trophy hunting tourism, evaluating what may be considered as a sustainable (though controversial) form of niche tourism. Consideration will be given to the economic, social and environmental implications of trophy hunting tourism in Namibia. The aim is to stimulate debate on whether trophy hunting can be considered as a sustainable form of environmental management, and a valuable niche tourism product for the areas involved.

Introduction

Over the past century, the African continent has seen an impressive growth in nature-related tourism activities, where wildlife observation in its natural habitat has been a strongly inspirational and attractive focus of tourism since the colonial time. The modern wildlife tourism context may be recognised in the known forms of *tourism safaris*, *hunting tourism* and *conservation tourism*. Further distinction can be

Table 14.1 'Trophy' hunting: aims and prizes

Defining a trophy	Any part of an animal that can be displayed as a sign of the catch Antelope: horns and skin Elephant: tusks
Quality parameters	According to species: Size (length/diameter) Weight
The hunters' aim	Trophies from: mature, big, older animals no longer reproductive (ethical hunting)

made in relation to the non-consumptive (i.e. photographic safaris and observation of animal behaviour for conservation purposes) and consumptive (i.e. trophy hunting) nature of the above.

The African wildlife tourism market has grown dramatically since the mid-1960s when increased interest, affordability and opportunities facilitated the access to relatively unspoiled and remote areas. Over the past 50 years, a number of tourism-based wildlife management projects have been developed in order to promote wild land and endangered species preservation, to take advantage of the lucrative international non-consumptive and consumptive tourism market and to find alternative sources of food and income in marginal areas where agriculture can no longer be a sustaining industry. Examples are the CAMPFIRE project in Zimbabwe (consumptive) and the Gorilla Sanctuaries in Uganda (non-consumptive). Controversy on the origins of African wildlife tourism (i.e. the creation of game parks), on the management (i.e. nature conservation) and on the ethics (i.e. hunting and animal rights issues) of certain projects have been widely discussed (see Dieke, 2000; Hulme and Murphree, 2001; Newsome *et al.*, 2002; Tourism Concern, 1997). However the aim of this chapter is to look at the intrinsic value of *trophy hunting* as a micro-tourism niche within the wildlife macro-tourism context, focusing on the Namibian experience. In this context, trophy hunting (Table 14.1) will be considered as an activity-based form of recreation and tourism, which provides the hunter with an outdoor experience, based on elements of adventure, thrill of the chase, challenge of shooting and uniqueness of the landscapes.

Background

Namibia is situated in the South Western coast of Africa, occupying approximately 825,000 square kilometres. The country is mainly characterised by a semi-arid to arid environment, which does not prevent the country from having an astonishing variety of flora and fauna, contrasting landscapes and an untouched wilderness. It is sparsely inhabited with a population of 1.8 million growing at around 3% per annum. The country is characterised by a strong need for development and has high unequal distribution of assets and income partly due to the legacy of South African *apartheid* (Ashley and Barnes, 1996). The Namibian economy is primarily natural resource-based. Mining, agriculture and fishing contribute around 40% of Gross Domestic Product (GDP). Tourism is the fastest growing sector and contributes 2.3% of GDP (Standard Bank of Namibia, 2003), which may be the result of the 1991 government strategy that declared tourism a priority sector.

A key role has been played by international aid donors in supporting tourism related projects. Since 1992, the European Commission has supported a Tourism Development Programme including drafting of the 1993 Tourism Development Plan, followed by the 1994 White Paper on Tourism (Jenkins, in Dieke, 2000), and a range of other initiatives, such as the 1998 Namibia Tourism Development Programme, currently being implemented. Since 1995, the World Wildlife Fund (WWF) and the United States Agency for International Development (USAID) have been involved in significant community-based conservation projects, shaping a development strategy linked with the priorities of the Ministry of Environment and Tourism (i.e. the LIFE project described in USAID, 2004).

Namibia has 21 parks and reserves, which cover 14% of its land, with a total of 12 government-owned resorts established in these parks (Ministry of Environment and Tourism, 2000). The main attractiveness of Namibia lies in its natural environment, but its diverse cultures and indigenous communities, such as the Himba community, offer additional value to the experience of tourists visiting the country.

From a land management point of view, there are three primary forms of land tenure in Namibia: privately owned commercial farms (comprising 43% of total land area), state owned communal land (40% of total land area) while proclaimed state land for conservation makes up 17% of total land area. Although communal areas belong to the state, recent legislation and policy allows the transfer of property rights, for management and use of wildlife and other natural resources, to communities. These initiatives are seen as empowerment processes to provide incentives for conservation in communal areas (Barnes, 2003). In terms of numbers, protected and communal areas each hold about 14% of the wildlife, while commercial farms on private land contain the majority (about 72%). The semi-arid to arid rangelands on private land have produced a multi-million pound industry based on both consumptive and non-consumptive use of wildlife.

Development of trophy hunting in Namibia

Trophy hunting is part of the Namibian tourism industry, offering economic benefits through generation of income, earning of valuable foreign exchange and creation of employment. Another prime benefit, though not economic, is that of offering incentives for wildlife conservation. The economic importance of ecotourism, game hunting and game farming has increased awareness of conservation. Namibia is one of the few countries in the world to have explicitly adopted environmental conservation in its constitution. Trophy hunting in Namibia takes place on both public and private land and is primarily aimed at upper-income recreational hunters from Europe and the USA.

Namibian private land owners can register as game farmers and stock their farms with wildlife and hunters can pay to hunt the annually produced surpluses. Between 2,000 and 3,000 hunters visit Namibia each year, with the sector being regulated both by government and by private agents. Before a hunt, the farm involved must obtain a permit from the government and it is only permitted to hunt under supervision of a registered hunting guide. There are three types of hunting guides in Namibia. The ordinary *hunting guide* may guide hunts on a particular farm on which he/she is registered. The *master guide* may guide hunts on a farm on which he/she is registered and on two other farms with permission from the government. A *professional hunter* may guide hunts anywhere in the country, where hunting is permitted, including on public land. The trophy-hunting season in Namibia is open from February to November each year and hunters are limited to two animals per species (Barnes, 1996). As a rule, sustainable off-take of trophy quality animals means that less than 3% of the game population is normally hunted per annum.

In Namibia, the hunter can only choose between predetermined hunting packages containing varying numbers of animals from each species. According to Barnes (1996) there are marked differences in the species composition of animals hunted on private and public land. On private land, hunting bags are dominated by highly valued trophies such as elephants, lions and buffaloes. After the hunt, the hunters must obtain export permits from the government in order to take their trophies home.

Private nature reserves can be registered as well, but then only the owner can hunt on it, and only on a limited scale. Conservation areas, known as conservancies, are becoming increasingly popular. As mentioned by Jones and Murphree (2001: 42) 'Driven by the need to remove discrimination and a belief that what worked on commercial land could work on communal land, the post-independence government developed a new conservation approach for communal land' to be found in the Policy on Wildlife Management, Utilisation and Tourism in Communal Areas of the Ministry of Environment and Tourism. According to this policy, the rural community would gain similar rights and benefits from the use of wildlife and over tourism concessions as the operational commercial farms. These rights would be given to a community that could form a 'collective management institution called a conservancy'. The Nature Conservation Amendment Act (1996) made the policy effective, and the Ministry of Environment and Tourism was the body in charge of declaring communal areas conservancies (Figure 14.1), once they meet the legal requirements (Jones and Murphree, 2001).

There are currently two types of conservancies: commercial and communal. The commercial conservancies consist of groups of commercial farms that combine

Figure 14.1 Conservancy signposting (*Source*: Novelli October 2003 collection).

for the objectives of holistic environmental management. Communal conservancies are driven by rural communities on public land. Communal conservancies are supported by the state and official foreign assistance and are the areas where the big trophies are hunted. Hunts are driven by concession holders and a portion of the income accrues to local communities and conservation. Commercial conservancies do have the support of the government and are seen as management units. However, these entities still do not have jurisdiction over hunting quotas and permits in their areas. Currently there are 24 commercial conservancies, making around 5 million of hectares under private conservation management. This comprises a total of 900 farms and makes up 42% of total conservation areas. Around 29 communal conservancies are registered in Namibia, totalling an area of more than 74,000 square kilometres (Weaver, 2003).

Earliest records of trophy hunting in Namibia date back to 1962 when a few game farmers first allowed professional hunting. Since then, trophy hunting has grown phenomenally, with as many as 3,640 hunters visiting the country during the 2002 hunting season. German hunters make up to 40% of the total hunting clients visiting Namibia. The most popular species hunted are gemsbok, kudu, warthog, springbok and hartebeest. Those members of the 'Big Five' that can be hunted in Namibia are elephant, lion, buffalo and leopard.

Economic aspects of trophy hunting

In Namibia, studies on the economic value of trophy hunting are emerging. Ashley and Barnes (1996) synthesised data from various tourism surveys to crudely estimate that the net value added to Namibia's national income from trophy hunting in 1996 was N$20 million (US$2.9 million). Humavindu and Barnes (2003) present a more comprehensive study on estimates of trophy hunting economic values. The work employed specific hunting statistics and hunting enterprise models to estimate the income generated in the Namibian trophy hunting industry during 2000. The aim was to determine the magnitude of the direct use value of hunting, to assess its relative economic importance by comparing this value with those of other activities in the tourism sector and the economy, and to identify the important beneficiaries of the income earned through trophy hunting.

The study provides measures of gross output (direct hunting client expenditures) as well as the gross value added (expenditures on internal factors of production such as land, labour, capital entrepreneurship, made by operators and suppliers) associated with trophy hunting. All economic activities in the industry generated some N$134 million (US$19.6 million) in gross output, and some N$63 million (US$9.2 million) in gross value added. Trophy hunting makes up an estimated 14% of the whole tourism industry in Namibia, which itself makes up 2.3% of the whole Namibian economy. Furthermore, the work estimated trophy hunting to contribute 18% of the economic value of the wildlife-based component of the tourism industry. The results of the two measures are shown in Table 14.2.

There are indications that the trophy hunting industry has grown since these 2000 estimates were made. Erb (2003) estimates the trophy hunting income for the 2001 season at N$120 million (US$17.5 million). If the estimated direct trophy hunting related income is added (comprising 70% of N$120 million), the total becomes N$204 million (US$29.8 million) in gross output, an increase of 52%.

Table 14.2 Total income and average client expenditures in the trophy hunting industry in Namibia – 2000 hunting season

Values	N$	US$
Direct expenditure (gross output)		
Trophies income	52,242,075	7,648,913
Accommodation and other services	26,585,037	3,892,392
Subtotal	78,827,112	11,541,305
Estimated other	55,178,983	8,078,914
(70% of direct		
expenditures)		
Total	134,006,096	19,620,219
Direct gross value added		
Sales of hunting permits	98,050	3,922
Estimated other	62,956,078	9,217,581
(to 47% of		
gross output)		
Total	63,054,128	9,221,503
Average expenditures		
Average expenditure per client	36,774	5,384
Average expenditure per day	8,675	1,270
Total	45,449	6,654

Source: Humavindu and Barnes (2003).

Table 14.3 Estimated allocation of income generated by different earners in the trophy hunting industry in Namibia – 2000 hunting season

	Allocation by	
Category	Percentage	Amount (N$ million)
Government	21	28.3
High income employees	11	14.7
Low income employees	12	16.1
Local communities	12	16.1
Owners of capital	44	59.1
Total	100	134.0

Source: Humavindu and Barnes (2003).

However, Erb's estimate might not be comparable with the work done by Humavindu and Barnes (2003). A better way might be to extrapolate, using figures on trophy hunting volumes. These show an increase of 35% between 2000 and 2002. This would suggest an annual increase of roughly 16% in trophy hunting volume and by imputation, in direct expenditures as well. Thus trophy hunting gross output for 2002 may be estimated at N$180 million (US$26.3 million).

Distributional analysis to explore where the income derived from trophy hunting goes to is highlighted in Table 14.3. About 24% of the income earned in the sector accrues to poor segments of society, through wages and rentals or royalties. Government also benefits significantly through taxes, amounting to an estimated 21% of income earned.

Table 14.4 Breakdown of incomes/benefits generated in conservancies

Source of income/benefit	%
Community-based tourism enterprises/campsites	35
Joint ventures with private tourism enterprises	27
Trophy hunting and meat	21
Thatching grass sales	7
Crafts sales	4
Game donations	2
Own use game meat	1
Interest income	1
Live sale of game	1
Miscellaneous	1

Source: USAID (2004).

The trophy hunting industry thus appears to be a significant economic sector in Namibia, and this seems to be confirmed by a recent USAID study (USAID, 2004), highlighting the percentage of income/benefit generated by 'trophy hunting and meat' (21%) in communal land conservancies (Table 14.4).

Eight communal land conservancies have agreements with companies organising trophy hunting. 'The joint ventures, along with trophy hunting concessions, and the privately owned enterprises that will benefit from increased tourism, will have a significant impact on the broader Namibian economy' (USAID, 2004). This argument seems to be reinforced by the nature of the trophy hunting sector, which can be defined as 'low volume-high value' in terms of number of visitors in relation to its economic role.

Social aspects of trophy hunting

There is no doubt that the future of Namibia mainstream tourism and niche tourism such as 'trophy hunting' rests on the success of the 'conservancy' strategic planning and implementation. In this context, the indigenous communities have been encouraged to turn much of their land into nature conservancies, where wildlife is strategically managed in order to preserve both the heritage of the area and specifically for local economic gain.

Empirical research conducted by the authors in Namibia in October and November 2003, highlighted the changing face of the trophy hunting niche segment generally recognised as elite-run. Through the 'conservancy' policy (involving both commercial farms and communal land) and the 'community-based tourism' strategy developments, the involvement and empowerment of the indigenous community seems to be a growing element of the sector (Krafft, 2003; Louis, 2003; Matthaei, 2001; Meier, 2003). The Ministry of Environment and Tourism was the author of the Community-based Natural Resource Management (CBNRM) conservancy initiative whereby a sense of responsibility and value for wildlife was developed through the indigenous communities, involving them in the decision-making process where possible. This programme was aimed at building awareness within the indigenous communities of the potential economic gain, which could derive from a sustainable consumptive and/or non-consumptive use of local wildlife.

Attempts to actively involve and empower the indigenous communities in the trophy hunting industry have recently been envisaged in the 'Hunting Guide' training and qualification initiative offered by the Namibian Professional Hunter Association (NAPHA), which now involves an oral examination rather than a written one making it more accessible to people with low or no literacy levels (Grellmann, 2002; Meier, 2003; Strauss and Strauss, 2003). Moreover, the newly organised community agreements on the best sustainable use of hunted species (i.e. the trophy for the tourist and the meat for the community), seem to have a more sustainable outcome as the income generated by the local wildlife and tourism enterprises stays in the area where it is generated and belongs.

Trophy hunting is accountable for the creation of employment for under-privileged Namibians living in the rural areas, creating opportunities for trackers, skinners, cooks, cleaners, drivers, etc. (Morris, 2001). Education is also being promoted at various levels, from the simple learning of English to communicate with the visitors to the more specific training for hunting guides and taxidermists (Meier, 2003).

It must be said that in a phase of 'intra-communal institutional development' (Jones and Murphree, 2001), an important achievement is the increasing awareness of the value of wildlife by the indigenous community, which has started to look at their natural resources not only as a source for subsistence (i.e. food and skin), but also as a priceless supply of income through consumptive and non-consumptive tourism related activities.

Environmental aspects of trophy hunting

Both the conservancies and the community-based development approaches adopted as core strategies for the growth of the Namibian economy are to be considered as two of the most favourable factors in facilitating the country's path to sustainable development. From a wildlife management perspective, the community-oriented approaches to wildlife conservation, adopted in Namibia, highlight a strong economic rationale reflecting sustainable utilisation of the wildlife for the benefits of the local community.

The African continent has seen a number of wildlife conservation initiatives aimed at local development, that for the most part excluded consumptive approaches. More recent attempts in wildlife conservation have employed strategies based on the principles that 'communities must benefit from wildlife if they are to be willing and able to conserve it' (Emerton, 2001: 208) and a wider variety of options is being considered in relation to the potential direct economic benefits of wildlife (e.g. game sales, meat, skins and trophies, scientific research, education, tourism). When tourism becomes the preferred option, whether consumptive or non-consumptive, it is often the case that the first becomes the less liked of the two by the public, giving origin to a variety of conflicting arguments and discussions. However, in the case of Namibia, it has been possible to evaluate how some of the consumptive tourism operations are planned and managed in a rather more ethical manner than the non-consumptive ones. This judgement is obviously limited to the personal experiences of the authors, who have travelled widely through the central and north part of Namibia and observed both consumptive tourism operations (i.e. trophy hunting safaris in Dordabis) and non-consumptive

Figure 14.2 Touring Namibia (*Source*: Novelli October 2003 collection).

ones (i.e. wildlife observation and photographic safaris in Etosha National Park) (Figure 14.2).

The selection of bulls for trophy hunting is often a concern highlighted by environmentalists, who worry that the culling might involve the strongest male specimens, therefore weakening the reproduction potential. However, statistics show that the number of animals is growing and that the trophy hunting industry is not negatively impacting the wildlife populations. On the contrary, it 'is increasing the diversity of species that can be harvested by visiting hunters' (Weaver, 2003). Trophy hunting quotas are kept extremely low, keeping wildlife numbers healthy at all times. In June 2003, a ground-based wildlife survey covering almost 6 million hectares in the north-west of the country showed a dramatic increase since the early 1980s – e.g. springbok from 3,000 to 74,000; gemsbok from 400 to 15,000, zebra from less than 1,000 to 12,500 and desert-adapted elephant from 200 to 800 (Anon, 2003).

Thus land-use planning in Namibia has tended to result in the establishment of large wildlife areas, where the primary land use is for game production for hunting and tourism. In relation to this, the revenue from trophy hunting and tourism has been reinvested in the area also for conservation purposes, such as the purchase and translocation of game species where needed (Weaver, 2002). While one must acknowledge the presence of environmental problems, such as growing desertification, it seems that in certain areas the reintroduction of wildlife by farmers has also produced a better balance between bushes and grasses with the animals helping to control bush encroachment.

Final considerations

The importance of trophy hunting in Namibia is linked to the recognition of Namibia as a prime tourism destination in southern Africa. Regionally, Namibia possesses advantages that make it an attractive trophy-hunting locale. Macroeconomic and political stability have been the norm since independence. The game farms are large with only limited fencing. Species in demand for hunting are found in all areas, providing a good platform for trophy hunting. However, the most important advantage is the recognition of the economic incentives for trophy hunting. The notion that trophy hunting can be an effective tool for conservation is increasingly gaining hold. The major insight is that funds emanating from hunting activities can be used for conservation measures. A good example of this is the hunting concessions allocated, albeit on a limited scale, to hunt in national parks. The revenue that flows from these activities is then used for environmental management. The creation of economic incentives for management is perceived by many as the key to maintaining existing wildlife habitats on both commercial and communal lands in Namibia.

Trophy hunting faces considerable opposition internationally, mostly from animal rights groups, who in any case oppose almost any form of wildlife utilisation. However, trophy hunting tourism numbers seem to be stable and linked to an activity-based niche market, which will remain strongly attached to the hunting tradition and personal relationship between the farmer and the client. This was recently demonstrated in countries like Zimbabwe whose mainstream tourism suffered from its political instability. There, the trophy hunting industry was less affected, with the clientele visiting the country's hunting farms regardless (Gebhardt, 2003).

The government plays a crucial role in managing and regulating trophy hunting in the country. This is happening through its co-operation with NAPHA's initiatives such as: testing of hunting guides, professional hunters and hunting assistants; establishment of quality-control and bow-hunting committees; implementation of hunting code of ethics; and general control of the sector (Meier, 2003; Strauss and Strauss, 2003).

The description of trophy hunting in Namibia as niche tourism is incomplete without some comparisons with non-consumptive tourism. From a wider Namibian perspective, attention should be given to the links that trophy hunting has with other initiatives taking place in the country, such as the 'community-based tourism' development strategy supported by the government and by organisations like the Namibia Community-Based Tourism Association (NACOBTA). Although not directly involved in activities such as trophy hunting, NACOBTA is certainly linked to what the country's tourism portfolio offers to the hunters and their families during their visit (Louis, 2003).

The international community recognises Namibia's rich patrimony and tourism potentials. Indigenous communities are increasingly benefiting from this and are increasingly being empowered in the control of the wildlife. However, far more work needs to be done in order to mitigate possible conflict, which may arise from different stakeholders' interests, cultural diversities and traditions, from different ways of perceiving and interpreting the natural environment, and from problems with the coexistence of people, livestock and wildlife in the same area.

Acknowledgements

I am grateful to all those who contributed to the research for this chapter. Firstly, the co-author who agreed to work with me and facilitated access to information and relevant contacts in Namibia; the Gebhardt family who allowed me to share moments of true Namibian life; the Strauss family who offered me the opportunity to experience the adventure of 'trophy hunting' and all those people who offered their expertise and time, in particular: Jon Barnes (MET – Environmental

Economics Unit), Michele Cervone (European Union Delegation in Namibia), Peter Erb (MET – Permit Office), Patrik Klintenberg (Desert Research Foundation of Namibia), Michael Krafft (Krafft Hunting Farm, Dordabis), Maxi Louis (NACOBTA), Felix Marnewecke (Camelthorn Safaris, Okahandja), Thorsten Meier (NAPHA), Nils Odendaal (Namibia Nature Foundation), Danie and Ansie Strauss (Kowas Adventure Safaris), Chris Thouless (MET – Namibia Tourism Development Project), Chris Weaver (WWF – Life Project), and all the others met in the visited communities.

Marina Novelli

References

Anon (2003) Wildlife utilisation benefits Namibia. *Huntinamibia 2003*, 2.
Ashley, C. and Barnes, J.I. (1996) A preliminary note on the contribution of wildlife to the economy of Namibia. Unpublished paper. Directorate of Environmental Affairs. Ministry of Environment and Tourism, Windhoek, Namibia.
Barnes, J.I. (1996) Trophy hunting in Namibia. In P. Tarr (ed.) *Namibia Environment*, Volume 1, Ministry of Environment and Tourism, Windhoek, Namibia, pp. 100–103.
Barnes, J.I. (2003) Wilderness as contested ground. In D. Harmon and A.D. Putney (eds) *The Full Value of Parks: From Economics to the Intangible.* Lanham, Maryland: Rowman & Littlefield, pp. 269–280.
Dieke, P.U.C. (2000) *The Political Economy of Tourism in Africa.* New York: Cognizant Communication Corporation.
Emerton, L. (2001) The nature of benefit and the benefit of nature. Why wildlife conservation has not economically benefited communities in Africa. In D. Hulme and M. Murphree (eds) *African Wildlife and Livelihoods. The Promise and Performances of Community Conservation.* Portsmouth: Heinemann.
Erb, P.K. (2003) Consumptive wildlife utilization as a land-use form in Namibia. MBA thesis. The University of Stellenbosch Business School, Stellenbosch, South Africa.
Gebhardt, K. (2004) Manager at Bwana Tucke-Tucke, Windhoek. Personal communication, 23 October 2003.
Grellmann, V. (2002) From assistant to hunting guide. *Huntinamibia 2002*, 28–29.
Humavindu, M.N. and Barnes, J.I. (2003) Trophy hunting in the Namibian economy: an assessment. *South African Journal of Wildlife Research*, 33(2), 65–70.
Jenkins, C.L. (2000) The development of tourism in Namibia. In P.U.C. Dieke (ed.) *The Political Economy of Tourism in Africa.* New York: Cognizant Communication Corporation, pp. 113–128.
Jones, B. and Murphree, M. (2001) The evolution of policy on community conservation in Namibia and Zimbabwe. In D. Hulme and M. Murphree (eds), *African Wildlife and Livelihoods. The promise and performances of community conservation.* Portsmouth: Heinemann, pp. 38–58.
Krafft, M. (2003) Professional Hunter, Dordabis Commercial Hunting Farm. Personal communication, 1 November 2003.
Louis, M.P. (2003) Director of Namibia Community Based Tourism Association (NACOBTA). Personal communication, 13 November 2003.
Matthaei, J. (2001) Conservancies – a concept for sustainable utilisation. *Huntinamibia 2001*, 12–13.
Meier, T. (2003) Professional Hunter, NAPHA Committee. Personal communication, 24 October 2003.
Ministry of Environment and Tourism (2000) *State of Environment Report on Parks, Tourism and Biodiversity.* Draft Report, May 2000.
Morris, K. (2001) Hunting – a boost to the economy. *Huntinamibia 2001*, 17.
Newsome, D., More, S.A. and Dowling, R. (2002) *Natural Area Tourism: Ecology, Impacts and Management.* Clevedon: Channel View Publications.
Standard Bank of Namibia (2003) *Namibia in Figures 2002/2003.* SBN.

Strauss, A. and Strauss, D. (2003) Kowas Adventure Safaris, Dordabis, Namibia. Personal communication, 31 October 2003.

Tourism Concern (1997) *In Focus*. Spring issue.

USAID (2004) www.usaid.org.na/project.asp?proid=3, accessed 23/02/04.

Weaver, C. (2002) Exclusive wilderness ventures into Africa benefits communities. *Huntinamibia 2002*, 25–26.

Weaver, C. (2003) Chief of Party LIFE Project, WWF. Personal communication, 29 October 2003.

Questions

1 What are the reasons why trophy hunting can be considered as a sustainable form of environmental management and valuable niche tourism product?
2 What are the key policies implemented in Namibia, which are determining a visible improvement in the organisation of local resources and community empowerment?

Further reading

Hulme, D. and Murphree, M. (eds) (2001) *African Wildlife and Livelihoods. The promise and performances of community conservation*. Portsmouth: Heinemann.

Namibia Association of CBNRM Support Organisations – NACSO (2003) *Proceedings of the Regional Conference on CBNRM in Southern Africa: Sharing the Benefits*. Windhoek, March 3–7.

Ritvo, H. (2002) Destroyers and preservers. Big game in the Victorian empire. *History Today*, January 2002, 33–39.

Websites

European Union in Namibia www.delnam.cec.eu.int
Namibia Professional Hunting Association www.natron.net/napha
USAID Mission in Namibia www.usaid.org.na

15

Volunteer tourism

Deconstructing volunteer activities within a dynamic environment

Michelle Callanan and Sarah Thomas

Introduction

Volunteer tourism, coined 'voluntourism', is one of the major growth areas in contemporary tourism. This niche market is an inevitable consequence of a restless society, jaded from the homogenous nature of traditional tourism products, and seeking alternative tourism experiences. As such, the 1990s saw the 'cultural and adventure tourism rush' and the late 1990s and early 2000s are now experiencing the 'volunteer tourism rush' influenced by an ever increasing 'guilt-conscious' society.

Within a short timeframe, volunteer tourism has arguably become a 'mass niche' market facilitated by a number of factors: the growth in volunteer projects, the variety of destinations promoted, the range of target markets, the type of players involved (for example: charities, tour operators and private agencies) together with the increasing competitive nature of this sector. In addition, volunteer tourism focuses on the altruistic and self-developmental experiences that participants can gain during their time working on such projects. As such, there is an urgent need to examine this niche market further and to deconstruct it accordingly.

The aim of this chapter is to provide an overview of the historical context of volunteer tourism, including an analysis of the key factors that have shaped its development and growth, predominantly in the past 30 years. The authors will also examine the parameters of the eclectic volunteer tourism product within today's dynamic and consumer society. Finally, the chapter will provide a new framework for the study of volunteer tourism.

Defining volunteer tourism

Volunteer tourism has its roots in 'volunteerism', which implies that individuals offer their services to change some aspect of society for the better; in other words, to participate in goodwill activities. As Bussell and Forbes (2002: 246) conclude: 'a volunteer must have some altruistic motive'. In fact, they advocate that 'to be considered a volunteer, altruism must be the central motive where the reward is intrinsic to the act of volunteering. The volunteer's motive is a self-less one' (Bussell and Forbes, 2002: 248). Similarly, volunteer tourism focuses on such goodwill/altruistic activities whilst on holiday. In this context, Wearing (2001: 1) provides a definition of volunteer tourists as:

> Those tourists who, for various reasons, volunteer in an organised way to undertake holidays that might involve aiding or alleviating the material poverty of some groups in society, the restoration of certain environments or research into aspects of society or environment.

In addition, Wearing (2001) contends that the volunteer tourism experience offers an opportunity to examine the potential of travel to develop oneself, in the belief that experiences have the potential to have a more lasting impact than the average package holiday that lasts 2 or 3 weeks.

Accordingly, volunteer tourism is perceived in a two-dimensional manner; at the centre of this definition is the fact that 'holidaymakers' volunteer their time to work on projects that are established to enhance the environment of an area or a local community. The second dimension focuses on the development of the participant through the intrinsic rewards of contributing to such projects.

In an effort to refine definitions of volunteer tourism, whilst acknowledging its link to many different types of tourism and leisure activities, Figure 15.1 depicts volunteer tourism as having discrete yet related components.

Wearing (2001: 12) formally categorises voluntary tourism as a form of alternative tourism, which 'tourism appears able to offer an alternative direction where profit objectives are secondary to a more altruistic desire to travel in order to assist communities'. Thus the importance given to altruistic desires over profit motives presents volunteer tourism primarily as alternative to mass tourism. On a sub-level, volunteer tourism can also be linked to 'social tourism' (Relph, 1977, as cited in Suvantola, 2002: 81), 'charity tourism', 'moral tourism' (Butcher, 2003), and 'serious leisure' (Stebbins, 1992) owing to its link with tourists working on local projects with local groups.

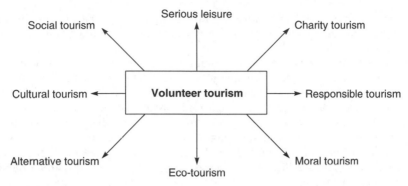

Figure 15.1 Categorising volunteer tourism.

Historical context of volunteer tourism

The growth of tourism as a social phenomenon changed dramatically during the second half of the 20th century. Voluntary activities, however, have their roots in the altruistic and missionary movements of the 19th century; the key driving force of this movement was to curb the explicit class divisions in society. Over time, various social institutions were established to address social problems and create social good. Many institutions relied on their workers to volunteer their time to engage in such social activities; for example, the Red Cross.

The late 20th century was a significant time period in the growth of both the volunteer sector and international tourism. Mass tourism was growing at a phenomenal rate, exposing tourists to international cultures albeit in an uncontrolled and exploitative manner. Arguably, the 1980s was a key turning point both in tourism and in society. Concepts like *eco-tourism*, *responsible tourism* and *sustainable tourism* emerged during the 1980s as the alternative to mass tourism. The media played a key role in exposing the exploitation of resources and communities on a global scale and the explicit divisions between the 'haves' and 'havenots' of society. The success of international initiatives, such as the global exposure of Band Aid/ Live Aid, provided a new promotional outlet for the voluntary and charity sectors with established icons of society popularising charitable contributions. This growing attention to goodwill activities has prompted charities to exploit new opportunities available to them to promote their cause.

In recent years, many charities have teamed up with tour operators to create combined fundraising and adventure holidays. According to Marriott (1999: 48) 'over the past 2 years, sponsored charity tours have become one of the fastest growing sectors of the holiday market'. The two key strands of charity involvement with tourism operators are fundraising travel events or volunteer projects. According to McCallin (2001) charities are increasingly 'looking to business to diversify their revenue stream' due to the increasing 'public concern that there are too many charities on the beat' and increasing competition for limited financial resources. Simultaneously, the motive for tour operators and many other businesses to get involved in social and community projects is to promote an image of ethical and social responsibility. According to Patten (1991: 6) 'investing in the community is not simply an optional, charitable extra for companies; it is part of core business and sound commercial reasons and like crime prevention, should be on the agenda of directors as well as staff'.

The motive for tourists to engage in voluntary tourism stems from a new breed of discerning tourists, who have become jaded with standardised package holidays and are searching for more alternative types of travel offering a range of experiences. Volunteer tourism provides opportunities for experiential travel. Frankl's (1962, 1997) theory on *Man's Search for Ultimate Meaning* has significance in this context. Frankl suggests that meaning within leisure lies in four dimensions: physical, mental, social and spiritual, and thus there is a pursuit of inner freedom, perceived self-worth, significance and sense of values, all of which can be pursued within volunteer tourism.

One particular target market of charities and the volunteer sector is the gap year market, coined simply as the 'gappers'. Over the past decade there has been a dramatic rise in 'gap year' travel. According to Melrose (2003) about 250,000 people from the UK, aged 18–25, set off on a year's break in autumn 2003. Raleigh International claims that 40% of their project participants are 'gappers' (Turner *et al.*, 2001). More recently, Prince William's volunteer work in Chile and Prince Harry's in Malawi, during their gap year, were high profile cases further promoting overseas voluntary work. The gap year experience predominantly focuses on the individual's self-development and enhancement of their curriculum vitae. In fact, according to Ramrayka (2001) who refers to a study conducted by Reed Executive, employers prefer to recruit candidates with volunteering experience on their curriculum vitae. Such volunteer tourism projects have 'symbolic' value given their 'alternative nature' (within a social setting) and also they can appear 'worthy' activities on a participant's curriculum vitae, a concept Urry (1990) refers to as 'symbolic consumption'. However, even with increasing interest in volunteer activities by gappers, Ramrayka (2001) contends that the charity sector must do more to make volunteering a more attractive option for this market. Thus the promotional activities of charity and volunteer tourism organisations have become more important than ever.

Volunteer projects and the tourism context

Given the multi-dimensional nature of volunteer tourism and its phenomenal growth in recent years, this chapter sets out to examine the range of *volunteer projects* on offer and to ascertain whether they align to how volunteer tourism is presented in current literature. Based on the above, a new conceptual framework for volunteer tourism will be presented.

The study offered in this chapter is not attempting to be representative of all organisations providing volunteer tourism experiences; however it does aim to be more inclusive in terms of the proliferation of projects offered, the destinations promoted and the appeal to different types of volunteers. Therefore, a broad examination of organisations offering volunteer projects via the Internet was undertaken to gain a richer insight into the diversity of projects offered across the globe. The term 'volunteer projects' was entered in the on-line search engine 'Google' and consequently access was gained to a database of volunteer projects through the organisation 'Go Abroad.com'. This database held information on 156 countries from Afghanistan through to Zambia and it was possible to enter each country in turn and view a range of projects operated by different organisations within the selected country. This study accessed 698 projects across 156 countries representing 289 different organisations. The number of projects that can be accessed is constantly changing as the database is frequently updated.

It must also be recognised that there are other organisations that provide databases of volunteer projects on the Internet such as 'Do-it-overseas'. In this instance, it was decided that the Go Abroad.com database provided a more exhaustive list of projects and supplied relevant information with minimum difficulty.

In conjunction with the Go Abroad.com database, a separate database was constructed in Access to store information retrieved from the volunteer database. In order to select appropriate information from the volunteer database to transfer onto the Access database, a framework was developed. There was a clear need to record the organization's name and contact details together with the name, nature, duration and destination of the project. In addition to the above, there was a need to record the requirements of these projects in terms of the prospective volunteer having specific skills, knowledge and experience. Particular attention was given to information concerning the minimum age of a volunteer and whether there were any criteria for the suitability of the project work in terms of the individual's age, knowledge, skills or experience of the volunteer. This information was relatively simple to identify and was transferred to Access. Due to the variety of language used by each of the organisations to describe their projects, there was a need to code all the information into a common language in order to clarify the activities and allow for comparison across the projects and destinations. A comprehensive list of codes was inductively developed which facilitated the identification of similarities and differences among the projects.

The product

The 698 project entries have a number of associated project activities listed in Table 15.1. A total of 1,222 itemised project activities were identified; for ease of examination these activities have been categorised into 11 definitive project cluster groups. However, it is to be noted that each project has a variable number of sub-activities associated with it, therefore, it is very difficult to convert the case numbers into meaningful percentages for comparison with other categories, such as duration and volunteer requirements.

Hence, in further discussions the numerical values will remain as number of cases rather than as a percentage. Table 15.1 also shows how many cases were identified in each cluster group; the most frequently cited group was 'Community welfare' with 295 cases, closely followed by 'Teaching' with 252 cases. The least cited group was 'Journalism' with 15 cases. This may be due to the narrower range of activities associated with 'Journalism' and the increased level of knowledge required to undertake these activities. For example, six of the 15 cases for 'Journalism' required professional experience coupled with either linguistic skills or technical qualifications. Only five of the 15 cases expressed 'No requirement' for this type of activity, which is a relatively small proportion in relation to other cluster group activities.

Table 15.1 Project cluster groups and their sub-activities

Name of cluster groups	*Sub-activities*	*Total number of cases*
Community welfare	Care for the elderly Care for children Refugees Social services Legal assistance Counselling Youth work Non-violent conflict Disability Supporting peace actions AIDS education	295 cases
Teaching	Teaching a foreign language In-class instruction Vocational training, i.e. IT skills Indigenous issues	252 cases
Business developments	Farming business (organic, sustainable) IT/finance projects Local businesses	126 cases
Environmental regeneration	Conservation work – enhancement Wildlife – breeding programmes Plants, i.e. rainforest conservation Gardening and landscaping	120 cases
Building projects	Constructing new buildings, i.e. hospitals, schools Renovating buildings Architecture	109 cases
Cultural developments	Progs personal dev. – empowerment of women Cultural work exchange progs Indigenous progs Arts progs	100 cases
Environmental research and education	Interpretation trails Animal and plant research Learning about looking after the environment Land mapping for zoning	72 cases
Environmental protection	Preservation – maintaining current form Land care Wildlife monitoring and rehab care Ranger work	66 cases
Medical	Working in a hospital/doctor's practice Working with AIDS patients	35 cases
Other/Miscellaneous Journalism	 Working with local press Development of language/ communication	32 cases 15 cases

From examining the number of projects available, the most popular duration is 'Less than 6 months' and accounts for 211 projects, with the least popular duration period being 'More than 1 year', accounting for 68 project cases (Table 15.2). However, on closer examination of the range of activities offered the most popular duration shifts from 'Less than 6 months' to 'Less than 4 weeks'. This is because each project has a number of activities attached to it and, on examination of each activity the most frequently cited duration in terms of range of activities is 'Less than 4 weeks'. During this time period the most frequently cited activity was 'Community welfare' with 115 cases, followed by 'Building' activities with 90 cases and 'Environmental regeneration' work with 68 cases. They may be the most popular activities for 'Less than 4 weeks' duration because these activities require less skill and no specific qualifications. As such they are ideal for a short alternative tourism experience or as part of a longer travel experience where the individual participates in a project for a specific period of time and contributes something to the community, whilst also taking the time to explore the destination. Referring back to the work of Frankl ([1962], 1997), the overall experience of the traveller can have more 'meaning' or value through participation in such projects.

Table 15.2 Breakdown of projects and their durations

The breakdown of projects and their durations are as follows:
Projects that have time duration of less than 4 weeks account for 188 project cases (26.9% of projects).
Projects that have time duration of less than 6 months account for 211 project cases (30.3% of projects).
Projects that have time duration of less than 12 months account for 110 project cases (15.8% of projects).
Projects that have time duration of more than 1 year account for 68 project cases (9.7% of projects).
Projects that had no clear indication of timeframe or duration accounted for 121 project cases (17.3% of projects).
The matrix below shows the range of project activities in relation to four time durations.

Project activity	Less than 4 weeks	Less than 6 months	Less than 12 months	More than 1 year
Building	90 cases	12 cases	1 case	1 case
Community welfare	115 cases	78 cases	42 cases	23 cases
Teaching	39 cases	71 cases	61 cases	46 cases
Environmental regeneration	68 cases	34 cases	4 cases	3 cases
Business	40 cases	33 cases	24 cases	22 cases
Cultural development	44 cases	28 cases	7 cases	1 case
Environmental research and education	16 cases	26 cases	8 cases	1 case
Environmental protection	21 cases	23 cases	4 cases	11 cases
Medical	3 cases	16 cases	2 cases	7 cases
Other miscellaneous	4 cases	13 cases	5 cases	4 cases
Journalism	1 case	3 cases	4 cases	4 cases
Total number of cases for each duration	441 cases	337 cases	163 cases	123 cases

This certainly appears to be the case in terms of 'Cultural development' activities where the most cases occur in the 'Less than 4 weeks' duration period (44 cases) and show a sharp decrease in availability as the time period increases, whereas only one case is shown in the 'More than 1 year' duration category. 'Cultural development' activities are focused more on the volunteer's experience, often linked to the improvement of their linguistic skills and social understanding of a geographical region.

Many of the 'Cultural development' projects promote the benefits of this type of experience in terms of the volunteer gaining academic credit and achievement. The focus of these projects is clearly on the self-gain of the volunteer with the likely ego-enhancement of the individual on their return home.

Where a volunteer experience has the 'hallmarks' of self-gain, short duration (Less than 4 weeks), and no specific qualifications or skills required of the volunteer, it is not clear how the 'packaged' activities directly contribute to the host community and severely challenges the perception of volunteer work as being partly or solely altruistic in nature. Accordingly, based on Bussell and Forbes' (2002) definition of volunteerism, these activities would not be considered as 'voluntary' in the real sense given that the volunteer's motive is not a selfless one and altruism is not the central motive.

Those activities requiring professional qualifications and experience, such as 'Medical' and 'Teaching' are most popular for the duration period 'Less than 6 months'. This may take the form of secondment periods from work with the need to spend a greater amount of time at the destination before their contribution begins to make a difference. It would be quite unfair for children to experience a teacher for less than 4 weeks, as some stability is required in the community for the children to gain from the experience.

It is quite reasonable to expect the frequency of project activities to decline in relation to the duration of the project. This may be partly due to the marketability of the projects; the longer the project time the less likely people will want to participate in the project. Therefore, to sustain a volunteer's motivation to work on a project for more than a year, their intentions are arguably more altruistic in nature. Although all activities have at least one case operating for this time period, it is interesting to note that 'Medical' and 'Environmental protection' appear to increase in the number for activities for the duration of 'More than 1 year', after dipping in the 'Less than 12 months' category. This raises the issue of whether these particular activities focus more on an individual's altruistic tendencies than other activities. 'Teaching', 'Business' and 'Community welfare' maintain their number of cases across each of four time periods, despite a general decline as the duration increases. Whilst other activities flourish in the short time period of 'Less than 4 weeks', they then experience a sharp decline in availability, e.g. 'Building' has only two cases in total for the longer durations.

Whilst Table 15.3 depicts all the destinations used by the Go Abroad.com database and the number of project cases listed at each destination (found at the time of collecting information), the 'Top Ten' destinations, in terms of the highest number of projects cited at each destination, are listed in Table 15.4, where several points of interest can be found. Firstly, in the range of destinations included within the 'Top Ten' the majority of the destinations featured would be categorised as developing countries, with India claiming the number one position, except for two developed countries, Italy and England, at positions ten and eleven in the table.

Table 15.3 List of destinations and number of projects

Country	Project	Country	Project	Country	Project
Afganistan	1	Hawaii	1	Slovakia	1
Albania	3	Honduras	28	Slovenia	1
Algeria	1	Hungary	3	Solomon Islands	1
Angola	1	Iceland	6	South Africa	3
Antigua & Barbuda	1	India	51	Spain	2
Argentina	6	Indonesia	13	Sri Lanka	2
Armenia	4	Ireland	8	St Kitts & St Nevis	1
Australia	12	Israel	6	St Lucia	1
Austria	2	Italy	15	St Vincent & Grenadines	1
Azerbaijan	2	Ivory Coast	4	Suriname	1
Bahamas	1	Jamaica	4	Swaziland	1
Bahrain	1	Japan	8	Sweden	1
Bangladesh	4	Jordan	1	Switzerland	1
Barbados	1	Kazakhstan	2	Taiwan	1
Belarus	4	Kenya	21	Tanzania	2
Belgium	7	Kiribati	1	Thailand	3
Belize	9	Korea (South)	8	Tibet	1
Benin	4	Kosovo	1	Togo	1
Bolivia	11	Laos	5	Tongo	1
Bosnia	3	Latvia	1	Trinidad & Tobago	1
Botswana	4	Lebanon	1	Tunisia	1
Brazil	15	Lesotho	1	Turkey	1
Bulgaria	4	Lithuania	1	Turkmenistan	1
Burkina Faso	4	Macedonia	1	Uganda	2
Cambodia	1	Madagascar	1	Ukraine	1
Cameroon	7	Malawi	1	United States	1
Canada	11	Malaysia	1	US Virgin Islands	1
Chile	7	Mali	1	Uzbekistan	1
China	23	Mauritania	1	Vanuatu	1
Colombia	2	Mauritius	1	Venezuela	1
Cook Islands	1	Mexico	2	Vietnam	1
Costa Rica	43	Micronesia	1	Wales	1
Croatia	3	Moldova	1	Western Samoa	1
Cuba	3	Mongolia	2	Yugoslavia	1
Cyprus	1	Morocco	1	Zambia	2
Czech Republic	4	Mozambique	1		
Denmark	5	Namibia	2		
Dominica	1	Nepal	2		
Dominican Republic	3	Netherlands	2		
Ecuador	47	New Zealand	3		
Egypt	1	Nicaragua	1		
England	13	Nigeria	2		
Estonia	5	Northern Ireland	1		
Ethiopia	5	Norway	1		
Fiji	5	Pakistan	1		
Finland	7	Palau	1		
France	12	Palestine	1		
Gabon	1	Panama	2		
Gambia	5	Papua New Guinea	1		
Georgia	1	Paraguay	1		
Germany	6	Peru	1		
Ghana	37	Philippines	1		
Greece	4	Poland	1		
Greenland	1	Portugal	1		
Greneda	1	Puerto Rico	1		
Guatemala	26	Romania	1		
Guayana	3	Russia	2		
Guinea	3	Scotland	1		
Haiti	4	Senegal	1		

Table 15.4 'Top Ten' Destinations

Destination	Total number of projects	Building	Community welfare	Teaching	Environmental regeneration	Business	Cultural development	Environmental research and education	Environmental protection	Medical	Other/ miscellaneous	Journalism
India	51	1	17	19	1	3	9	2	0	3	0	2
Ecuador	47	6	15	10	1	5	5	14	8	1	2	1
Costa Rica	43	4	9	11	10	9	10	13	8	1	0	0
Ghana	37	2	17	19	1	8	4	3	1	4	0	3
Honduras	28	4	9	12	4	2	1	3	1	0	1	0
Guatemala	26	5	10	7	2	4	2	5	3	4	3	1
China	23	1	3	18	1	4	3	0	0	1	0	1
Kenya	21	5	9	6	3	1	3	3	0	1	2	0
Brazil	15	4	7	4	3	3	2	2	2	1	1	0
Italy	15	3	4	2	3	4	0	1	1	0	2	0
England	13	3	6	1	3	6	1	1	2	1	3	0
Indonesia	13	1	3	6	2	1	2	2	1	0	0	0

Often volunteer work is associated with destinations of poverty and severe social, political and/or environmental conditions that constrain and often prevent economic development. Therefore, it is surprising to see two European countries on this list, both of which are leading political powers within the European Union. It is even more interesting to see that both countries require volunteers most in the project areas of 'Community welfare' and 'Business'.

In the other destinations, 'Teaching' and 'Community welfare' are the most frequently advertised activities. This could be accounted for by the lack of investment in social services and educational systems coupled with an increasing demand on these systems due to issues such as: increasing birth rates, increase in number of refugees and orphaned children due to either disease or conflict, the widespread intensity of people with AIDS and a deficit in the amount of professionally skilled and experienced individuals in these countries to work within the educational and social services.

It is also worth considering the popularity of these project areas in relation to the destination marketing of volunteer projects. Many organisations offering volunteer projects promote the environmental aspect of the destination, such as stunning sunsets across clear shorelines or groups trekking through the area's beautiful forests and mountains. These images are key markers of paradise destinations where volunteering here is about adventure and experiencing the beauty of the destination. These images appear to be in sharp contrast to the actual nature and involvement of the volunteers in activities such as 'Community welfare' and 'Teaching' in countries such as India, Ecuador, Ghana and Honduras. In contrast, only two countries within the 'Top Ten' offered a large proportion of 'Environmental research and educational' based projects; these were Ecuador and Costa Rica. 'Environmental regeneration' and 'protection' activities were not popular in the 'Top Ten', yet it is these types of projects and images that are frequently used to promote volunteer projects. This further supports the argument that organisations have a tendency to glamorise destinations and projects, but in turn this further questions the motives of volunteer tourists, in terms of the amount of time they spend exploring the destination in relation to their level of involvement in volunteer activities. It also raises the issue of whether third-party organisations, such as Go Abroad.com may mislead potential volunteers by increasing the volunteer's expectations beyond the project's capability. This may result in the volunteer moving on to their next destination earlier than scheduled, leaving the host community and the project organisation without sufficient help and poor public relations.

The participants

The focus and language used to describe 'Community welfare' projects can range from being very vague such as 'social work' to the very specific social welfare projects, such as caring for AIDS victims and people with mental and physical disability. In many cases no specific qualifications are required and no mention of training prior to working on such projects is offered, yet 147 of 295 cases that refer to 'Community welfare', target 'Young' individuals, from a minimum age of 15 years. It is questionable whether these teenagers are really equipped to manage the emotional and physical strain of these situations.

An example of a 'Community welfare' project is demonstrated by a Cross-Cultural Solutions project in Peru, where 'no special skills or experience are required' in order to undertake the following programme:

> The volunteer work is on sustainable community development projects with infants and children, teenagers, adults, the elderly and people with special needs like HIV/AIDS patients, or the mentally or physically disabled (Cross-Cultural Solutions, 2003).

This particular programme has a number of durations from '1–2 weeks' to '3–6 months'. The typical volunteer duration for the above programme is '5–8 weeks'.

Since 'Community welfare' work often involves either one-to-one or small group sessions with members of the community, it would be reasonable to expect the volunteer to be able to speak the local language. From 295 'Community welfare' cases, only 71 cases (24.06%) require volunteers to have linguistic skills. This questions the level of volunteer involvement and clearly challenges the perception that a volunteer can actually make a valuable contribution to the community and local area, particularly with projects of short duration.

Following on from this, the second highest category of projects was 'Teaching', yet only 32 cases (12.6%) from the 252 teaching projects required individuals to have a professional teaching qualification. This percentage is low, possibly due to the high number of projects targeting 'Young' people, who would not have had the opportunity to acquire professional teaching qualifications. From the 252 teaching projects, 83 cases (32.9%) specifically stated that they were suitable for young people; of those, three cases required some tutoring experience and only two cases required professional teaching qualifications. Therefore, one has to question the learning experience of the children and the value of the work to the volunteers, especially if no pre-training is provided. Many of the teaching projects require volunteers to work informally in the community but also within primary and secondary schools along with youth and adult education. This again raises the question of whether these individuals have sufficient skills to be engaging in this type of work and whether they can make a real contribution to the community. In spite of this concern, some organisations, such as Brazil Community work with the local NGO and Ecuador Community Development will prepare the volunteer for a TEFL course as part of their placement fee, so that the volunteer can go abroad and have initial skills to teach English.

The 'real' value of volunteer work to the host community is, in some cases, very questionable. Cross-Cultural Solutions is an example of an organisation that appears to have a clear mission and philosophy to international volunteering that is compatible with an altruistic approach of volunteering. For example, they regard international volunteering as consisting of three components: learning; service; and getting involved back home. The service component of volunteer work involves a cultural exchange through travelling and immersing oneself in a country where the local culture is different from that of the volunteer. Volunteers learn from the communities in which they work and from the experience of exploring a country and meeting new people. Emphasis is placed on the volunteer taking the time to respect and apply local customs and methods, and learning about the historical and cultural context of each. Finally, volunteers are encouraged to participate in projects on their return home. These three components are far closer to the philosophical altruistic perspective, yet the operational project descriptions, durations and requirements of the volunteers undertaking the project appear to belie the organisation's mission and approach to international volunteer work. There would appear to be a difference between the organisation's espoused desire to follow and communicate an altruistic approach to international volunteering and the actual operational projects advertised.

A more general observation is that the majority of organisations advertise their projects as being suitable for 'Young' people, categorised as '18 30 years old'. The majority of the projects would probably attract the younger end of the age range, such as '18–24 year olds', because many of the projects would be suitable as part of a Gap Year or placement from an educational institution. As previously mentioned, many of the projects do not require volunteers to have any specific skills, qualifications or experience (186 cases, 26.6% of total projects); the projects are available in a range of formats regarding activities and durations and many can be used to acquire academic credit. These features increase the appeal of volunteer work as an attractive 'alternative' travel experience for a young person.

To advocate the value of volunteer work to a 'Young' person, the Peace Corps heavily endorse the experience as something to draw upon for the rest of your life. They state that:

> Career benefits in the global marketplace to today's business world, the overseas experience, cross-cultural knowledge and language skills that you gain as a Volunteer are extremely valuable and highly sought by employers. From government to business literature, returned Volunteers have used their Peace Corps experience as a foundation for successful careers in a variety of areas (www.volunteerabroad.com).

In contrast to the amount of projects attracting a 'Young' person, there were a few discerning projects that specifically stated that the projects would be more suitable for a mature person, or alternatively the skills and experience required would not have been sufficiently developed by a young person. One such example is the Mondo Challenge (2003), where 'the average age of a Mondo volunteer is 32. Couples and families are welcome and receive a 10% discount'. These projects are in the minority with only seven cases (1% of total projects) requiring middle-aged volunteers (31–54 years) and five cases (0.7% of total projects) specifically utilising individuals who are retired (55 + years).

A conceptual framework for volunteer tourism

The findings of this study suggest that there is a proliferation of volunteer tourism products available at many destinations, some provided by charities/non-governmental organisations (NGOs), and others provided by private companies. As such, volunteer tourism is becoming increasingly ambiguous in definition and context. The concept does not differentiate between say, a 16-year-old participating on a 2-week project, with no specific skills and qualifications, who 'observes' the work of others and with no direct contribution to the local community/environ-ment, compared to a 30-year-old qualified builder who engages in a 6-month project training the local community how to build local facilities, where there is a clear, direct and active contribution to the local community/environment. In addition, current literature does not consider the altruistic actions of some tourists whilst on a typical package holiday; for example, the assistance that tourists provided following the terrorist attack on Bali in October 2002 (BBC News, 2002).

Rather than offer new definitions of volunteer tourism, it is more appropriate to deconstruct the concept based on a number of factors: the duration of the participant's visit, the extent of involvement in a particular project (from passive to active), the skills/qualifications of the participant with reference to the project itself and the extent to which the project focuses on self-development or/and the altruistic contribution of the experience to the local community. As such, people are not 'real' volunteers if they simply visit a project regardless of how much of their 'holiday' payment has contributed to local community projects.

Accordingly, a new conceptual framework of volunteer tourism is needed. Such a framework can draw on the work of Arne Naess (1972), cited in Acott et al. (1998: 241), who classified ecology into 'Deep' and 'Shallow' ecology. Sylvan (1985), as cited in Acott et al. (1998: 241) refines and extends this classification into three groups: 'Shallow', 'Intermediate' and 'Deep'. As such, Sylvan's classification can be applied to volunteer tourism. The two key strands of volunteer tourism are volunteer tourists and volunteer tourism projects; as such two separate frameworks are proposed. It is not assumed that all volunteer tourists or volunteer tourism projects can be 'neatly' classified within the simple classifications below; the aim of these frameworks is to provide a general conceptualisation of the range of volunteer tourism projects and volunteer tourists around.

As presented in Table 15.5, at one end of the volunteer tourist spectrum is the 'Shallow volunteer tourist' who focuses predominantly on their self-development and how their experience can be used for academic credit, enhancing their curriculum vitae and for 'ego-enhancement' (MacCannell, 1976). The 'volunteer' usually participates in a project for a short duration of time, has no specific skills or qualifications relating to the project and makes little direct contribution to the local community/environment. The destination of the project is of paramount importance and should offer interesting off-site trips. This typology is closely associated with the mass tourist who visits an alternative destination.

At the other end of the spectrum is the 'Deep volunteer tourist' where self-interest motives are secondary to altruistic ones. This volunteer has acquired certain skills and/or qualifications that can be used in the project. They tend to stay for a longer period of time (6 months) and thus there is a clear and direct contribution to the local community/environment.

In the middle of this spectrum is the 'Intermediate volunteer tourist', who focuses both on altruistic and self-development motives, stays on the project for a reasonable length of time (2–4 months), directly contributes to the project but still ensures that they have some 'holiday time' for exploring the destination.

As presented in Table 15.6, at one end of this spectrum is the 'Shallow volunteer tourism project'. Such projects promote the experience to be gained from the trip, offer flexible durations (from as little as 2 weeks), and do not require specific skills and/or qualifications even to engage in projects such as teaching and building work and offer little/no pre-project training. In addition, the actual project is promoted as secondary to the actual destination, with details about the various travel experiences to be gained whilst in the destination.

Table 15.5 A conceptual framework for volunteer tourists

	Shallow VT	Intermediate VT	Deep VT
Importance of the destination	The destination is important in the decision-making	Focuses on both the project and the destination	More attention is given to the project than the destination
Duration of participation	Short-term, typically less than 4 weeks in duration	Medium-term, typically less than 6 months in duration	Medium to long-term, 6 months or intensive shorter term projects
Focus of experience: altruistic v. self-interest	Self-interest motives are more important than altruistic ones	Self-interest motives are of similar importance to altruistic ones	Altruistic motives are more important than self-interest ones
Skills/Qualifications of participants	Offer minimal skills or qualifications	May offer generic skills	May offer some technical/professional skills and experience and/or time
Active/Passive participation	Tends to be more passive in nature	Mixture of passive and active participation	Tends to be more active in nature
Level of contribution to locals	Minimal direct contribution to local area	Moderate direct contribution to local area	High level of direct contribution to local area

Table 15.6 A conceptual framework for volunteer tourism projects

	Shallow VTP	Intermediate VTP	Deep VTP
Flexibility in duration of participants	High degree of flexibility & choice for volunteers	High degree of flexibility & choice for volunteers	Time periods typically determined by organisation rather than volunteer
Promotion of project v. the destination	Strong promotion of the destination and additional travel opportunities	Promotes the project within the context of the destination	Strong emphasis on the project, the activities, the local community and area and the value of the project to the area
Targeting volunteers – altruistic v. self-interest Markers	Promote the experience and skills to be gained with specific reference to academic credit	Promote the experience and skills to be gained with specific reference to academic credit as well as the contribution to local area	More focus on the value of the work to the local community and area. Promote cultural immersion, intrinsic rewards and reciprocal relationships
Skills/Qualifications of participants	No/limited skills required	Limited to moderate skills required but desirable	Focus on skills, experience, qualifications or time
Active/Passive participation	Passive participation	Moderate participation	Active participation, immersion in local area
Level of contribution to locals	Contribution of volunteers is limited on an individual basis but collectively can be of value to the local area. Limited information provided on local involvement in decision-making	Contribution of volunteers is moderate on an individual basis but collectively is of clear value to the local area. Limited information provided on local involvement in decision-making	Contribution of volunteers is explicit with a direct impact on the local area. Clear information on how locals are involved in the decision-making process of the project

At the other end of the spectrum is the 'Deep volunteer tourism' project. Such projects typically seek individuals with specific skills and qualifications, actively encourage volunteers to commit to as long a time period as possible, and provide extensive pre-departure material about the project and/or pre-departure training. The destination is also promoted as offering many interesting travel opportunities, but this is secondary to the information of the project itself.

In the middle of this spectrum is the 'Intermediate volunteer tourism projects'. These projects focus on promoting both the project and the additional travel opportunities available to the volunteer. They generally seek a range of qualifications, skills and experiences, with some projects targeting the younger, less skilled market. These projects focus on both the financial success of the project as well as the project's contribution to the local area.

Final considerations

Volunteer tourism is an ambiguous term owing to the proliferation of volunteer tourism projects available, the types of volunteers they target and the various degrees of direct contribution to local communities. As such, it seemed necessary to develop two conceptual frameworks to address these issues, the basis of which can be used for future primary research in this area.

Given the extensive range of volunteer tourism projects, a number of questions arise that have implications for project managers and third-party organisations: Are there any official codes of conduct/guidance for such projects? Should such codes be devised along the same line as The Ecotourism Society's code of conduct for ecotour operators? These codes could be developed along the same lines as Tourism Concern's Himalayan Tourist Code on cultural and environmental good practice (Tourism Concern, 1995) and 'Danger tourists', Survival International's cultural guidelines for tourists (Survival International, 1996). As these projects are linked to charities/social development activities, should they be regulated? Should explicit criteria for skills and experience be used more extensively by such organisations? Is there a need for organisations to actively screen and select candidates to participate in projects that match their skill profile?

References

Acott, T.G., La Trobe, H.L. and Howard, S.H. (1998) An evaluation of deep ecotourism and shallow ecotourism. *Journal of Sustainable Tourism*, 6(3), 238–251.

BBC (2002) Tees photographer treats Bali victims, *BBC News*, 14th October, www.bbc.co.uk.

Bussell, H. and Forbes, D. (2002) Understanding the volunteer market: The what, where, who and why of volunteering. *International Journal of Non-profit and Volunteer Sector Marketing*, 7(3), 244–257.

Butcher, J. (2003) *The Moralisation of Tourism Sun, Sand . . . and Saving the World?* London: Routledge.

Cross-Cultural Solutions (2003) www.crossculturalsolutions.com, accessed November 2003.

Frankl, V.E. (1997) *Man's Search for Ultimate Meaning*, New York: Perseus Book Publishing.

MacCannell, D. (1976) *The Tourist: A New Theory of the Leisure Class*. New York: Schocken Books.

Marriott, E. (1999) Charity now begins abroad. *Evening Standard*, 5th March.

McCallin, J. (2001) Charity management: the issues explained. *The Guardian*, 20th March (www.guardian.co.uk).

Melrose, K. (2003) Top 10 destinations for the UK 'Gap' market. *Telegraph*, Friday, 27th June.

Mondo Challenge (2003) www.mondochallenge.com, accessed November 2003.

Patten, J. (1991) Government, business and the voluntary sector: A developing partnership. *Policy Studies*, 12/3, 4–10.

Peace Corps (2003) www.volunteerabroad.com. accessed November 2003.

Ramrayka, L. (2001) Charities urged to woo gap volunteers. *The Guardian*, 16th August.

Stebbins, R.A. (1992) *Amateurs Professionals and Serious Leisure*. Ulster: McGill – Queens University Press.

Survival International (1996) *Parks & People: tribal peoples and conservation*. Survival International pamphlet, October, London.

Suvantola, J. (2002) *Tourist's Experience of Place*. Hants: Ashgate.

Tourism Concern (1995) *The Himalayan Code*. London: Tourism Concern.

Turner, R. Miller, G. and Gilbert, D. (2001) The role of UK charities and the tourism industry. *Tourism Management*, 22, 463–472.

Urry, J. (1990) *The Tourist Gaze*. London: Sage.

Wearing, S. (2001) *Volunteer Tourism: Experiences that Make a Difference*. Oxon: CABI.

Wearing, S. and Wearing, B. (2001) Conceptualising the selves of tourism. *Leisure Studies*, 20, 143–159.

Questions

1 What factors will influence a volunteer's altruistic motives and level of involvement in volunteer projects?

2 Examine how organisations that organise and promote voluntary tourism projects operate in a more socially responsible fashion.

Websites

www.goabroad.com

www.crossculturalsolutions.com

16

Adventure tourism

Hard decisions, soft options and home for tea:
adventure on the hoof

Graham Shephard and Sarah Evans

Introduction

In an era where product diversification is the key
to business success, the service industry has been
experiencing great variations in its supply profile.
Over the past 10 years, the travel and tourism sectors
have seen several variations in the product and
services offered to visitors according to a more varied
sets of needs and wants. Newly defined portfolios of
activities, such as adventure tourism, have allowed
the identification of what is seen as a true niche
market within the global tourism context.

The rise in interest towards activity-based tourism
has allowed many players to enter what is now a
highly specialised and lucrative market characterised
by an enormous variety of products, ranging from
whale watching trips in the Scottish Hebrides to
guided ascents to the summit of Mount Everest, from
cycling trips to surfing holidays, from canoeing to
heli-hiking. Wilderness experiences have developed
in a way that almost every adventure activity has
been capitalised upon to provide some form of
tourism experience.

This chapter will attempt a definition of adventure
tourism and will examine how it is perceived both
by the tourists taking part in it and the operators
supplying the services.

Adventure tourism

It would seem a very straightforward task to define the term 'adventure tourism'. However, considering the wide variety of opportunities for adventure seekers, a definition may depend very much on the participant's characteristics. Adventure levels can be based on the personal perception of risk and the type of travel which is perceived to be adventurous; and this will be inherent to the traveller, his/her background and previous life experiences (Evans, 2003; Weber, 2001).

For example, the highly organised whale spotting trip in the Scottish Hebrides may be perceived as great adventure for a tourist with little travel experience, while this may not hold the same value to a yachtsman who has travelled the seas and in doing so has had ultimately various experiences in deep sea wildlife spotting. As Weber (2001: 371) highlights, 'previous travel experience is a further aspect that is likely to affect an individual's perception of a holiday as an adventure'.

Swarbrooke et al. (2003) emphasise this problem of definition by suggesting that there are ten core characteristics of adventure (Table 16.1) which, once combined, can be related to tourism, thus creating an expectation and fulfilment within the adventure tourism context.

In any definition of adventure tourism, the fact that there may be combinations of the elements shown in Table 16.1 could create difficulties in classifying adventure tourism in absolute terms. As adventure is broadly about uncertainty of outcome, then 'adventure by numbers', or the creation of specific criteria for a product to be an 'adventure', cannot exist (Price, 1978 in Beedie and Hudson, 2003). This might also indicate that any predetermined and closely defined adventure tourism product may be by definition not a true adventure product and that any adventure should be undertaken with no predetermined expectation as it may end in a way quite different from that planned. The difficulty in establishing a definition for adventure tourism also comes from the need for adventure tourism operators to achieve a balance within their particular adventure tourism niche, where the paying client can have their expectations met whilst remaining within their accepted envelope of safety and risk. It would not only be irresponsible for adventure tourism operators to knowingly push their clients into risky situations but it would also create financial and legal implications due to

Table 16.1 Characteristics of adventure

1	Uncertain outcome
2	Danger and risk
3	Challenge
4	Anticipated rewards
5	Novelty
6	Stimulation and excitement
7	Escapism and separation
8	Exploration and discovery
9	Absorption and focus
10	Contrasting emotions

Source: Swarbrooke *et al.* (2003).

potential litigation resulting from accident and other unexpected harmful events. Achieving the balance between safety and accepted levels of risk is very difficult, leading to situations where the client has become dissatisfied with the experience, or he/she has been unnecessarily exposed to risk and situations beyond their experience and competence. For example, white water rafting, often marketed as an adventure experience or as part of an adventure tourism operator's portfolio, sometimes may not meet expectations as the actual rafting element is undertaken in a closely supervised manner and often bears little resemblance to the dynamic, wet and wild and action packed perception the clients may have initially had.

Another example may be taken from New Zealand, where true wilderness trekking and an expectation of the portrayed isolation does not always occur, as walkers and trekkers quite literally form a queue for most of the day as they walk from mountain hut to mountain hut. This has resulted not only in tourist dissatisfaction, but also in physical hardship and personal risk for some tourists who, in order to avoid levels of overcrowding, have undertaken side trails or gone on their own, becoming lost or stranded as a result of the area's hostile terrain and swiftly changing weather conditions.

Adventure tourism then would appear to come at different levels, with the danger and risk ranging from very low to very high. At the same time, while in cases where the risk is limited, there is a chance of the participant experiencing at least some of their expected emotions associated with the chosen adventure product, at the other end of the spectrum – with a high level of danger – skilled or adventure specialists would be involved, dependent on the tourists' levels of competence. In fact, risk takes on a major and central role as 'satisfaction with the experience and a desire to participate may decrease if risk is absent' (Ewert, 1998, in Weber 2001: 361).

The spectrum of adventure activities ranging from non-hazardous to high risk has led to the concept where adventure tourism can be categorised as either 'Soft adventure' or 'Hard adventure'. *Soft adventure* would involve very low risk and may be undertaken by anybody physically fit and able, yet they would not necessarily need to have any previous experience in their chosen holiday. Accommodation would be provided and there would be little or no need for participation in anything other than the chosen holiday. Motivation for this would be more to the experience rather than the expectation of an encounter with any risk. On the other hand, *hard adventure* would require previous experience, recognised levels of competence, ability to cope with the unexpected and skills associated with type of holiday. While this might imply some sense of risk seeking, Ewert and Hollenhorst (1994: 188) are at pains to suggest that 'although adventure recreators seek out increasingly difficult and challenging opportunities, they paradoxically do not necessarily seek higher levels of risk'.

Table 16.2 specifies those activities which should be the primary sources on which to analyse adventure segments. By analysis of the most commonly provided activities, Sung *et al.* (2000) identified six groupings (Table 16.3).

From this it can be understood that there are various deriving levels of adventure tourism activities, but, as suggested earlier, their perception and fulfilment will depend much on the participant characteristics rather than on the actual type of tourism undertaken (Adventure Travel Society, 2004).

Table 16.2 Examples of adventure categories

Soft adventure tourism might include	Hard adventure tourism might include
Wilderness jeep safaris	Climbing and mountaineering
Supervised and escorted trekking	Long distance back country trekking
Cycling holidays	Downhill mountain biking
Sailing holidays	Paragliding
Learning to surf and to windsurf	Heli-skiing holidays
Camping	Canoeing and kayaking

Source: Sung *et al.* (2000).

Table 16.3 Adventure category groupings

Soft nature
Risk equipped
Question marks
Hard challenge
Rugged nature
Winter snow

Source: Sung *et al.* (2000).

Adventure tourism can mean different things to different groups of participants at various levels of risk. In order to establish an overall definition, adventure tourism can be associated with:

a leisure activity that takes place in an unusual, exotic, remote or wilderness destination. It tends to be associated with high levels of activity by the participants, most of it outdoors. Adventure travellers expect to experience varying degrees of risk, excitement and tranquillity and to be personally tested. In particular they are explorers of unspoilt exotic parts of the planet and also seek personal challenges (Mintel Report, 2001: 5).

Adventure tourism, whether soft or hard, fits very well into the concept of niche tourism, attracting groups of people with specific interests in a common theme and originating a product recognised worldwide.

Adventure tourism in the Yukon Territories, Canada

The Yukon Territories, traditionally thought by many to be a large, isolated and sparsely inhabited part of Canada, possesses enormous potential for adventure tourism. This area offers opportunities for both summer and winter adventure activities, ranging from hiking, wilderness back-packing, fishing and river exploration in the summer, to dog sledding, skiing, ice fishing and snow-mobiling in the winter. Both seasons offer the potential for

---

testing adventure tourists of all levels in a true wilderness environment, with a high chance of encounters with wildlife, including grizzly bears and moose.

The Yukon Territories is known for the abundance of rivers within this vast and inhospitable area, with the Yukon River being the most famous. The tenth longest river in the world at 2,300 miles long (3,680 kms), it starts from humble beginnings in Atlin Lake in the coastal mountains of the border of British Columbia and Alaska, only 16 miles (25 kms) from the Pacific Ocean, finishing in the wide marshy deltas of the Bering Sea. Although not alone in offering excellent opportunities for adventure tourism, the Yukon River holds a special fascination for many tourists as it was the major route way to Dawson City and the Klondike gold fields in the era of the Gold Rush from 1894 to 1896. While the 'Rush' was short-lived at the time, many optimistic Klondikers suffered unimaginable hardships, and most of them arrived to find all the claims already staked out and little or no opportunity left for them to achieve the riches they sought. From the lakes above Carcross or Caribou Crossing to Dawson City, the Yukon River and banks contains several relics of the Gold Rush. Many of them just lie untouched. The sternwheeler river boat, *SS Evelyn/Norcom* is still on the stocks where she was left for the winter in 1913 at Hootalinqua, where the Teslin River meets the Yukon.

This sense of travelling through a living museum holds a fascination for tourists and the Yukon River itself offers a challenge for canoeists to follow the steps of those hopeful Klondikers of over a 100 years ago. Whereas anxious and gold-fevered Klondikers wished to reach Dawson City as quickly as possible, most canoe trips take between 10 and 14 days to make the 460 mile (736 kms) trip.

Indeed, due to the interest in the historical character of the stretch traditionally known as the 'Thirty Mile River' by the sternwheeler captains, from the end of Lake Laberge to Hootalinqua, where the Teslin River merges, this area of the wilderness has become one of the 'must see' sights of the world. It is along this stretch that many of the more poignant relics lie untouched and unchanged since the Gold Rush days and has resulted in the Thirty Mile River being awarded with the Canadian Heritage River Status (CHRS).

The adventure trail down the Yukon River to Dawson City can only be wholly achieved by boat or canoe. Sea-plane and helicopter options exist, but these are often beyond the financial consideration of the average adventure tourist and, due to their mechanised nature, these are sometimes seen to contradict the wilderness experience sought.

The river trail starts at Whitehorse, scene of the notorious Whitehorse Rapids that claimed many a hopeful gold seeker's ambition, either by tipping them and their supplies into the river or, more tragically, drowning the inexperienced explorers. Now tamed by a hydro-electric dam, the rapids offer short-lived thrills to white-water kayakers who test their skill in the spillway below the dam. Having realised the potential for providing adventure tourism activities, there are now several adventure outfitters in and around Whitehorse, who can supply everything from a guided, fully provisioned and supervised trip down the Yukon River, to just providing the basic necessities of canoe, paddles and lifejackets.

Kanoe People Ltd are a small, family-run company, combining enthusiasm and passion for the Yukon Territories with enormous experience of wilderness travel, to cater for a growing niche tourism market interested in the river. Established in 1974, they have enormous experience in providing all the requirements for summer river trips either guided or not. They also offer other river trail experiences in the area such as the Teslin and the Big Salmon River, where they can supply either a fully guided service or just canoes and transportation to both the travellers' 'put in point' where the journey begins and back from the 'take out point' where the journey ends. Kanoe People Ltd's fully guided service offers clients a first-hand and close experience of the Yukon wilderness and the river whilst at the same time ensuring the safety and security of their clients (Kanoe People Ltd, 2004).

All clients have to paddle their own canoe and must to an extent be prepared to put up with the privations of wilderness travel such as no toilet facilities, no running water and also the chance encounter of wildlife and the guaranteed presence of mosquitoes and blackfly. However, clients are provided with camp site facilities, including a fire, cooking area and supplied meals. During the adventure, the tourist comes across practices of 'No Trace Camping', where all rubbish is either burnt or sterilised in the fire and then packed out from the campsite. The other benefit of the guided trails is the assistance offered should anything happen. At certain times, the isolation of the river is such that it would take travellers up to five days to walk to a main road, which is anyway actively discouraged. The final and important benefit is that the guides also possess excellent knowledge of the river, the Yukon wildlife and the Gold Rush history and are able to provide highly informative descriptions of areas of interest along the river.

Some adventure tourists, on the other hand, may decide to tackle the trip unsupervised and unaided. Although a long trip lasts 14–16 days if the full Whitehorse to Dawson City trip is attempted, the Yukon River itself holds no major technical difficulties in the way of rapids or whitewater apart from the legendary Five Finger Rapids just below Carmacks. However, these are easily negotiated with a modicum of care and caution. Unsupervised adventure tourists need to be aware of the skills of paddling and handling their chosen canoe, whether traditional Canadian style or long-distance kayak. Self-sufficiency for up to 15 days, including drinking water and fuel for fires is required, although many tourists might use open fires for warmth and to keep the mosquitoes at bay. There is a need to forage for firewood, and there is also a tradition of replacing any found cut firewood at the campsites which has been used.

Guide books to the river are available and much has been written on the Gold Rush so the lack of a formal guide is not an issue and does leave the independent adventure tourist free to explore (see Karpes, 2004).

Safety and security is the major factor as there are no rescue services immediately available and the only line of communication is other river travellers or satellite phone. There is little or no chance of paddling back up river as the Yukon flows at a steady 6–8 miles an hour and only a highly skilled canoeist could make any headway against that. The chance of wildlife encounters in smaller groups is much greater and thus requires equal care in storing food and setting up camp and an understanding of what to do should a bear encounter take place – i.e. the need for a large can of pepper spray and the wearing of a bear bell may mean the difference between life and death in an extreme encounter. For the lone adventure tourist there is very much an element of self-reliance and independence available as a result of both the opportunities offered by the wild environment and by the amount of information and support that the tourist wishes to have.

From the authors' experience, the examples of Kanoe People Ltd and the Yukon River independent experience are to be considered just as a brief introduction to the wide variety of adventure tourism niches being exploited to both the tourist and the providers' benefit. Rather than looking for the market wants, they would appear to have examined their own personal and cultural strengths, the geography and the history of the region and then combined and to have presented them in a variety of marketable packages from organised group travel to fully customisable individual products. These are presented and delivered in an attractive and professional way, responding to both groups and individuals seeking a unique adventure experience at a level that will meet and satisfy their own skills and desire to explore the Yukon Territories wilderness.

Some management issues

Adventure tourism is seen as a growth industry, both within Europe and worldwide. The Mintel Report 2001 on the European Adventure Travel market suggests that the adventure side of the package tourism business in Europe accounts for something in the region of 25% of the total package sales. This indicates that, excluding domestic travel, the total size of the European Adventure travel market is some 443,000 holidays per year (Mintel, 2003).

As tourists become more familiar with their environment and as their knowledge and understanding of destinations increases, coupled with an increasing interest in sport and leisure-based activity, so will the curiosity of tourists to explore these destinations increase further. As the examples used in this chapter show, the only way to experience the uniqueness of certain areas of the Thirty Mile River is to become an adventure tourist. Adventure tourism then becomes a far more demanding segment, as tourists seek more from destinations visited. If one views adventure tourism as a continuum from soft through to hard adventure, then it could be suggested that adventure tourists may start moving along the continuum as their curiosity increases and their perception of the risk and hardship involved at their level decreases. The example of the Thirty Mile River shows the potential for this change within this micro-niche of adventure tourism. Tourists who may initially engage in organised guided tour, may well in the future decide to undertake a similar trip without employing the services of a guide and maybe using a different river either in the Yukon Territories or elsewhere in the world. This may stimulate considerations on the level of risks and skills of the visitors. In some cases, the tourist, although experienced may seek further advice and guidance to move into a difference zone of experience. The provision of organised adventure tourism allows the tourist to return to a comfort zone where all is provided for and the elements of both high organisation and high risk are diminished by employing guides and organisers (Beedie and Hudson, 2003).

The management issues surrounding providing a niche product such as adventure tourism can be seen to be very varied and can come in different forms. These may depend on people's own perception of what is adventure and their expectations from an adventure experience, their ability to participate at expected level of engagement, either at the soft end or at the hard end of the spectrum.

One of the issues of adventure is that things can go wrong, obviously at different levels, but sometimes with great consequence for the individual involved. Someone on a cycling holiday may be as unlikely to veer off the road and break a limb as a paying climber on a fully organised guided climb to slip and fall, with consequences from superficial to fatal.

In relation to the management issues regarding care and risk management it can be argued that they constitute some of the most challenging issues in running an adventure-related business. Successful adventure operators will require strong preparation to meet these challenges and will have to be alerted to deal with both the expected and unexpected issues of performing in this niche market. Adventure tourists will expect a certain level of risk; however at the soft end they will expect it to be negligible or minimal as on a cycling holiday.

Final considerations

This chapter has argued that the level of adventure expected in an adventure tourism product is very much dependent on the person's level of expectation and experience of the particular sport or type of activity chosen. The same can be said for the level of risk anticipated by the person undertaking the tourism experience, if the activity chosen is something that is within the experience and capability of the person undertaking it; furthermore if it is well organised the participant will perceive the risk less than what appears. Indeed for the client seeking to maximise on the vast array of potential adventure tourism formats available to them, the hardest and perhaps riskiest decision they may have to actually take may well be choosing which adventure tourism format they wish to experience.

References

Adventure Travel Society (2004) Adventure Travel Defined. Available from: http://www.adventuretravelbusiness.com/travel_defined.htm.

Anon. (2003) *Tourism Highlights. Edition 2003*. Madrid: World Tourism Organisation.

Beedie, P. and Hudson, S. (2003) Emergence of mountain based adventure tourism. *Annals of Tourism Research*, 30(3), 625–643.

Evans, S. (2003) Quest for adventure and profit. Unpublished paper on development of adventure tourism amongst UK Tour operators.

Ewert, A. and Hollenhorst, S. (1994) Individual and setting attributes of the adventure recreation experience. *Leisure Sciences*, 16, 177–191.

Kanoe People Ltd (2004) http://www.kanoepeople.com/index.html accessed 25 February 2004.

Karpes, G. (2004) http://www.yukonweb.com/tourism/kugh/ accessed 25 February 2004, Yukon Books.

Mintel (2001) *Adventure Travel. Global Report November 2001*. Mintel International Group.

Mintel (2003) *Adventure Travel. European Report. October 2003*. Mintel International Group.

Sung, H., Morrison, A. and O'Leary, J. (2000) Segmenting the adventure travel market by activities. *Journal of Travel and Tourism Marketing*, 9, 1–20.

Swarbrooke, J., Beard, C., Leckie, S. and Pomfret, G. (2003) *Adventure Tourism. The New Frontier*. Oxford: Butterworth-Heinmann.

Weber, K. (2001) Outdoor adventure tourism. *Annals of Tourism Research*, 28(2), 360–377.

Questions

1 What style of adventure tourism is the canoe trip down the Yukon River from White Horse to Dawson City or any of the river's take-out options? Discuss in your answer whether there are clear differences between the styles.

2 Using Kanoe People (http://www.kanoepeople.com/) as a case study, discuss what you feel to be the major issues in supplying the adventure tourism

experience to their clients both at a fully guided level and for the independent traveller.

Suggested further reading

Adney, E. (1994) *The Klondike Stampede*. University of British Columbia Press.
Adventure Travel Society (1995) *An International Assessment of Adventure Travel and Eco-Tourism:* The Proceedings of the 1991 World Congress on Adventure and Eco-Tourism.
Berton, P. (2001) *Klondike: The Last Great Gold Rush, 1896–1899*. Anchor Books/ Doubleday.
Hudson, S. (ed.) (2003) *Sport and Adventure Tourism*. Haworth Hospitality Press.
Mann, M. (2003) *The Community Tourism Guide: Exciting Holidays for Responsible Travellers*. Earthscan.

Web sites

Canadian Heritage River Systems
http://www.chrs.ca/Rivers/Yukon/Yukon_e. htm
Explore North
http://www.explorenorth.com/library/weekly/aa100199.htm

Part IV
The future of niche tourism

The contributions offered in Parts I, II and III have provided the reader with a wide variety of practical examples of niche tourism segments in place. This fourth part intends to extend niche tourism investigation to markets which are not as yet developed and that are focusing their strategy on two main themes: technology and ethics. In relation to these, *the future of the niche tourism consumption process seems to* be in scientific projects and in businesses' strategic attempts at making tourism more of a sophisticated sector and possibly fairly managed. These elements will be reflected in the variety of issues discussed in the case studies. If on one hand, the chapters on 'space' and 'virtual' tourism look at some futuristic approaches to tourism as revolutionary experience, on the other the contribution on 'ethical' tourism assesses the extent to which niche tourism may be a more responsible option for modern holidaymakers. The overall aim of this part is certainly to expose new fields of research and stimulate further investigations and debates.

17

Space tourism
Small steps, giant leaps: space as the destination of the future

David T. Duval

The trouble with being a space tourist is that there really isn't very much to do. The astronauts hog all the good stuff (Sample, 2000: 50).

Introduction

Space, or perhaps more properly, *non-terrestrial environments*, presents a remarkable opportunity for providers of unique and niche holiday experiences. For many potential travelers, space represents the ultimate in adventure tourism. The willingness to take part in such an experience is quite strong, although the reality is that it is currently strictly within the limits of those of high net-worth. There is room for speculation, however, that the exclusivity associated with space tourism may lessen over time. With technological advances in transport, we have seen how some of the world's most exclusive destinations have literally 'opened up' to the masses. The question remains whether or not space tourism will follow a similar trajectory – if you will pardon the pun.

The desire to travel in space is not recent. Since the first organized tours under the guidance of Thomas Cook, curiosity about travel to space has been relentless, especially given that over half-a-million people in the United States formally apply each year to become astronauts (Tito, 2003). To some degree, space tourism, or rather its potential, is analogous to a single thin branch on a large tree: it has a limited capacity for hosting travelers at present due to technological and cost barriers, but represents considerable danger despite great advances in our knowledge of the composition of this environment. The question remains, however, whether or not space as a medium and a destination can offer unique experiences to a niche market (as early tours managed to do) or will it become another casualty of mass tourism inflicting considerable damage to the natural environment? Will the branch thicken in order to support more travelers or will it (and should it) remain out of the grasp of the hordes?

The goal of this chapter is to position space as a tourist destination and outline potential issues involved, including safety and security considerations, environmental impacts on quite possibly the most sensitive environment ever exposed to travel and tourism, and supply issues relating to competition, market demand, and segmentation. The chapter seeks to address the management of space for tourism, the potential safety frameworks that will likely be needed, and the potential for negative environmental impacts. Whether or not the boundaries of holidaymaking become re-defined through significant advances in technology, thus facilitating the use of space, either as a transport medium or a destination, remains to be seen. Also discussed is the current trend toward using space as a means of travel to various points on earth. This includes development plans for high-speed air transport vehicles that have been proposed. The chapter concludes with some future considerations for the management of space tourism.

Niche context

Space tourism, as a concept, occupies several 'layers' within the niche tourism context. First, it represents travel to a particular environment which is sensitive. Space tourism, in effect, shares this aspect of fragile environments with many other niche forms of tourism which also have these kinds of environments as their central focus (e.g. Valentine, 1992). Space tourism, therefore, is not entirely unlike those forms of tourism which are inherently designed and packaged for certain types of travelers. Ecotourism is perhaps most similar as it has, as its explicit purpose, the delivering of tourists to (often) fragile natural environments. Second, it fulfils the risk element so often found in niche tourism contexts. In other words, many niche forms of touristic activities have embedded within them an element of danger or lack of safety that can actually act as a motivator (Hall and Weiler, 1992). Many sub-forms of adventure travel are perfect examples, and space tourism fits neatly within this characterization. Third, space tourism can be further contextualized by the need of many travelers to undertake holidays which are inherently experience-based (for elaboration, see MacCannell, 2002).

Space tourism

Space tourism is actually not a new concept. Stanley Kubrick's movie *2001: A Space Odyssey* from 1968 saw tourists traveling to the moon in a PanAm SST (Morgan, 2001). More recently, Richard Branson of Virgin Atlantic has registered the name 'Virgin Galactic Airways', suggesting that Virgin may well be planning space tourism-based travel in the future (see www.spacefuture.com/tourism/timeline. shtml). While the economics of space travel and tourism are discussed below, it is important to point out beforehand that space tourism is already in full swing. Dennis Tito was the first 'tourist' in space. Tito spent US$20 million for the opportunity to ride a Russian Soyuz rocket and capsule that eventually docked with the International Space Station. Critics of this endeavour were quick to point out that only individuals of high net-worth could afford such adventures.

Mark Shuttleworth was the second space tourist, spending 1 week aboard the International Space Station and the same amount as Dennis Tito for the privilege. In April 2002, Shuttleworth followed in Tito's footsteps, but added to his experience by actually conducting a variety of experiments, most notably experiments on the HIV virus. Space Adventures, a company based in the United States, has entered into a relationship with Rosaviakosmos, the Russian space agency, to fly at least two more individuals to the International Space Station within the next couple of years (eTurbo News, 2003).

Space tourism is currently limited to those with substantial amounts of money to spend on such exclusive experiences, and whether or not this changes remains to be seen. The average individual who works 50 weeks of the year for a 2-week cruise holiday in the Caribbean, according to some critics, would never be able to afford such a trip at the current prices. Yet major space agencies, such as the National Aeronautic and Space Administration (NASA) in the United States, are banking on the future of space tourism. In NASA's case, negative publicity over failed missions involving the Space Shuttle, the Hubble Telescope and unmanned vehicles on Mars has put heat on the agency to develop a more positive public image. With space tourism as the leverage, it could be the break they are looking for, and some suggest that the recent problems plaguing the space agency may actually be good for tourism (TravelBiz, 2003). These ideas are supported by research and polls suggesting that the average person would thoroughly enjoy a trip into space (CNN, 1998). In fact, a number of recommendations were issued in 1998 by NASA and the Space Transport Association:

- National space policy should be examined with an eye toward encouraging the creation of space tourism.
- The expansion of space camps, space-themed parks and other land-based space tourism should be encouraged.
- The federal government should cooperate with private business to reduce the technological, operational and market risks – much as it has done with aviation and satellite communications.
- The government should sponsor research and development to dramatically lower the cost of space travel and demonstrate ways to reduce the effects of space sickness (CNN, 1998).

While most people associate space tourism with travel into orbit, or perhaps even to other planetary bodies in our immediate solar system, there are, in fact, various forms of space tourism (Crouch, 2001). Of course, the most prominent, and perhaps the most desired, is the action of traveling to either near-earth orbit or through the immediate planetary system. We can refer to this type of space tourism as extra-terrestrial space tourism to distinguish it from other forms of tourism which are terrestrial-based, yet have mild relationships to the images that such travel conjures up. For example, launches of the US's space shuttle program draw enormous crowds to the Florida launch site. Several tour operators were offering tours to locations around the world where recent solar eclipses would be visible. At least one operator, Carlson Wagonlit (through www.eclipsetours.com), refers to such activities as 'astro-tourism' and is already planning tours for the upcoming 'almost total' solar eclipse in Panama in April 2005. While many tour operators are forced to plan ahead with the best available means of estimating (and guessing) demand, Carlson Wagonlit's eclipse tours are already planning beyond 2024, and thus capitalizing upon a unique scientific/nature-based experience.

High-speed aircraft, utilising low-earth orbit in their flight paths, need to be considered in the context of space tourism. Boeing announced its Sonic Cruiser in March 2001. The plane was designed to fly at supersonic speeds, thus significantly reducing the amount of time it takes to fly great distances (see http://www.boeing.com/news/feature/concept/background.html). In essence, the key to the development of the Sonic Cruiser was, in reality, minimizing the amount of time the traveler spent in an aircraft. To accomplish this, the aircraft would need to fly significantly higher (virtually skirting the lower atmosphere) than 'traditional' jumbos such as the Airbus A340 or the Boeing family of large jets. In December 2002, however, the company announced that the project would be put on hold in favor of developing aircraft that would use significantly less fuel (Clark, 2002). Other developments abound: Vela Technology in Virginia is planning a mid-air-launched vehicle that would travel in sub-orbit; the British Ascender spaceplane is another example (see Clash, 1999); and more recently the founder of Amazon, Jeff Bezos, announced that his company, Blue Origin, will hopefully be shuttling passengers into space within 4 years. This suggests that the potential for future development of similar low-orbit (or sub-orbit) travel is quite high, although travelers would have to weigh the high cost of rapid travel with the low cost of more traditional forms of transport such as jet airliners. Further, the development of rapid, low-earth orbit vehicles would also need to consider the increased environmental damage to sensitive atmospheric layers that would potentially be exposed to such travel.

Implications for management

Many forms of tourism are criticized for being associated with the destruction of the very resource(s) used to attract tourists. When planning for ecotourism, for example, much of the academic literature rightfully addresses the potential for biophysical impacts resulting from hordes of tourists congregating within a particular area of 'wilderness' or 'nature'. Of course, numerous factors determine the amount of people that a particular area can or should reasonably support, including the number, the type, and the frequency of visitation. Thus, we have an extensive literature on environmental and social carrying capacity (however defined) and the associated tenets of limits of acceptable change. By extension, it is not surprising to see a significant amount of literature on management of tourism in sensitive or 'critical' environments (e.g. Singh and Singh, 1999). With space tourism, the actual management of tourism in space will depend on how it is positioned in the context of existing environmental regulatory frameworks. Further, it can be suggested that management implications for space tourism essentially fall under several broad categories: cost structures, demand variables, safety concerns and impacts. These are not unlike those management challenges that face other critical or sensitive environments associated with tourism.

Cost structures and demand implications

Cost structures are perhaps the most critical, and even these can be broken into categories. Vehicles designed for orbit require different fuel (liquid hydrogen), which is enormously expensive. Part of the substantial cost structure associated with extra-terrestrial travel could be mitigated if particular technologies and logistical considerations are taken into consideration. For example, the use of RLVs (reusable launch vehicles), not unlike the space shuttle, could help keep costs down (see http://www.hobbyspace.com/Links/RLVCountdown.html).

Supporters of the development of space tourism products point to substantial rates of visitation to specific tourist attractions centered upon astronomically-related educational themes as evidence of the public's support for space-based holidaymaking. Yet this cannot immediately be used to accurately forecast demand for a space tourism product. Demand for a product is to some degree, although often indirectly, linked with price, and more extensive market research is clearly needed, as Crouch (2001) points out, in order to determine how much a potential tourist might be willing to spend on a trip into space. Researchers in the market research profession have known for decades that interest does not always translate into purchase. Thus, it is not entirely clear whether space tourism will benefit from the economies of scale that have come to characterize mass forms of tourism product on the ground.

The immediate reality is that the enormous cost of propelling a vehicle into space would likely translate into substantial prices for tourists, which could translate into depressed, or very specific, demand. Investment in space tourism programs could suffer as private companies opt to offer products and services to larger market segments. This begs the question: what is the appropriate amount someone would pay to have a holiday in space? An article in *Aerospace Daily* in 1999 highlighted research conducted by DaimlerChrysler Aerospace (DASA). The study suggested that space tourism could be a business worth in excess of one billion dollars if ticket prices were reasonable. Reasonable, according to research, is between US$50,000 and US$250,000. The research by DASA (*Aerospace Daily*, 1999) suggests that approximately 4,000 people spend US$250,000 or more for a car each year, and there are millions of people worldwide who take annual cruises costing up to US$50,000. The theory is, then, that if someone is willing to pay this much money for luxury products and experiences, they would be more likely to fly into space for a holiday.

The Aerospace Corporation conducted a survey in 1995 that asked how much consumers would be willing to pay for a ticket to travel into space (Sample, 2002). Their analysis suggested that a US$15,000 price tag would generate about one million visitors to space each year. Penn and Lindley (2003) outline a program by which high cost structures associated with space flight might be mitigated. They argue that a two-stage system could be used to propel tourists into orbit. The first stage would be recoverable and thus re-used on future flights. The capsule would be designed for re-entry. Penn and Lindley (2003) suggest that up to 9,500 flights per year could be possible, thus achieving a degree of economy of scale.

Safety concerns

Perhaps one of the biggest concerns with respect to orbital or sub-orbital transport is safety. Safety concerns are already prevalent in many forms of tourism, but considerations of safety need to be conceptually separated from risk. Safety considerations involve legislated and regulatory frameworks imposed on tourist activities. For space tourism, these might include regulations with respect to the overall fitness of the space tourist (i.e. minimum standards of health), the type of aircraft or spacecraft, and the on-board and pre-flight equipment used.

The dangers of space travel are evident, and stark reminders of this quickly make for worldwide headlines. The disaster befalling the space shuttle Columbia on 1 February 2003 is just such an example: the tragic events of the shuttle Challenger in 1986 is yet another. Before that was Apollo 13 from the early 1970s, the events of which were captured in a major Hollywood motion picture. The world's fascination with space certainly plays a role in the media attention devoted to situations that are perilous. When the NASA shuttle program was in its infancy, launches were generally broadcast live across the United States and Canada (and indeed the world) by non-cable networks such as ABC, NBC and CBS. Today, it is only the major news corporations (such as CNN) that would quickly cover the first few minutes of the launch and then return to other news segments. In many respects, this follows the pattern of early air travel. In New Zealand, for example, the arrival of some of the earliest planes to remote airstrips was met with much fanfare in the early 20th century (Wright, 2002). Today, aircraft are common, and the romance and fantasy associated with air travel has all but been replaced, in recent years, by fear and anxiety as a result of 11 September.

In general, space travel will require safety protocols at a variety of 'spot points' throughout the experience:

- *Proper training of space tourists*: the issue is how much training is necessary in order to be a space tourist, especially given the amount of physical and operations training that typical astronauts currently receive.
- *Launch, initial burn, and re-entry safety protocols*: these are much scrutinized by the world's many country-specific space agencies, and represent possibly the riskiest portion of the flight. It was during these stages that NASA lost the Shuttles Challenger and Columbia.
- *In-space safety protocols*: dangers in space include collision with orbiting debris, human error in judgement relating to safety procedures or otherwise, and mechanical failure. In the future, it is possible that some of these can be counteracted through enhanced computer systems, such as collision-avoidance systems. Multiple backup contingencies will also help to minimize substantial risk.

To some extent, the risk of extra-terrestrial space tourism appears very similar to the risks associated with modern aviation: large jet aircraft are theoretically most at risk of accident or loss during take-off or landing; significant safety protocols exist while in transit (seat-belts, etc.), and some modern jets have been fitted with collision-avoidance systems. What remains to be seen is whether extra-terrestrial space travel follows a similar trend. In other words, will space, particularly near-earth orbit, become as congested as some of the air passenger services routes in, for example, Europe? Will such forms of space tourism follow a similar trend of ever-increasing safety protocols and services programs?

Impacts

Because space tourism is positioned in this chapter as a form of niche tourism, special consideration is needed with respect to the range of impacts that are possible. In fact, the impacts of space tourism need to be considered both on earth and in space. For example, to be considered is the cumulative impact of numerous space vehicles plying through the fragile layers of the earth's atmosphere. These vehicles could produce substantially greater emissions (assuming new forms of fuel are not identified) at higher altitudes where the atmosphere is less resilient to such incursions. Similarly, while much attention has been given to the environmentally destructive behavior of many types of 'alternative' and 'mass' tourists on earth, the degree and types of impacts in space are technically unknown.

So what are the implications for management of impacts in the extra-terrestrial environment? How do tourism planners and providers assess the impact of tourism in such an environment? Indeed, space may almost be considered the most fragile and sensitive environmental candidate for human play, so undoubtedly those tasked with managing such an environment will face considerable hurdles. If past experience on the ground is any measure, there is room to consider that the first few decades of space tourism might well be fraught with environmental mismanagement, ignorance and perhaps even catastrophe.

Perhaps we should add to this the immediate orbit surrounding earth. One reason is that from a political jurisdiction viewpoint, it belongs to no one country, and therefore no single law (or groups of laws) will, at present, be legally binding in such an environment. What we are essentially relying upon, then, is the goodwill and environmental values established and acted upon by companies providing space tourism adventures for paying customers. We will have to rely upon, at least in the interim, their ability to want to employ a sustainable operation and management approach to their business. But is this asking too much? After all, we have no benchmark with which we might measure the potential change as a result of space tourism activities.

Final considerations

Space as a holiday destination represents a remarkable form of space–time compression with respect to transport and mobility. It has only been 100 years since a human first learned to fly. Conspiracy theories aside, not 70 years later a program for walking on the moon was already in place. What this demonstrates is that technological advances allow for constriction of the amount of time it takes new technologies to have a direct impact on social structures and individuals. Thus, while air travel may have been limited to daydreams of many in the early part of the 20th century, it is currently within reach for many in developed countries. Perhaps space tourism, in a hundred years, will be commonplace. Such technological advances also have an impact on the spatial distances that people travel. Cook's Tours were highly regarded because they took tourists to places only imagined previously. In short, modes of transport have significantly impacted upon tourism in the past, and with the coming age of space tourism this influence will be equally as strong.

As with most niche tourism products, however, critical concerns over management can be raised in the context of space tourism. As noted in this chapter, these concerns can be considered along three lines: (1) who manages the actual destination of space for tourist consumption, (2) what are the safety and regulatory frameworks that need to be established, and (3) how are the negative environmental impacts managed in space as a result of tourism? Upon returning to earth, Dennis Tito remarked of his space adventure: 'It was perfect. It was paradise' (CNN, 2001). It is now incumbent upon those charged with managing space tourism to ensure that such a paradise does not follow in the footsteps of other localities initially described in a similar manner. Those with even a passing concern for the sustainability of the 'space environment' can, for now at least, rest easy. For at least the immediate future, the cost of sending passengers into low-earth orbit en route to a terrestrial destination or to a fixed orbiting structure could seem to suggest that such an experience would be limited to individuals who can afford such a luxury.

Two primary concerns can be outlined with respect to the future of space tourism. The first is the jurisdiction of management over the environment in which space tourism will be offered. For example, who will control and be held accountable for infringements in extra-terrestrial environments? What form of global agreement will (or should) be necessary in order to move forward on actually establishing such management? Given the ability of the globe as a whole to embrace wide-ranging emission targets, one would be forgiven for being rather dubious. The second concern is the number, size and frequency of launches carrying space tourists. At issue is the level of capacity that 'space' can handle, and this can be further broken into low, middle and high orbit around earth, within the immediate planetary system (assuming the technology is eventually developed), and beyond. Also at issue is the impact of multiple flights (no one is sure of the critical capacity limit at present) of orbital vehicles pounding through the earth's sensitive atmospheric layers.

How might one classify the future of space tourism? Clearly there are a number of considerations to be made: safety, scale of operations, management within fragile environments, cost, demand, and impacts. Space tourism is very much embedded within a niche context because of the extremely slim market segment currently participating. In fact, segmentation of space tourism markets will not likely be necessary for quite some time because, in effect, the media coverage provides in-depth profiling of any and all space tourists (and hopefuls). The extent to which space becomes the destination of the future is not known, unfortunately, but with the pace of technological change in the past 100 years, science fiction may soon give way to reality.

References

Aerospace Daily (1999) DASA's space tourism market research (http://www.panix.com/ ~kingdon/space/dasa.html).

Clark, A. (2002) Boeing puts Sonic Cruiser on hold. *The Guardian*, 23 December 2002 (http://www.guardian.co.uk/airlines/story/0,1371,864707,00.html).

Clash, J. (1999) Ticket to ride. *Forbes*, 5 July 1999, 143.

CNN (1998) NASA says space tourism is on its way but skeptics doubt it, 25 March 1998 (http://www.cnn.com/TECH/space/9803/25/space.tourism/#1).

CNN (2001) Tourist finds 'paradise' in space, 6 May 2001 (www.cnn.com/2001/TECH/space/ 05/06/space.tourist.05/).

Crouch, G. (2001) The market for space tourism: early indications. *Journal of Travel Research*, 40, 213–219.

eTurbo News (2003) *Russia Ponders Space Tourism Deal*, 23 July 2003 edition (eturbonews.com).

Hall, C.M. and Weiler, B. (1992) What's special about special interest tourism? In B. Weiler and C.M. Hall (eds) *Special Interest Tourism*. London: Belhaven Press, pp. 1–14.

MacCannell, D. (2002) The ego factor in tourism. *Journal of Consumer Research*, 29, 146–151.

Morgan, D. (2001) The legacy of *2001*: The visionary film will turn 33 years old – but is it dated? (ABCnews.com) (http://abcnews.go.com/sections/scitech/DailyNews/ 2001_001223.html).

Penn, J.P and Lindley, C.A. (2003) Requirements and approach for a space tourism launch system. *Acta Astronautica Journal*, 52(1), 49–75.

Sample, I. (2000) Earth eleven. *New Scientist*, 29 July 2000, 50.

Sample, I. (2002) Holiday in orbit for the price of a car. *New Scientist*, 2 November 2002, 10.

Singh, T.V. and Singh, S. (1999) (eds) *Tourism Development in Critical Environments*. New York: Cognizant Communications.

Tito, D. (2003) Why I won't invest in rockets for space tourism ... yet. *Aviation Week and Space Technology*, 159(4), 66 (28 July 2003).

TravelBiz (2003) Shuttle disaster may increase space tourism appeal: researcher. 6 February 2003 (http://www.travelbiz.com.au/articles/66/0c013f66.asp).

Valentine, P.S. (1992) Review: nature-based tourism. In B. Weiler and C.M. Hall (eds) *Special Interest Tourism*. London: Belhaven Press, pp. 105–128.

Wright, M. (2002) *Wings over New Zealand: A Social History of New Zealand Aviation*. New Zealand: Whitcoulls.

Questions

1 If we assume that space tourism, specifically extra-terrestrial, near-earth orbit experiences aboard, for example, orbiting space stations, flourishes over the next 20 years, what impacts do you see this having for other forms of niche tourism on earth?

2 What are some of the significant safety concerns facing extra-terrestrial space tourism?

Further recommended reading

Crouch, G. (2001) The market for space tourism: early indications. *Journal of Travel Research*, 40, 213–219.

Smith, V.L. (2000) Space tourism: the 21st century 'frontier'. *Tourism Recreation Research*, 25, 3, 5–15.

Websites

www.spacetourismsociety.org
www.spacetransportation.org
www.spacefuture.com
www.space.com

18

Virtual tourism
A niche in cultural heritage

David Arnold

Introduction

This chapter will examine the potential areas in which technology may be moving the goalposts for potential markets of cultural heritage in tourism and for other forms of visitors. Some projects offering early adoption of different technologies will be highlighted and consideration will be given to the obstacles currently faced by these early adopters.

If 'niche' is defined as a sub-area offering a specialised provision which addresses a minority interest then cultural heritage as a sector of tourism can hardly be described as a 'niche'. In a recent study (Ecosystems Ltd, 2003) 'historic interest' was cited as the fifth most common reason for the choice of tourist destination (by 32% of those surveyed), behind (1) 'scenery' (49%), (2) 'climate' (45%), (3) 'cost of travel' (35%), and (4) 'cost of accommodation' (33%). The citation of scenery here may also have a cultural heritage component.

Technology has an increasingly ubiquitous role – virtually all aspects of human endeavour are increasingly reliant on technological underpinning – so the idea that mainstream technology in a mainstream area of tourism represents a 'niche' seems unlikely. However, although the volume of cultural heritage tourism will be shown to be extensive the use of the most novel technologies is still in its infancy (by definition) and in these areas the technology is only just beginning to show the possibilities for new types of cultural heritage venue, new types of experiences in traditional cultural heritage venues, and new revenue streams for heritage related products and services.

In these areas the use of technology is very definitely only reaching a small percentage of the potential market. In addition the new venues that have emerged, where technology is used extensively as an essential component of the experience, remain relatively rare. They are also not necessarily linked to traditional cultural heritage centres, since the technology can be housed in appropriate accommodation anywhere. In these respects such venues might be considered as meeting the definition of 'niche' as well as the specific interest in virtual reality as part of the tourism consumption process.

The cultural heritage tourism market

In Europe, the tourism industry is a very important economic sector and raises significant revenues from visitors from other parts of the world.

> According to 1998–2000 figures, 12% of Europe's Gross Domestic Product (GDP) is generated by tourism and tourism-related activities and over 20 million jobs have been created in this sector, essentially within small and medium-sized enterprises (SMEs). This sustained growth is predicted to continue well into the future. According to forecasts by the World Tourism Organisation (WTO), the number of tourists in Europe is expected to double in the next 25 years. By 2020, there will be more than 700 million cross-border tourist arrivals a year. In economic terms, this corresponds to an annual growth rate of 3% and an increase of 100,000 new jobs a year, as experienced in the past few years (Ecosystems Ltd, 2003).

In 2002, the World Tourism Organisation (WTO, 2002) reported that

> Worldwide receipts amounted to US$462 billion in 2001 ... half of all receipts are earned by Europe, the Americas have a share of 26%, East Asia and the Pacific 18%, Africa 2.5%, Middle East 2.4% and South Asia 1.0%.

Within this, the market size for cultural heritage can be measured in many ways. The numbers of visitor centres (i.e. monuments, sites and museums) in each major European country is measured in thousands. For example, in the late 1990s the UK had around 10,000 such venues, of which only half were charging an entrance fee (Arnold, 2001). France is approaching 50,000 cultural heritage venues mainly consisting of historic buildings. On the other hand, over 200 UNESCO World Heritage Sites are to be listed in Europe (Ecosystems Ltd, 2003). Even if cultural heritage venues do not directly charge entrance fees, they may be acting as pulling factor and motivator for people to visit a certain destination, being responsible for revenue generation in support of the local economies through the provision of other tourism services.

Within the cultural heritage context, a further area of economic interest is its relevance to the educational sector, where increasing importance is placed on cultural identity and on the celebration of both cultural diversity and common roots. This socio-economic importance attached to cultural heritage often translates into a steady stream of schools visits to sites of importance and increasingly to a direct linkage to specific curriculum objectives. The economic value of this contribution to the education agenda does not appear to have been quantified, but will be the subject of some evaluation within a project named Excellence in Processing Open Cultural Heritage (EPOCH).

Potential areas of impact for technology

Although cultural heritage is an undoubtedly important facet of a healthy tourist industry without technological enhancement, there are many areas in which a clever use of technology could enhance the experience of the visitors as well as offering additional opportunities for a better utilisation of resources. The elements which would enhance the visitors' experience involve helping them in understanding more about the remaining physical artefacts. Hence ruins, which may only be visible at ground level but are the remains of substantial man-made environments, may require visual interpretation of their significance before the lay-visitor is able to appreciate the implications of the remaining physical evidence.

The additional utilisation is extremely important as, in many cases, the richness of cultural heritage coexists with areas of modern economic decline and hence regions in which additional economic activity is desperately needed. The Council of Europe (2002) has expressed concern that this additional economic activity could threaten this heritage, if it is not seen as part of the solution – the implication being that other sources of wealth creation (i.e. manufacturing) would threaten the surviving heritage either through competition or pollution.

> ... it is a question of either remedying inadequate exploitation of heritage resources by the market or counterbalancing excess industrialisation, which may jeopardise heritage conservation itself (Council of Europe, 2002).

Primary markets for monuments, sites and museums involve the audiences to whom they market on-site. Secondary markets involve alternative marketing of their cultural assets. There are really two broad categories of primary market and many secondary markets for cultural heritage. All are candidate markets for enhancement using technology. The categories of primary market are:

- *Cultural Heritage Tourism*, including day visitors and domestic tourists, but also potential visitors from outside the region, who bring travel and accommodation spends as additional injections to the local economies.
- *Education*, providing for schools visits and other specifically educational activities.

Both groups look at the appreciation of cultural diversity and its origins and history are important aspects of the visitors' experience. Engendering under-standing of common roots between apparently diverse modern social groupings is part of the political agenda for supporting developments. The technology of the information age has the clear potential to enhance this understanding by drawing together disparate sources of information and common threads. The internet, as a source of information, has obvious potential including on-line museum and collection information.

Among the secondary markets, there are many opportunities to use the cultural assets in other forms, from publications to cinema sets, e-tourism to merchandising. Finally, securing an international reputation for European industry's expertise in these technologies will provide another avenue of exploitation. Here the technological potential is also clear, ranging from e-commerce opportunities, e-ticketing and tour planning technologies to marketing of digital assets in forms as diverse as printed images to components of digital games and film special effects. The experience with on-line publications would suggest that on-line publication of digital assets is likely to enhance the demand for physical visits to the originals.

Education, citizenship and socio-economic priorities

In 2002 the Council of Europe, in its report *Forward Planning: The Function of Cultural Heritage in a Changing Europe*, stated that:

> European co-operation has done a great deal to heighten awareness, among decision-makers and the general public, of the interest of heritage, conservation methods, research and technical co-operation between countries. Consideration must now also be given to the societal implications. In this respect, cultural heritage is a key component of the multiple identities that shape Europe. Juxtaposition of these identities raises the question of intercultural dialogue and mutual understanding between communities.

The report concludes:

The forward-looking work initiated in 2000 should be pursued in a number of directions:

- the "common heritage" concept, in connection with the Council of Europe's political role and the meaning to be given to Article 1 of its Statute;
- the function of cultural heritage in an information society for the benefit of all. . . .
- diversification of means of participation and of public access to culture and heritage in the context of globalisation.

> Research in these fields cannot be compartmentalised along traditional academic or administrative dividing lines, but should be pursued at an interdisciplinary, cross-sectoral level.

In relation to this, if the communication of cultural heritage can meet the objective of using positive messages to convey the cultural commonalities of European societies, then this will have both societal and economic benefits. By addressing the youth niche of Europe as well as the wider population, the first typically open to technological solutions and the second generally interested in technology as a means, any initiatives will have longer-term implications in shaping society. This would also contribute to the creation of a more-informed public demand for cultural heritage preservation, presentation and sustainable uses, and will help create and reinforce the industry sector engaged in producing experiences and digital reconstructions. This integrated effect on our perception of the value and significance of our shared heritage would represent an important aspect of the increasing use of technology and would enhance its positive economic and educational impact on our society in the coming decades.

Scenarios for integrating technology

A range of opportunities is available for the integration of technology and tourism consumption in relation to cultural heritage sites. Technology can be used to:

- enhance the experience of traditional monuments, sites and museums,
- create new venues for experiencing cultural heritage, and
- use remote access to virtual venues and secondary marketing opportunities.

Embryo technological developments in mainstream sites

The Jorvik visitor attraction in York, England, is a well-known early adopter of simulation as an enhancement of limited physical remains. The remaining artefacts showing the evidence for the Viking way of life in the area are displayed in a gallery attached to the visitor experience. The context is demonstrated via simulation/ reconstructions of aspects including physical models of a 'Viking' street and sensations (e.g. smells). The centre has been a phenomenal success, building on York's reputation as a short break destination. It also exhibits some of the dichotomies that all simulations must experience – the balance between reproducing an accurate depiction of the content (if this can indeed be known) and the need to provide an acceptable experience (Anon, 2004). In this case it is questionable whether a truly accurate simulation of all the smells of a Viking settlement would be as popular with visitors as a suitably sanitised version.

The early technologies adopted in Jorvik would probably not be recognised by the current visitors as a manifestation of 'Technology' which would now be thought of as requiring networked computer systems, internet access and impressive graphical special effects. While the world of IT has invented such delights as the Head Mounted Display (including 'smell-enabled' versions) more recent examples of technology used to enhance traditional cultural heritage experiences have tended to concentrate on the enhancement of the information content, using this to bring a new dimension to the venue.

The Ename Center for Public Archaeology and Heritage Presentation, established in 1998, is a pioneering centre of advanced technology and expertise in the field of heritage presentations for sites throughout Europe and the world. The Ename Center is a Belgian non-profit organisation founded to encourage and enable the dissemination of culture and history to the general public. The centre hosts a team of scholars, interpretive experts, and VR specialists, and has a twofold mission. On one hand it coordinates site-specific interpretive projects, international conferences, scholarly exchange programmes, and special training courses for site managers and heritage interpreters from 'partner sites' throughout Europe and other regions. On the other hand, it conducts research on the technology and methodology of heritage presentation. It has built an extensive know-how on interpretive techniques for monuments, sites and historical landscapes, and on the use of Virtual Reality and multimedia to support these interpretive techniques. The Ename Center was established on the basis of the expertise gained in the Ename 974 Project, which presents the heritage of Ename, incorporating an archaeological site, a standing monument, an innovative museum and a historical landscape, part of which is a nature reserve. In addition to developing a number of innovative heritage presentation systems for the Ename 974 Project at the archaeological site and museum in Belgium, the Ename Center is currently involved in the development of interpretive technologies at sites in The Netherlands, Belgium, Germany, Israel and the United States. One example of the technologies deployed in Ename is the TimeScope system at the archaeological site, which uses an innovative augmented reality method to show the way buildings would have appeared on site, viewing them on kiosk arrangements *in situ* (Pletinckx *et al.*, 2001).

The Archeoguide project (Vlahakis *et al.*, 2001; Archeoguide, 2004) has sought to take this approach one stage further by deploying mobile technologies to allow roaming augmentation, in a variety of formats ranging from PDAs to head-mounted augmented-reality viewing. These facilities can be used for several purposes, from a personally tailored replacement of guidebooks to mobile TimeScope similar to the Ename approach.

The technology uses a GPS system to record where the visitor is and wireless technologies to handle the interactions. This experimental technology has been deployed at the site of Olympia. Future developments of these prototypes will need to target issues of the size and weight of the portable equipment, accuracy of positioning, information content, reliability of networking connections, and all-weather use. The potential remains clear as the technology has the potential to bring to life sites with relatively little remaining physical evidence and we can anticipate systems which will include virtual humans and perhaps re-enactments, for example, allowing the visitor to an ancient battle site to view the deployment of the forces and the developing strategic situation. At Olympia, the Archeoguide team have so far confined this aspect to re-running some races.

Virtual tours can also be used to help preserve heritage and/or improve opportunity by giving visitors access to a simulation, rather than placing the original at risk of wear and tear. Examples of this potential are still at an experimental stage but would include sites where the possible volume of tourists would cause serious erosion or other damage to the surviving evidence. A typical site might be one where there is a mixture of environmentally sensitive and more robust remains – an archaeological site with delicate mural paintings or mosaics. By limiting access to the physical site the managers of the site can control the areas hosting the main visitor traffic whilst still allowing the visitors to visualise more sensitive areas in context.

The balance of access is clearly part of the design of the visitor experience, and will impact on the venue's attractiveness to potential visitors. However, visualisation can be used to enhance access to places that might otherwise need to be completely closed to the public. Other circumstances in which this facility would be useful include situations where the heritage centre may be unavailable due to intensive use for other purposes.

With the advent of ubiquitous networked centres and the potential use of smart cards, another development involves coordinated access to dispersed collections. This would enable the linking of a number of tourist attractions so that visitors to one venue would be equipped with a smart card to record their progress through the collection and store information about their visit on the card or on the network. In the case of re-visiting the same venue or accessing another one in the connected set, the visitors would be prompted with information about the location of the exhibits of interest to them, based on demonstrated interests on previous visits. Such individually tailored visits to thematically linked visitor centres can be expected to grow and to address increasingly specialised niche markets with interests in history, heritage, archaeology, nature and so on.

Technological venues with cultural themes

'Origins' is the name of a visitor centre at the Norfolk and Norwich Forum. The Forum is the result of a UK Millennium Lottery Fund proposal and is housed in a new building in the centre of Norwich. The Origins centre presents visitors with a variety of technologically assisted exhibits displaying aspects of the region's heritage. There are relatively few physical artefacts, but extensive guidance to direct the visitor to regional venues where the artefacts and monuments can be seen. 'Origins' is also connected to the Norwich Tourist Information Centre.

The Foundation of the Hellenic World (FHW) is a privately funded not-for-profit cultural institution whose constitution was ratified in 1993 by the Greek Parliament. The Foundation's vision is to preserve and disseminate Hellenic history and culture, to create an awareness of the broad scope of Hellenism and its contribution to cultural evolution. The FHW staff team includes multidisciplinary teams composed of computer scientists, graphic designers, 3-D graphic designers, and virtual reality engineers, as well as archaeologists, historians and museologists. Over the last 3 years the FHW has operated the cultural centre 'Hellenic Cosmos' in Athens, receiving thousands of visitors per year, to house its activities and present them to the public. The facility contains two high-end Virtual Reality (VR) exhibits, the 'Kivotos' (a Reactor^{TM} or CAVE®-like immersive display) and the 'Magic Screen' (an ImmersaDesk^{TM}). This is an innovative 'museum', which offers cultural tours through high-end VR systems. Future developments are planned to include a dome shaped theatre of 120 seats, where high quality cultural content will be displayed. The dome will use graphic computers to provide real-time interaction within the fully immersive experience. The Foundation now has a body of operational experiences of running a cultural heritage centre which is not sited in an established cultural heritage venue and where there are relatively few physical artefacts. What the centre offers is a technological environment, which provides accessible information to cultural heritage content.

E-tourism, cultural heritage and the internet

The internet offers three distinct new avenues for supporting the tourism sector. The first is the use of the internet for planning tourist activities on a personal basis. Although significant and having a measurable impact on the market for package holidays, it is not a topic for this chapter. The second area is the increasing use of internet-based experiences either as tasters for future visits (a use which is in a sense part of the marketing/tour planning category) or as a separate visualisation for those unable to visit. A classic example of this type would be the reconstructions included on the BBC virtual tours website (BBC, 2004).

The final category is the use of on-line facilities for secondary marketing – both for on-line ordering of reproduction physical artefacts from postcards to pottery and for the purchase of digital artefacts. This is a growing area of business with new sites appearing regularly (USA Museum Directory, 2004; British Museum, 2004; Natural History Museum, 2004; Victoria and Albert Museum, 2004). We can increasingly expect to see digital artefacts based on real monuments, sites and museum collections permeating other areas of digital media, for example being used within computer games or multimedia educational products. The balance here will be between the benefits of the 'authentic' artefact versus the potential additional licensing costs and the functional suitability of the models for inclusion in the product.

The rate at which the use of digital heritage permeates this wider audience and indeed the rate at which digital technologies permeate and add value to on-site experiences, will depend on the proper integration of technology at all stages of the pipeline of processing cultural heritage information from discovery (whether in archives or archaeological sites) to dissemination in visitor experiences beyond. The EPOCH Network of Excellence (Arnold, 2003) has been brought together to further the progressive integration of approach in applying technologies in this area. The project started in March 2004 and is due to run for 4 years. The consortium involves technologists, archaeologists and other heritage professionals, curators of museums, regional and national political groups and policy advice groups. Part of the work will be to produce best practice advice for policy makers and politicians and the programme of work will also involve education, training, standards activities and development of a common infrastructure to support the development of visitor experiences.

Final considerations

In this chapter we have looked at the variety of areas in which technology is interacting with cultural heritage and enhancing and broadening tourist experiences and related marketing opportunities for cultural heritage. Although largely experimental at this stage, the rate of development and potential change is clearly accelerating. Technically, realising the potential will rely on the improved data acquisition and reduced costs of developing reliable digital products.

The remaining barriers are many and complex, varying from the time, and hence cost, taken to develop new experiences to the need to bring together the aspirations and philosophy of cultural heritage professionals with the economic regime of the entertainment industry and the pedagogic needs of the education sector. There will also need to be substantial attention paid to the operational needs in terms of visitor throughput and reliability, combined with the presentation of engaging experiences. All of these aspects need to be brought together holistically before the technologies will become an integrated and widely used part of cultural heritage experiences. Contributing to and accelerating these developments is the topic of the EPOCH network of excellence.

References

Anon (2004) 'Jorvik' http://www.jorvik-viking-centre.co.uk/jorvik-navigation.htm, accessed February 2004.

Archeoguide (2004) http://archeoguide.intranet.gr/project.htm, accessed January 2004.

Arnold, D.B. (2001) Virtual heritage: challenges and opportunities. In R. Earnshaw and J. Vince (eds) *Digital Content Creation*. Springer Verlag.

Arnold, D.B. (2003) Plans for the EPOCH Network (Excellence in Processing Open Cultural Heritage). In *Pre-proceedings of VAST 2003 the 4th International Symposium on Virtual Reality*. Archaeology and Intelligent Cultural Heritage, pp. 161–162.

BBC (2004) Virtual tours http://www.bbc.co.uk/history/multimedia_zone/virtual_tours/, accessed February 2004.

British Museum (2004) http://www.britishmuseum.co.uk/, accessed February 2004.

Council of Europe (2002) *Forward Planning: The Function of Cultural Heritage in a Changing Europe*. Brussels.

Ecosystems Ltd (2003) *Using Natural and Cultural Heritage to Develop Sustainable Tourism in Non-Traditional Tourist Destinations*. European Commission Study.

Natural History Museum (2004) http://www.nhm.ac.uk/shop/, accessed February 2004.

Pletinckx, D., Silberman, N. and Callebaut, D. (2001) Presenting a monument in restoration: the Saint Laurentius Church in Ename and its role in the Francia Media Heritage Initiative. In *Proceedings of VAST 2001: Virtual Reality, Archeology, and Cultural Heritage*, pp. 197–204.

USA Museum Directory (2004) http://www.museumstuff.com/museums/usa/, accessed February 2004.

Victoria and Albert Museum (2004) http://www.vandashop.co.uk/, accessed February 2004.

Vlahakis, V., Karigiannis, J., Tsotros, M., Gounaris, M., Almeida, L., Stricker, D., Gleue, T., Christou, I.T., Carlucci, R. and Ioannidis, N. (2001) ARCHEOGUIDE: First results of an augmented reality, mobile computing system in cultural heritage sites. In *Proceedings of VAST 2001: Virtual Reality, Archeology, and Cultural Heritage*, pp. 131–140.

World Tourism Organisation (2002) News release, Madrid, 18 June 2002.

Questions

1 What is the value of virtual reality in heritage site development and management?
2 To what extent does technology play a key role in managing heritage?

Websites

USA Museum Directory
http://www.museumstuff.com/museums/usa/
Natural History Museum
http://www.nhm.ac.uk/shop/

19

Ethical tourism
Is its future in niche tourism?

Clare Weeden

Introduction

This chapter provides an overview of some of the challenges faced by UK niche operators who want to provide holidays that limit the damage commonly associated with mass tourism. It highlights constraints such as the operators' beliefs that these are negatively perceived by the consumer as 'worthy' and 'moralistic', and addresses the problem of whether consumers' ethical intentions translate into the purchasing of ethical holidays. For some organizations, 'ethics in business is not an option...but an absolute requirement for success' (Brennan, 1991 in Pitts and Cooke, 1991), and consideration is given to the circumstances that such tour operators have to face in a highly competitive industry. Further reflections are made regarding the moral obligations of the founder-directors, the promotion and adoption of ethical codes of conduct and how important these are to both tourists and tour operators. Finally, thought will be given to the question of whether ethical tourism will remain a niche product or whether its future lies in the mass-market adoption of its guiding principles.

Niche context

The global tourism industry has long been characterized by rapid growth and this is set to continue, even subsequent to the aftermath of 9/11. However, this success and rapid growth has given cause for concern, because tourism has become, for some developing countries, the principal focus of their economic well-being. This seeming over-reliance upon tourism has led some authors to question the ethics of development in general (Goulet, 1985) and the ethics of tourism development in particular (Lea, 1993).

The structure of the sector's operations has also attracted criticism; the global tourism industry is fiercely competitive and dominated by transnational corporations, mainly located in the North. These organizations leverage power over the suppliers of the tourism product, hence potentially creating unequal exchange and power relationships (Peet, 1991; Barrett-Brown, 1993). Within the UK, the market is dominated by a small number of very large, transnational organizations and competition is mostly characterized by an emphasis on cost pressures driving business forward (Page, 2003). Consequently, operators are forced to compete through international mergers and acquisitions, and survive on small margins by claiming benefits from the substantial economies of scale.

This 'hypercompetition' (Page, 2003), thus encapsulates the contemporary European business environment, and results in continuous new product development and aggressive marketing through lower prices (D'Aveni, 1998). The ensuing instability of the sector makes it difficult therefore for companies to plan for a more sustainable future, and Miller (2001: 590) argues that, 'against such a background taking steps to behave more responsibly has traditionally received a predictably low priority'.

For any independent specialist operator working within the UK holiday market there is a need to differentiate their product in order to compete effectively, and the provision of ethical tourism is seen as one such niche opportunity. For a tour operator, the adoption of ethical values can add quality and appeal to the product offering and enables them to compete on more than just price. For some tour operators, however, ethical policies may be considered a luxury (Krippendorf, 1991) and a cost rather than a long-term investment. Nevertheless, all businesses make decisions and choices directly related to moral issues, and tour operators are no exception (Ground, 1995). Indeed, against this background 'the concern for ethical conduct not only among the operators and members of tour organizations, but also among the tourists themselves has become a fundamental concern' (Malloy and Fennell, 1998: 453).

Defining ethical tourism

For some UK-based organizations such as Tourism Concern, who campaign for ethical and fairly traded tourism, and the development charity Tearfund, the term 'ethical tourism' is regarded as well established. However, among the wider public there remains confusion over exactly what is meant by this term.

Fundamentally, ethical tourism is a theme that has been developed, predominantly by the North, in response to global concerns about the impact of mass tourism and is an attempt to manage tourism for the benefit of all stakeholders. It takes its lead from sustainable development literature and highlights the importance of limiting the negative impact of tourism on destinations whilst simultaneously retaining the positive economic benefits for the host populations (Butler, 1992).

However, it is difficult to give a specific example of an ethical holiday. To date, specialist niche operators have preferred to develop packages that demonstrate commitment either to environmental, social and/or wildlife responsibility. Ethical tourism seems to be a step too far, not least because of the challenges involved in providing a tangible product to reflect what might be described as esoteric and intangible philosophies. Consequently, a completely ethical holiday is difficult for operators to provide, given the disparate nature of the product, the multicultural aspect of tourism and the complex chain of suppliers used in its delivery. Nevertheless, the World Tourism Organization (WTO) has tried to take a lead on this topic and committed itself towards a more equitable industry through its Global Code of Ethics for Tourism. This Code can be interpreted as a frame of reference for the responsible and sustainable development of world tourism, and the following passage, taken from Article One of the Code, illustrates the WTO's belief in an ethical approach to tourism:

> The understanding and promotion of the ethical values common to humanity, with an attitude of tolerance and respect for the diversity of religious, philosophical and moral beliefs, are both the foundation and consequence of responsible tourism (WTO, 1999).

Reading this Article it is clear that although ethical values are explicitly mentioned, and development is encouraged to be more ethical, the WTO stops short of advocating ethical tourism and instead uses the term 'responsible tourism'. Significantly, Ryan (2002: 17) suggests a reason for this; although it may be easy for tour operators to agree with the principles outlined by demands for an ethical approach to tourism development, it is sometimes hard to implement them because of the complex and 'pragmatic issues of management'. It could be argued that although laudable in intention, ethical tourism has been an extremely difficult niche product to provide.

This is a view supported by Harold Goodwin, director of the International Centre for Responsible Tourism (ICRT), who reports that 'currently what tour operators are looking for help with is ways to make themselves more responsible' (Goodwin, 2003). In other words, operators want to adopt responsible policies but are currently unable to understand how they can achieve this. The UK-based ICRT promotes responsible tourism, which is defined as 'tourism that attempts to minimize negative environmental, social and cultural impacts, and generates greater economic benefits for local people' (ICRT, 2003). It could be argued therefore that providing a responsible tourism product enables the suppliers of tourism to work individually towards tourism development that *aims to be more ethical by being responsible*.

Consumer behaviour

There has been a gradual emergence since the 1990s of the ethical consumer (Shaw and Clarke, 1999) and many companies now realize the importance to the consumer of social responsibility in business. There is increasing recognition that the majority of business decisions involve some form of ethical judgement and although companies are increasingly recommended to adopt socially responsible policies there remains the question of whether consumers really care about ethical business (Creyer and Ross, 1997).

For example, whilst recognizing that ethical and responsible tourism is a product that can satisfy a niche segment of the market (Goodwin and Francis, 2003), operators have had to acknowledge the tension between tourists' expressed interest in such products and their purchasing behaviour. In the UK, trends indicate an increase in the number of consumers actively seeking out ethical products, with more than one in four consumers declaring themselves to be strongly ethical, a rise of 5% since 1990 (Mintel, 1999). Within tourism specifically, 27% of tourists stated that a company's ethical policies were of high importance to them when choosing with which operator to travel (Tearfund, 2000).

However, the true picture is misleading, with evidence for increasing consumer concern in purchase behaviour being scarce (Creyer and Ross, 1997; Boulstridge and Carrigan, 2000). Although current market research indicates that ethical considerations are brought into tourist purchasing behaviour (Curtin and Busby, 1999; Cleverdon and Kalisch, 2000; Tearfund, 2000), the market for ethical holidays remains tiny. Only 7% of UK consumers explicitly seek a holiday provided by a tour operator with an ethical code of practice. A further 48% do not want to think about these issues on holiday and are more interested in the standard of accommodation or information about the weather (Mintel, 2001).

Part of the problem may lie with tourists' perception that ethical or responsible holidays are too 'worthy', when what they really want is a relaxing experience, away from the problems of the 'real world'. This 'escape' motivation may work against the ethical operators but it is clear that their clients buy holidays primarily for relaxation (Diski, 2003). One UK specialist, for example, takes the view that the 'company should take responsibility for doing the thinking', so that the tourist can relax and enjoy the experience (Matthews, 2003). Sophie Campbell (2003), writing in a recent *In Focus* article agrees, suggesting that as the developed world is consumed with guilt about many of its activities the last thing tourists want to think about on their holiday is how exploitative the tourism industry can be.

Apart from the problems of defining ethical tourism and the constraints associated with consumer behaviour, the holiday product is also problematic because of its complexity, and this too challenges the tour operator wanting to provide an ethical experience. As tour operators are but one element in the holiday experience, this makes it difficult for them to guarantee that all aspects of their holidays are ethically provided. For example, what specialist tour operators find particularly challenging is the length of their supply chain and the complexities of trying to persuade their subcontractors (accommodation suppliers for example) to adopt common ethical principles. As one UK specialist operator explains, even if the ground handler says they are working to the highest ethical standards 'it is very difficult for us to check they are actually doing what they say' (Matthews, 2003).

Moral obligation

Very often, specialist tour operators' founder-directors are driven by their personal enthusiasm for moral values in tourism and this determines the organization's achievements in this area. Of course, for a small company, the issues of power sharing and ethical development are not easy to forget – very often the directors lead trips and regularly come face-to-face with the impact of the tourism they promote (Loveridge, 2003). The importance of having a personal commitment to providing ethical tourism is highlighted by one specialist operator, who, when asked if the terms ethical and responsible tourism meant anything to him he replied:

> Do they have any relevance to me? Yeah, I mean I wouldn't be in it if I didn't think what I was doing was worth it, not only from my own point of view but worth it from a general wildlife point of view. It is very important to me as a person (Matthews, 2003).

Clearly, individual interpretations of ethical and responsible tourism will vary according to the personal beliefs and objectives of the owner-directors of these operators. It also rests on the ease and/or difficulty they perceive in implementing their ethical policies. However, whilst it is true that there have been calls for the development of tourism to become a more democratic and hence ethical process, it could be argued that tour operators in general have been slow to adopt responsible guidelines. Potentially this could be due as much to the challenges associated with their provision, as well as the very aspirational nature of the word 'ethical' and its accompanying complexities.

Also, although many specialists have identified moral values as important in their business activities they have had to temper personal motivation with commercial understanding. For example, both Rainbow Tours and Discovery Initiatives are examples of specialist operators who sell quality, tailor-made holidays and whose directors have a strong personal belief in the importance of trading ethically and responsibly. Thus, when starting up their businesses, the front covers of their first brochures depicted the images associated with ethical and responsible tourism. A specific example comes from Rainbow Tours, a London-based tour operator specializing in holidays to Southern Africa. Their first brochure in 1998 depicted a smiling South African boy holding a picture of Nelson Mandela. Five years later, their 2003 brochure for Africa and the Southern Ocean displays a spectacular wildlife photograph of a herd of zebra. As director Roger Diski explains, the moral aspects of their holidays are not attractive to potential clients and 'those who can afford to visit Southern Africa with a tour operator ... tend to lead pressured lives and want to go on holiday, not a crusade' (Diski, 2002: 6).

As a result, the directors of both these companies have learnt to mitigate their personal beliefs and how they publicize them, producing brochures and company material with images of the destinations, photographs of the wildlife and shots of luxurious tropical beaches, when appropriate. Certainly, these companies have realized that issues of ethical trading can make a difference in a decision about who to travel with, but in their experience, consumers do not ordinarily have the ethical policies of the operator at number one on their shopping list. Primarily, tourists want a quality experience and the choice as to which operator they travel with will be made according to this priority. If the operator also has an ethical policy then all well and good – it is the icing on the cake rather than the primary motivator. This highlights another constraint for ethical tour operators – that it is commercially difficult to stay close to their personal ethical values whilst simultaneously presenting an attractive but responsible holiday.

It is apparent from the preceding discussion that some parts of the industry have recognized that 'tourism needs to be developed in an ethical manner so that exploitation is not its hallmark' (Page, 2003: 18), and there are many specialist operators who clearly believe it important to be offering ethical tourism in one form or another. However, for other operators, offering 'ethical tourism' *per se* may be too difficult and restrictive. Not all specialists are comfortable with the terms 'ethical' and 'responsible', believing that the former is too vague and difficult to define, whilst the latter, if promised in a brochure can raise tourists' expectations falsely.

As integrity is paramount in business, so the promise of responsibility is serious, but does not always need to be made explicit in company material such as the brochure (Loveridge, 2003). One UK specialist, Wind, Sand and Stars, deliberately excludes mention of responsible tourism, believing that the company's attitude towards responsibility in business is implicit in all of the company's activities. This viewpoint is illustrated by the following quote taken from their 2003 brochure:

> Wind, Sand and Stars was started at the request of the local Bedouin who wanted someone to bring them direct trade so they could remain in their desert lands and avoid going to work in the coastal resorts springing up along Sinai's coastline.

It is clear from these few examples that the success of ethical tourism depends heavily on the personal values of the founder-directors, and it is their motivation and determination that ensures their companies' responsible attitude to holiday provision. As companies grow in size so the directors become more removed from the impact of their decisions and the difficulty of remaining true to responsible tourism becomes ever more challenging.

Codes of conduct

As Mason and Mowforth (1995: 11) explain: 'Codes of conduct for tourists are a relatively recent phenomenon', although several have been in existence for more than 20 years, such as the UK Countryside Commissions' Country Code. Generally, the purpose of codes is to raise awareness and educate the consumer, but they can also be aimed at the tour operator, at destination communities and to governments, to explain how it is possible for them to support the management of tourism whilst simultaneously conserving resources. Specifically, the codes most often brought to mind are directed at tourists, and are helpful in improving tourist behaviour in resorts as well as managing their expectations.

Codes are normally direct in style with advice or a list of instructions on what to do or not to do (Mason and Mowforth, 1995). In addition they also illustrate how the operators are encouraging and implementing local participation initiatives in the destination community. Responsibletravel.com gives an explanation and some instructions to operators on what to include and what not to include in their codes of conduct, thereby giving practical solutions to those companies who are either less confident in presenting their beliefs or perhaps those who are keen to adopt the responsible and ethical tourism banner. For the latter, responsibletravel.com emphasizes the importance of responsible policies to operators as a method of generating differentiation, thus highlighting the connection by some between these policies and commercial opportunity.

There is a plethora of codes aimed at the tourism industry, internationally as well as UK-based. On a global scale, the WTO have developed a Tourism Bill of Rights and a Tourist Code, as well as the Global Code of Ethics for Tourism. There are also codes produced by international conservation-oriented organizations (Mason and Mowforth, 1995) such as World Wildlife Fund for Nature. The United Nations Environment Programme (UNEP) also aims to encourage caring for the environment, and their publication *Environmental Codes of Conduct for Tourism* (1995) offers a detailed discussion of some of the voluntary environmental codes in tourism.

An additional initiative developed by UNEP, in conjunction with UNESCO and WTO, is the Tour Operators Initiative for Sustainable Tourism Development (TOI). This is a network of 25 operators who are keen to demonstrate how responsibility in sustainable development is at the core of their activities (UNEP, 2003). Members of the TOI include Discovery Initiatives (UK), British Airways Holidays (UK), Accor Tours (France), TUI Group (Germany) and Exodus (UK).

On a national, UK level, non-governmental organizations (NGOs) such as the tourism pressure group Tourism Concern, and development charities Voluntary Service Overseas (VSO) and Tearfund, have all conducted well publicized campaigns aimed at highlighting the problems associated with mass tourism, as well as developing advice and codes of conduct for tourists. So too have UK tourism trade associations. For example, the Association of British Travel Agents (ABTA) is currently encouraging both tour operators and tourists to take a more responsible stance to their holiday, and produce a 'Traveller's Code' to educate tourists about the impact of tourism (Richards, 2003). The Association of Independent Tour Operators (AITO) and the Federation of Tour Operators (FTO) also promote the benefits of environmental and ethical codes of practice to their members. A selection of some of the better known examples of codes developed by existing NGOs is shown in Table 19.1.

Although codes of conduct have their roots in the movement for human rights and are essential in order to help protect the needs of minorities (Smith and Duffy, 2003: 74), they are fraught with difficulty in such a complex and fragmented industry, not least because of the difficulty of implementation and measurement of success. In addition, these codes 'are often voluntary agreements that are little more than aspirational documents serving as indicators of best practice' (Smith and Duffy, 2003: 87).

Certainly, as the adoption of voluntary codes and guidelines became widespread in tourism during the early 1980s, critics were often sceptical of an organization's motives, suggesting they were mere advertising and PR activity. They were criticized for being a marketing tool rather than highlighting a genuine objective by organizations keen to illustrate how business can be both ethical and profitable (Forsyth, 1997). Of course, this scepticism remains to some extent but there are

Table 19.1 Examples of codes of conduct

Organization	Title of code
Ecumenical Coalition of Third World Tourism (ECTWT)	Code of Ethics for Tourism
Responsibletravel.com	Tips for Responsible Travellers
Tearfund	Suggested Actions for Tourists
Voluntary Service Overseas (VSO)	Every Holiday Has Hidden Extras Below the Surface
Tourism Concern	Going Travelling
	The Himalayan Tourist Code
RSPCA	Fun in the Sun – or is it?
RSPB	Code of Conduct for Birdwatchers
World Travel and Tourism Council	The WTTC's Environmental Guidelines
Survival for Tribal Peoples	Danger Tourists
WWF	Code of Conduct for Mediterranean Tourists
	The Ten Principles for Arctic Tourism
	Code of Conduct for Tour Operators in the Arctic
	Code of Conduct for Tourists in the Arctic

Source: http://www.responsibletravel.com

many tour operators and NGOs within tourism who genuinely advocate responsible business practice and use the codes of conduct to inform tourists, and the wider public, how their actions and behaviour can contribute to a more equitable exchange.

Currently, the wide proliferation of codes for environmental ethics or social responsibility gives tour operators an opportunity to highlight best practice as well as educating the consumer with regard to their expected behaviour. However, it is clear that just because an organization has these codes it does not mean that their clients will pay attention to them. That is purely a matter of personal motivation. 'It is important we say it, whether they use it or not is another matter' (Matthews, 2003). One UK specialist operator, Rainbow Tours, developed a code of conduct primarily 'because we believe in it' (Diski, 2003) and includes it in the brochure to explain what responsible tourism means to the company, and to illustrate the company's commitment to the concept.

Nevertheless, there is some concern among operators that the wide variety of codes will confuse tourists and that due to 'information overload' many tourists will screen out their message. Inevitably, responsible tourism should be about the actions of the tour operators, tourists and all the many subcontractors handling the business to and in the destination. However, consumers in general, and tourists in particular are suspicious of 'ethical wash' and if the industry is not seen to support their words with actions, then the codes may contribute to a continuing sense of scepticism and disbelief.

Can ethical tourism ever be anything more than a niche product? Historically, ethical tourism has been developed as a niche product by small, specialist independent organizations such as those highlighted in this chapter. As a result its success has been thought possible only in small-scale developments, in conjunction with local partnerships and community consent, whilst the mass market continues on its ubiquitous, destructive global march. Certainly this was a direct criticism of so-called 'alternative tourism', of which ethical tourism is one such example, which was advocated in the early 1990s as the panacea for the ills of mass tourism (Wheeller, 1997).

Recently however, there is growing evidence that some of the mass market operators, such as British Airways and First Choice, are adopting sustainable policies within their corporate objectives (Mintel, 2001), and whilst it is easy to criticize their motives for such activities, these initiatives make it inevitable that ethical tourism will eventually move from being a niche to a mainstream product. Of course, it must be acknowledged that the number of mass-market operators adopting such policies is still a minority and that any positive change will be a very slow process.

For many, ethical tourism should be part of an attitude towards tourism development and business rather than a niche product on offer to the market. Indeed, for these people, ethical tourism is seen not as a discrete product but as an approach to business and should run through all elements of tourism, rather than be classed a separate entity. The organization Tearfund, for example, 'sees "ethical" tourism as applying to mass tourism as well as to community tourism and eco-tourism' (Gordon, 2000). Harold Goodwin echoes this statement, believing that 'responsible tourism is not a niche product, it's an additional dimension' (Goodwin, 2003). Whilst he firmly believes that the term 'ethical' may be too fundamental and too personal to apply publicly to business activities, he clearly believes that 'any tour operator can do something responsibly – it's not a product range, it's a movement'.

To date, specialist operators have adopted ethical policies in order to compete effectively in the UK's oligopolistic marketplace. As they have done this, so the critics of ethical tourism have interpreted it as a small and therefore ineffective – solution to tourism's many negative impacts. In fact, this could be the root of the problem – by focusing on the niche opportunities of ethical tourism so the wider picture has been neglected. It is only when transnational companies adopt ethical and responsible policies for their holidays and tourism development that the benefits associated with ethical tourism will spread to the mass market.

Case Study – Discovery Initiatives

Discovery Initiatives (DI) is an example of an ethical tour operator whose aim is:

'to offer inspirational journeys that give you a privileged insight into cultures and the natural world whilst supporting their long-term survival and conservation. This is travelling as an investment – in all our futures'.

Julian Matthews established the company in 1997 with the specific objective of challenging the conventional approach to nature and wilderness travel. He wanted to demonstrate to the travel industry that it was no longer acceptable to think purely in terms of economic return, but to encompass the social and environmental concerns generated by global tourism. Essentially, Discovery Initiatives is a small group tour operator that offers tailor-made experiences, based on strong conservation principles. Their destinations are worldwide but primarily Africa-based and are characterized by wildlife conservation, and study and support tours. The company ethos is strong and clear and demonstrated by their working with local communities and conservation organizations in order to provide extraordinary experiences for travellers at the same time as actively contributing to local well-being.

The company works closely with organizations such as Conservation Worldwide, the Worldwide Fund for Nature, The Wilderness Trust and the Endangered Wildlife Trust in order to support and help fund important projects as well as raise awareness of the importance of conservation and its relationship to fairly traded nature tourism. The company further demonstrates its commitment by contributing between 6 and 7% of revenue (more than £250,000 in 2002) to various global conservation initiatives and uses the money paid for local services and accommodation to provide local communities with the economic, ethical and environmental incentives to conserve their environment and culture for future generations.

Discovery Initiatives has two codes of conduct: the Operator's Code of Conduct (illustrated in Table 19.2) and the Traveller's Code of Conduct (illustrated in Table 19.3). The purpose of these codes is to detail the ethos of the company and demonstrate what the company aims to do through its destination partnerships and promotion of community advocacy. The company has a third code under construction, for their ground handlers, although this has been problematic because of the expected difficulties surrounding the encouragement of a third-party organization to adopt ethical guidelines. In addition to these codes they also invite their clients to pre-holiday workshops where the guidelines for their holidays are discussed and preparations are made for a successful and positive experience for all stakeholders.

Table 19.2 Discovery Initiatives Operator's Code of Conduct

In order to provide a responsible tourism product Discovery Initiatives (DI) plan their trips while keeping the following objectives in mind:

To gain the full backing and cooperation of the host nation's authorities where necessary, and to obtain permission for our work and to undertake (by DI or their agents) full and proper reconnaissance of each area of operation.

Wherever possible, to use local accommodation, food and services in planning the programme.

To plan their ventures so that both the local people and the traveller participants achieve the maximum benefit in terms of cultural interaction, awareness and understanding.

To ensure that participants see the full picture, are made aware of the issues and concerns facing the tribal communities DI visit and the conflicts facing the conservation of wildlife and resources in each area.

To ensure that all participants have been fully briefed about the host country, its customs, cultures and its sensitivities and sensibilities, through pre-departure gatherings, tour leader briefings and/or tour dossiers.

To teach participants wherever necessary to act correctly and with due reverence and respect to cultures and customs, and encourage the learning of key words of the local language to facilitate this.

To involve the local community in planning and decision-making at all times, employing them wherever necessary at acceptable rates of pay.

Continually to assess the environmental, social and economic impact of their visit, so as to avoid over dependency.

To avoid patronizing, insulting or demeaning tribal people in marketing, advertising, or when interacting with them.

To avoid any activity that results in cruel treatment of animals, or interference in their natural way of life

To undertake each venture, wherever possible, with the maximizing benefits accruing to the host communities.

Table 19.2 Continued

To continue to support their work after their departure, and to raise awareness through talks, lectures and in the press of the issues raised or uncovered.

To garner support, backing and expertise of experts, learned institutions, non-governmental organizations and sponsoring companies for separate ventures as needed.

Source: Discovery Initiatives (2003) (http://www.discoveryinitiatives.com)

Table 19.3 Traveller's Code of Conduct

Act with courtesy and respect to local people, the authorities and to the other members of the team.

Avoid litter and the unnecessary use or wastage of natural resources.

Act with sensitivity regarding the dress code of the host nation. You are a visitor and will be treated as a guest if you show respect for their way of life.

Avoid taking excessive photographs, being intrusive with the camera and insensitive to those you are photographing. Always ask permission. A number of our ventures will have accomplished photographers on them and slides and pictures can be duplicated for participants to keep. Cameras with long lenses should take close-up photographs of people. In close confines with people, only one photographer should be chosen to take the pictures.

Endeavour to learn a few simple words of the language of your hosts.

Take time to get to know and understand your hosts.

Do not buy, collect or trade in wildlife products. It is frequently illegal and can lead to prosecution.

Source: Discovery Initiatives (2003) (http://www.discoveryinitiatives.com)

Final considerations

As can be seen in this chapter, ethical tourism is a complex and, at times, an ill-defined concept. The purchase of ethical and responsible holidays can be inconsistent with consumers' expressed intentions, and tour operators themselves have been reluctant to advertise their ethical policies for fear of appearing to be too 'worthy' and 'moralistic'. For the specialist operators who genuinely want to provide an ethical product the challenges are immense, not least due to the difficulties of the long tourism supply chain, but also because of their personal moral values. Codes of conduct are seen as an important tool in the education of consumers, tour operators and governments, but must be seen to be implemented if they are to be judged as effective. For a more positive contribution to global understanding, ethical tourism should be adopted by the mass-market operating industry, not as an alternative niche product, but as a guiding philosophy in all their future market development.

Acknowledgements

The author would like to acknowledge the following people for their enthusiastic help and cooperation: Roger Diski of Rainbow Tours, Dr Harold Goodwin of the International Centre for Responsible Tourism, Dr Emma Loveridge of Wind, Sand and Stars, and Julian Matthews of Discovery Initiatives.

References

Barrett-Brown, M. (1993) *Fair Trade*. London: Zen Books.

Brennan, B. (1991) Keynote speech. In R.E. Pitts and R.E. Cooke (1991). A realistic view of marketing ethics. *Journal of Business Ethics*, 10(4), 243–244.

Boulstridge, E. and Carrigan, M. (2000) Do consumers really care about corporate responsibility? Highlighting the attitude-behaviour gap. *Journal of Communication Management*, 4(4), 355–368.

Butler, R. (1992) Tourism, environment and development. *Environmental Conservation*, 18(3), 201–209.

Campbell, S. (2003) It may be ethical but is it news? *In Focus*, Summer, Issue 47(9).

Cleverdon, R. and Kalisch, A. (2000) Fair trade in tourism. *International Journal of Tourism Research*, 2, 171–187.

Creyer, E.H. and Ross, T.R. Jr. (1997) The influence of firm behaviour on purchase intention: do consumers really care about business ethics? *Journal of Consumer Marketing*, 14(6), 421–433.

Curtin, S. and Busby, G. (1999) Sustainable destination development: the tour operator perspective. *International Journal of Tourism Research*, 1, 135–147.

D'Aveni, R. (1998) Hypercompetition closes in. *Financial Times*, 4 February (Global Business Section). In S. Page (2003) *Tourism Management: Managing for Change*. Oxford: Butterworth-Heinemann.

Diski, R. (2002) Giving people what they want. *In Focus*, Autumn, 44(6).

Diski, R. (2003) Director, Rainbow Tours, Personal Interview. London, 19 September.

Forsyth, T. (1997) Environmental responsibility and business regulation: the case of sustainable tourism. *The Geographical Journal*, 163(3), 270–281.

Goodwin, H. (2003) Director, International Centre for Responsible Tourism. Personal Interview. London, 29 July.

Goodwin, H. and Francis, J. (2003) Ethical and responsible tourism: consumer trends in the UK. *Journal of Vacation Marketing*, 9(3), 271–284.

Gordon, G. (2000) Personal communications. November 2000.

Goulet, D. (1985) *The Cruel Choice: A New Concept in the Theory of Development*. Lanham: University Press of America.

Ground, I. (1995) Business ethics workshop. In J. Robson, and I. Robson, (1996) From shareholders to stakeholders. *Tourism Management*, 17(7), 533–540.

International Centre for Responsible Tourism (2003) Responsible tourism, available at http://www.icrtourism.org/resp.html, accessed 25 July 2003.

Krippendorf, J. (1991) Towards new tourism policies. In S. Medlik (ed.) *Managing Tourism*. Oxford: Butterworth-Heinemann.

Lea, J.P. (1993) Tourism development ethics in the Third World, *Annals of Tourism Research*, 20, 701–715.

Loveridge, E. (2003) Director, Wind, Sand and Stars, Personal interview. London, 19 September.

Malloy, D.C. and Fennell, D.A. (1998) Codes of ethics and tourism: An exploratory content analysis. *Tourism Management*, 19(5), 453–461.

Mason, P. and Mowforth, M. (1995) *Codes of Conduct in Tourism*. Occasional papers in Geography, No. 1. University of Plymouth, Department of Geographical Studies.

Matthews, J. (2003) Director, Discovery Initiatives. Personal interview. Cirencester, 9 September.

Miller, G. (2001) Corporate responsibility in the UK tourism industry. *Tourism Management*, 22, 589–598.

Mintel (1999) *The Green and Ethical Consumer*. Leisure Intelligence – UK report. Mintel International Group Ltd.

Mintel (2001) *Ethical Tourism*. Leisure Intelligence – UK report. October. Mintel International Group Ltd.

Page, S.J. (2003) *Tourism Management: Managing for change*. Oxford: Butterworth-Heinemann.

Peet, R. (1991) *Global Capitalism – Theories of Social Development*. London: Routledge.

Richards, K. (2003) The changing face of travel, *Geographical*, June. Available from http://infotrac.galegroup.com, accessed 16 October 2003.

Ryan, C. (2002) Equity, management, power sharing and sustainability – issues of the 'new tourism'. *Tourism Management*, 23, 17–26.

Shaw, D.S. and Clarke, I. (1999) Belief formation in ethical consumer groups: an exploratory study. *Marketing Intelligence and Planning*, 17(2), 109–119.

Smith, M. and Duffy, R. (2003) *The Ethics of Tourism Development*. London: Routledge.

Tearfund (2000) *Tourism: an Ethical Issue*. Market Research Report, January.

UNEP (1995) *Environmental Codes of Conduct for Tourism*. UNEP/IE Technical Report 29. UNEP/IE, Paris.

UNEP (2003) *Tourism and Biodiversity: Mapping Tourism's Global Footprints*. Washington: Conservation International. Available from http://www.unep.org/PDF/Tourism-and-biodiversity.pdf, accessed 14 November 2003.

Wheeller, B. (1997) Tourism's troubled times: responsible tourism is not the answer. In France, L. (ed.) *The Earthscan Reader in Sustainable Tourism*. London: Earthscan Publishing Ltd.

World Tourism Organization (1999) *Global Code of Ethics for Tourism*, available from www.world-tourism.org, accessed 1 May 2002.

Questions

1 Discuss some of the constraints that may be responsible for preventing tourists from carrying out their intentions to purchase ethical holidays.

2 Examine some of the issues commonly associated with the impact of tourism. Why might tourism development be seen as unethical?

Further recommended reading

Smith, M. and Duffy, R. (2003) *The Ethics of Tourism Development*. London: Routledge. For an extensive discourse on the development of human rights and codes of practice see pages 73–90.

Tourism Concern, *In Focus* – the magazine of Tourism Concern.

Recommended websites

Tourism Concern http://www.tourismconcern.org.uk

Discovery Initiatives tour operator http://www.discoveryinitiatives.com

Wind, Sand and Stars tour operator http://www.windsandstars.co.uk

Rainbow Tours tour operator http://www.rainbowtours.co.uk

Niche tourism

A way forward to sustainability?

Marina Novelli and Angela Benson

The concept of 'sustainable development' as a policy consideration in order to combat some of the environment problems was introduced as part of the World Conservations Strategy by the International Union for the Conservation of Nature and Natural Resources (IUCN, 1980). The World Commission on Environment and Development 1987 report named *Our Common Future* and often referred to as *The Brundtland Report* placed the concept of 'sustainable development' high on the world's agenda as a way of delivering meaningful strategies and policies in the interest of present and future generations (Murphy, 1994; Holden, 2000).

The term 'sustainable tourism' became popular in the late 1980s (France, 1997; Hall and Lew, 1998; Holden, 2000) and appears to be generally adopted in the literature as a key term and concept acknowledged by both researchers and practitioners. The proliferation of conferences, books, journal articles, dedicated journals (i.e. the *Journal of Sustainable Tourism*) and planning documents clearly indicates confirmation of this. However, despite the acceptance of the term generally, there is considerable variability and controversy concerning the interpretation of sustainability by tourism stakeholders, often leading to a delay in the implementation of the sustainable tourism agenda:

> Sustainable tourism development meets the needs of present tourists and host regions while

protecting and enhancing opportunities for the future. It is envisaged as leading to management of all resources in such a way that economic, social, and aesthetic needs can be fulfilled while maintaining cultural integrity, essential ecological processes, biological diversity, and life support systems (WTO 2001: 19).

This World Tourism Organization (WTO) definition is widely adopted and used as a template for the most varied sustainable tourism development programmes; however, it has often been criticized for its complexity.

It may be argued that the tourism sector's understanding of sustainable tourism has evolved over time and with this has come the sudden increase of niche tourism markets as an alternative to mass tourism. In fact, examples of this are the widely spread ecotourism, adventure tourism, nature tourism, green tourism and rural tourism, which have given a broader choice and a richer portfolio of opportunities to the consumer.

The modern tourism market seems increasingly characterized by a multiplicity of definitions linked to a varied set of recreational activities, demand for alternative locations, entertainments and attractions, and stimulating new tourism segments, which are characterized by an increasingly sophisticated tourist clientele. The selected cases presented in this book confirm that niche tourism can be defined in relation to its multitude of factors interacting and responding to an ever-changing tourism demand and market trends.

While certain niche segments, such as cultural heritage, sport and adventure tourism, are widely known and easily recognizable, there are others listed under newly born micro-niches, such as photographic, genealogy and research tourism. In relation to this, whether the niche is established or emerging, it attracts growing numbers of visitors to a variety of destinations and is increasingly perceived as a way forward to facilitate sustainable tourism. Despite this perception, the question is: 'Is niche tourism sustainable?', which still requires further investigation and debate. For the purpose of this book, the concept of sustainability has been considered in order to assess the extent to which certain forms of niche tourism can offer a viable option for environmental, social and economical equity. In relation to this, some consideration can be made on the way niche tourism may be strategically developed and managed in this direction.

Similarly to 'main stream tourism' strategic development and management approaches, the work by niche tourism developers is influential, in terms of the assessment of the resources available, the involvement of potential stakeholder groups and the planning of realistic action in the interest of the visitors and for the benefit of the hosting community. In fact, niche tourism seems characterized by a complex mechanism of issues. From a strategic point of view, the planning process involves elements such as: the presence of infrastructure; the availability of resources; the presence of private entrepreneurship and public initiative; the involvement of the community; the location of resources and activities; the predisposition to innovation and the implementation of ethical approaches regarding the products and the services offered (see also European Commission, 2002). In many cases, niche tourism is operated by small businesses and involves fragile environments, often requiring tailored management approaches that extend far beyond business practice and profitability and into stakeholder relationships.

It must be mentioned that mainstream tourism and niche tourism often share the same infrastructure-determining implications of varying nature, both positive and negative for the host destination. For example, one may argue that in certain cases, niche tourism would not require extra infrastructure development, therefore limiting the man-made action on the environment. On the other hand, niche tourism may cause pressure on the carrying capacity of destinations and over-exploitation of resources in the same region. Within the presented chapters, valuable examples of such scenarios were offered by the cases on 'Dark tourism' (P. Tarlow), 'Sport tourism' (B. Ritchie), 'Youth tourism' (G. Richards and J. Wilson) and 'Cultural heritage tourism' (E. Wickens).

Several chapters indicate that private entrepreneurship seems to be a key player in niche tourism, with the establishment of SMEs based on the local resources available, often responding to the interests of an identified market segment and sometimes stimulated by institutional initiatives in the form of funding and other financial support, thus aspiring to local development in a sustainable manner. At the same time, public initiatives play a key role with governments identifying tourism development strategies aiming at private collaboration and proactive stakeholder involvement. The chapter on 'Research tourism' (A. Benson) highlights elements of private entrepreneurship; the chapters on 'Tourism in peripheral regions' (R. Grumo and A. Ivona) and 'Wildlife tourism' (M. Novelli and M.N. Humavindu) look at both private and public initiatives; and the case of 'Genealogy tourism' (M. Birtwistle) reflects a public sector approach.

Community participation is central to many tourism development strategies, both in the developed and the less developed world and constitutes one of the key objectives for the sustainable management approach of resources. As indicated in chapters such as 'Photographic tourism' (C. Palmer and J.A. Lester), 'Tribal tourism' (P. Burns and Y. Figurova) and 'Gastronomic tourism' (C.M. Hall and R. Mitchell), although from different angles, the host and guest relationship is often a key part of the travel experience, therefore requiring a more adequate planning approach aiming at a fairer 'exchange' between the visiting and the local community. This is particularly difficult in the many cases where there are conflicting, paradoxical pressures for and on development.

The location of niche tourism activities often involves fragile destinations both in environmental and social terms. In common with mainstream tourism markets, business revenue interest often overtakes environmental and social effects, creating conflicts of interests and potential long-term implications. The cases on 'Adventure tourism' (G. Shephard and S. Evans), 'Geotourism' (T.A. Hose) and 'Transport tourism' (D. Hall) highlight, some more explicitly than others, the risks of attracting visitors to potentially unstable locations.

Innovation of tourism products and services, although very difficult to define, has recently entered the tourism academic arena touching on themes of sustainability in terms of product and services offered. In the context of this book, valuable examples are offered in the chapters on 'Space tourism' (D.T. Duval) and 'Virtual tourism' (D. Arnold).

Ethics are surely at the centre of several academic debates concerning a wide range of issues, such as: corporate social responsibility, fair trade, altruistic tourist behaviour and codes of conduct. Valuable contributions on some of the above are given in the chapters on 'Volunteer tourism' (M. Callanan and S. Thomas) and on 'Ethical tourism' (C. Weeden).

Each chapter has provided the reader with a set of theoretical, management and implication elements, a selection of specific themes and locations and an array of attempts at framing the niche tourism cases within a sustainable tourism agenda, making difficult, if not impossible, generalizations of any kind. In this context, any answer to the question 'Is niche tourism sustainable?' is left to the specificity and uniqueness of the resource, location, destination, activity, community, scale of operation and typology of tourist partaking in niche tourism, basically 'particularizations' (that give us insights into tourism on the ground) as opposed to 'generalizations'.

References

European Commission (2002) *Using Natural and Cultural Heritage to Develop Sustainable Tourism in Non-traditional Tourism Destinations.* Brussels: Directorate-General for Enterprise, Tourism Unit.

France, L. (1997). *The Earthscan Reader in Sustainable Tourism.* Guildford: Earthscan Publications.

Hall, C.M. and Lew, A.A. (eds) (1998) *Sustainable Tourism: A Geographical Perspective.* New York: Addison Wesley Longman.

Holden, A. (2000) *Environment and Tourism.* London: Routledge.

IUCN (1980) *World Conservation Strategy.* Gland, Switzerland: IUCN.

Murphy, P.E. (1994) Tourism and Sustainable Development. *Global Tourism: The Next Decade.* W.F. Theobald. Oxford: Butterworth-Heinemann.

WTO (2001) *Guide for Local Authorities on Developing Sustainable Tourism.* Madrid.

Index

Figures and tables in *Italic*
'n' after a number indicates material is a note